Henry James

THE PORTRAIT OF A LADY

Mark Twain

THE PORTRAIT OF A LADY

[Edited with Introduction, Author's Information, Complete Text, Summary and Analysis and Study Questions]

Aditya Nandwani
B.A. English (Hons) , Delhi University;
M.A. (English), IGNOU; Print Journalism (English) YMCA

ANMOL PUBLICATIONS PVT. LTD.
NEW DELHI - 110 002 (INDIA)

ANMOL PUBLICATIONS PVT. LTD.

H.O.: 4374/4B, Ansari Road, Darya Ganj,
New Delhi-110 002 (India)
Ph.: 23278000, 23261597

B.O.: No. 1015, Ist Main Road, BSK IIIrd Stage
IIIrd Phase, IIIrd Block
Bangalore - 560 085 (India)
Visit us at: www.anmolpublications.com

The Portrait of a Lady

First Published, 2009

PRINTED IN INDIA

Printed at Mehra Offset Press, Delhi.

Contents

Preface

Born in New York City on April 15, 1843, Henry James traveled extensively with his parents, Henry James, Sr. and Mary Walsh James, and their four other children. Before he reached the age of 20, James had been to Europe several times, living in Switzerland, France, Germany, and England.

Henry James, an American author, spent much of his life living in, and writing about, Europe. As a novelist, short-story writer, and critic, James was particularly interested in Europe's history and traditions and the formal manners of its upper class.

Author

Chapter 1

Introduction

Henry James, an American author, spent much of his life living in, and writing about, Europe. As a novelist, short-story writer, and critic, James was particularly interested in Europe's history and traditions and the formal manners of its upper class. His tales of independent, yet naive, Americans encountering the cultivated, subtle influences of European society made him famous, although his work was not fully accepted until years after his death. Influenced by European authors such as George Eliot, Honoré de Balzac, Gustave Flaubert, and Ivan Turgenev, James was a prolific writer, publishing 22 novels and over a hundred short stories. In addition, he is the author of a number of plays, autobiographical writings, and noted critical essays.

Born in New York City on April 15, 1843, Henry James traveled extensively with his parents, Henry James, Sr. and Mary Walsh James, and their four other children. Before he reached the age of 20, James had been to Europe several times, living in Switzerland, France, Germany, and England. His broad education, provided mainly by his parents and private tutors, included the study of literature, philosophy, languages, and religion. Henry, Sr., a wealthy, eccentric essayist and philosopher, knew a number of famous authors and thinkers of the day, including Henry David Thoreau and Ralph Waldo Emerson. This created a unique atmosphere, and exposed young Henry to an impressive array of intellectual and artistic ideas as he was growing up.

In 1860, James suffered a debilitating back injury while fighting a fire at the family home in Newport, Rhode Island.

The injury would have a profound influence on him for the rest of his life, affecting his limited romantic relationships, and keeping him from fighting in the Civil War. Unable to participate in the war, James continued his education, studying with private tutors until he entered Harvard Law School when he was 19. His time at Harvard was not a success, however—he was unable to adapt to the rigors of formal education, and he left the school after his first year. Now James began to write seriously and he soon published a short story, anonymously, followed by a series of book reviews and other works of short fiction written under his own name. Much of James's early work reflects his interests in the supernatural, the individual's role in society, and the psychological influences that affect human behavior.

James traveled alone to Europe for the first time in 1869, visiting England, Switzerland, and Italy. Three years later he returned to Europe, touring with relatives at first, then remaining to write and travel on his own. He finally returned to the United States in 1874 and a year later published two books, one a collection of travel essays, and the other a book of short stories. In 1876, he wrote his first novel, Roderick Hudson. That same year, James decided to move to Europe, settling first in Rome and then Paris before moving to England where he lived until his death in 1916.

In his early work, such as Daisy Miller and The Portrait of a Lady, James explored the theme of Americans encountering European culture. It was Daisy Miller, his novella about a young American innocent in Europe, that first earned him widespread recognition and would become his most famous work. In other novels, including The Portrait of a Lady, James developed similar themes and characters, but Daisy Miller would remain his most popular piece of writing, becoming something of a phenomenon both in America and Europe.

Later, in novels such as The Bostonians and The Princess Casamassima, James wrote about revolution and political unrest. His short novels, such as The Aspern Papers and The Turn of the Screw, brought him further acclaim, and in the early 1900s, he wrote his last novels, The Wings of the Dove, The Ambassadors, and The Golden Bowl, works considered by many to be his masterpieces.

Although a resident of England for many years, James remained a U.S. citizen until 1915 when, as a political protest over America's refusal to go to war with Germany, he became a British citizen. After James died in 1916, his works were largely ignored until the 1930s, when he was rediscovered in England and the United States. Even today, some readers find his work too abstract and difficult to follow, but others appreciate James's ability to reflect deep thought and human emotion.

James is considered to be a major influence on the work of many authors, including James Joyce, Virginia Woolf, and William Faulkner. He has long been admired for his great literary skill, and his ability to create profound and innovative psychological portraits.

Chapter 2

Biography

Henry James

American-born writer, gifted with talents in literature, psychology, and philosophy. James wrote 20 novels, 112 stories, 12 plays and a number of literary criticism. His models were Dickens, Balzac, and Hawthorne. James once said that he learned more of the craft of writing from Balzac "than from anyone else".

"A novel is in its broadest sense a personal, a direct impression of life: that, to begin with, constitutes its value, which is greater or less according to the intensity of the impression." (from The Art of Fiction, 1885)

Henry James was born in New York City into a wealthy family. His father, Henry James Sr., was one of the best-known intellectuals in mid-nineteenth-century America, whose friends included Thoreau, Emerson and Hawthorne. James made little money from his novels. Once his friend, the writer Edith Wharton, secretly arranged him a royal advance of $8,000 for THE IVORY TOWER, but the money actually came from Wharton's royalty account with the publisher. When Wharton sent him a letter bemoaning her unhappy marriage, James replied: "Keep making the movements of life."

In his youth James traveled back and forth between Europe and America. He studied with tutors in Geneva, London, Paris, Bologna and Bonn At the age of nineteen he briefly attended Harvard Law School, but was more interested in literature than studying law. James published his first short story, 'A Tragedy of Errors' two years later, and then devoted himself to literature. In 1866-69 and 1871-72 he was contributor to the Nation and Atlantic Monthly. From an early age James had read the classics of English, American, French and German literature, and Russian classics in translation. His first novel, watch and ward, appeared first serially in the Atlantic. James wrote it while he was traveling through Venice and Paris. Watch and Ward tells a story of a bachelor who adopts a twelve-year-old girl and plans to marry her.

After living in Paris, where James was contributor to the New York Tribune, he moved to England, living first in London and then in Rye, Sussex. "It is a real stroke of luck for a particular country that the capital of the human race happens to be British. Surely every other people would have it theirs if they could. Whether the English deserve to hold it any longer might be an interesting field of inquiry; but as they have not yet let it slip the writer of these lines professes without scruple that the arrangement is to his personal taste. For after all if the sense of life is greatest there, it is a sense of the life of people of our incomparable English speech." During his first years in Europe James wrote novels that portrayed Americans living abroad. James's years in England were uneventful. In 1905 he visited America for the first time in twenty-five year, and wrote 'Jolly Corner'. It was based on his observations of New York, but also a nightmare of a man, who is haunted by a doppelgänger.

Between 1906 and 1910 James revised many of his tales and novels for the so-called new york edition of his complete works. It was published by charles scribner's sons. His autobiography, a small boy and others was continued in notes of a son and brother. The third volume, the middle years, appeared posthumously in 1917. The outbreak of world war i was a shock for james and in 1915 he became a british citizen as a loyalty to his adopted country and in protest against the us's refusal to enter the war.

James suffered a stroke on December 2, 1915. He expected to die and exclaimed: "So this is it at last, the distinguished thing!" However, James died three months later in Rye on February 28, 1916. Two novels, The Ivory Tower and THE SENSE OF THE PAST, were left unfinished at his death.

Characteristic for James novels are understanding and sensitively drawn lady portraits; James himself was a homosexual, but sensitive to basic sexual differences and the fact that he was a male. His main themes were the innocence of the New World in conflict with corruption and wisdom of the Old. Among his masterpieces is daisy miller, where the young and innocent american daisy finds her values in conflict with european sophistication. In the portrait of a lady again a young american woman is fooled during her travels in europe. James started to write the work in florence in 1879 and continued with it in venice. The definitive version appeared in 1908. "I had rooms on riva sciavoni, at the top of a house near the passage leading off to San Zaccaria; the waterside life, the wondrous lagoon spread before me, and the ceaseless human chatter of Venice came in at my windows, to which I seem to myself to have been constantly driven, in the fruitless fidget of composition, as if to see whether, out in the blue channel, the ship of some right suggestion, of some better phrase, of the next happy twist of my subject, the next true touch for my canvas, mightn't come into sight."

The protagonist is Isabel Archer, a penniless orphan. She goes to England to stay with her aunt and uncle, and their tubercular son, Ralph. Isabel inherits money and goes to Continent with Mrs Touchett and Madame Merle. She turns down proposals of marriage from Casper Goodwood, and marries Gilbert Osmond, a middle-aged snobbish widower with a young daughter, Pansy. "He had a light, lean, rather languid-looking figure, and was apparently neither tall nor short. He was dressed as a man who takes little other trouble about it than to have no vulgar thing." Isabel discovers that Pansy is Madame Merle's daughter, it was Madame Merle's plot to marry Isabel to Osmond so that he, and Pansy can enjoy Isabel's wealth. Caspar Goodwood makes a last attempt to gain her, but she returns to Osmond and Pansy.

The bostonians, set in the era of the rising feminist movement, was based on alphonse daudet's novel l'évangéliste. What maisie knew depicted a preadolescent young girl, who must chose between her parents and a motherly old governess. In the wings of the dove a heritage destroys the love of a young couple. James considered the ambassadors his most "perfect" work of art. The novel depicts lambert strether's attempts to persuade mrs newsome' son chad to return from paris back to the united states. Strether's possibility to marry mrs newsome is dropped and he remains content in his role as a widower and observer. "The beauty that suffuses the ambassadors is the reward due to a fine artist for hard work. James knew exactly what he wanted, he pursued the narrow path of aesthetic duty, and success to the full extent of his possibilities has crowned him. The pattern has woven itself, with modulation and reservations anatole france will never attain. But at what sacrifice!"

Although James is best-known for his novels, his essays are now attracting audience outside scholarly connoisseurs. In his early critics James considered British and American novels dull and formless and French fiction "intolerably unclean". "M. Zola is magnificent, but he strikes an English reader as ignorant; he has an air of working in the dark; if he had as much light as energy, his results would be of the highest value." In partial portraits james paid tribute to his elders, and emerson, george eliot, and turgenev. His advice to aspiring writers avoided all theorizing: "Oh, do something from your point of view". H.G. Wells used James as the model for George Boon in his Boon. When the protagonist argued that novels should be used for propaganda, not art, James wrote to Wells: "It is art that makes life, makes interest, makes importance, and I know of no substitute whatever for the force and beauty of its process. If I were Boon I should say that any pretense of such a substitute is helpless and hopeless humbug; but I wouldn't be Boon for the world, and am only yours faithfully, Henry James."

James's most famous tales include 'The Turn of the Screw', written mostly in the form of a journal, was first published serially in Collier's Weekly, and then with another story in THE TWO MAGICS. The protagonist is a governess, who works on a lonely estate in England. She tries to save her two young charges, Flora and Miles, two both innocent and corrupted children, from the demonic influence of the apparitions of two former servants in the household, steward Peter Quint and the previous governess Miss Jessel. Her employer, the children's uncle, has given strict orders not to bother him with any of the details of their education. Although the children evade the questions about the ghosts but she certain is that the children see them. When she tries to exorcize their influence, Miles dies in her arms. The story inspired later a debate over the question of the "reality" of the ghosts, were her visions only hallucinations. In the beginning of his career James had rejected "spirit-rappings and ghost-raising", but in the 1880s he become interested in the unconscious and the supernatural. James wrote in 1908 that "Peter Quint and Miss Jessel are not "ghosts" at all, as we now know the ghost, but goblins, elves, imps, demons as loosely constructed as those of the old trials for whichcraft; if not, more pleasingly, fairies of the legendary order, wooing their victims forth to see them dance under the moon." Virginia Woolf thought that Henry James's beings have nothing in common with the violent old ghosts-"the blood-stained captains, the white horses, the headless ladies of dark lanes and windy commons." Edmund Wilson was convinced that the story was "primarily intended as a characterization of the governess".

Chapter 3

Chronology

American novelist and, as a naturalized English citizen from 1915, a great figure in the transatlantic culture. His fundamental theme was the innocence and exuberance of the New World in clash with the corruption and wisdom of the Old, as illustrated in such works as Daisy Miller, The Portrait of a Lady, The Bostonians, and The Ambassadors.

April 15, 1843, born New York, N.Y., U.S.

- Father an important theorist and lecturer, very wealthy family
- Older brother the famous American philosopher, William James
- Traveled in Europe extensively when young
- Lived in Newport and Boston much of early life

1862	Harvard Law School, but mostly read literature
1864	First short story, published anonymously, in New York Continental Monthl becomes good friends with William Dean Howells, help begin era of American literary realism
1865	Early stories depict the leisurely life of the well-to-do
1869	Goes to Europe extensively as an adult
1875	Publishes Roderick Hudson
1875	Transatlantic Sketches, collected travel writings
1875-76	Lived in Paris
1877	Novel, The American mid-1870s, came to know and be influenced by Turgenev, Flaubert, Zola, de Maupassant
1876	Moved to London, associates with Tennyson, Browning, Meredith, Stevenson

1878	Daisy Miller
1881	The Portrait of a Lady
1881	Washington Square
1886	Writes two novels dealing with social reformers and revolutionaries: The Bostonians The Princess Casamassina 1890, The Tragic Muse 1890-1895, "Dramatic Years," tries to win success writing for the stage
1891	The American, met with modest success
1895	Guy Domville, theatrical failure Post "Dramatic Years," spends several years trying to reinvent his writing, begins to use alternating "picture" and dramatic scenes, and other writing methods
1895-97	James's old international theme of innocence in a corrupting world, now set in an English setting
1897	The Spoils of Poynton
1898	The Turn of the Screw and In the Cage
1899	The Awkward Age Turn of the century; James writes three novels that lead the way for the "20th-Century Novel," known as his "major" phase
1903	The Ambassadors
1902	The Wings of the Dove
1904	The Golden Bowl
1904-05	Lives in retirement in 18th-century house at Rye in Sussex, England. Does return to U.S.
1907	The American Scene (poetic volume of observations in America) Spends three years revising works, "to shore" them up for publication in "New York Edition," published in 24 volumes James's edition contains 15 prefaces dealing with his theories of fiction
1915	Receives the Order of Merit from King George V and official British citizen, opposing U.S.'s failure to enter WWI. Feb. 28, 1916, dies in London, Eng. James' General Writing Style and Reputation:

Henry James is considered a very prolific writer,

authoring many novels, short stories, and essays on a variety of topics. His topics are diverse and all encompassing. For James, nothing is to be excluded from his realm of discussion. His overall regions of writing stretch from the United States to Europe. James has gained a reputation as "a master of character portrayal." He frequently writes in a "stream of consciousness" method, namely in his fictitious pieces. James is considered to be a realistic fiction writer for the most part. However, he also has been known to write a number of quite intriguing ghost tales taking the psychological aspects of ambiguity to new limits.

Chapter 4

Major Works

Henry James, American-born writer, gifted with talents in literature, psychology, and philosophy. James wrote 20 novels, 112 stories, 12 plays and a number of works of literary criticism.

Henry James was born on April 15, 1843 in New York City into a wealthy family. His father, Henry James Sr. was one of the best-known intellectuals in mid-nineteenth-century America. In his youth James traveled back and forth between Europe and America. He studied with tutors in Geneva, London, Paris, Bologna and Bonn. At the age of 19 he briefly attended Harvard Law School, but preferred reading literature to studying law. James published his first short story, "A Tragedy of Errors" two years later, and devoted himself to literature. In 1866-69 and 1871-72 he was a contributor to the Nation and Atlantic Monthly.

From an early age James had read the classics of English, American, French and German literature and Russian classics in translation. His first novel, Watch And Ward, was written while he was traveling through Venice and Paris. After living in Paris, where he was contributor to the New York Tribune, James moved to England, living first in London and then in Rye, Sussex. During his first years in Europe James wrote novels that portrayed Americans living abroad. In 1905 James visited America for the first time in twenty-five years, and wrote "Jolly Corner".

Among James' masterpieces are Daisy Miller, where the young and innocent American, Daisy finds her values in conflict with European sophistication and The Portrait Of A

Lady where again a young American woman becomes a victim of her provincialism during her travels in Europe. The Bostonians was set in the era of the rising feminist movement. What Maisie Knew depicted a preadolescent young girl, who must chose between her parents and a motherly old governess. In The Wings Of The Dove a heritage destroys the love of a young couple. James considered The Ambassadors his most 'perfect' work of art. James's most famous short story must be "The Turn of the Screw", a ghost story in which the question of childhood corruption obsesses a governess. Although James is best known for his novels, his essays are now attracting a more general audience.

Between 1906 and 1910 James revised many of his tales and novels for the New York edition of his complete works. His autobiography, A Small Boy And Others, appeared in 1913 and was continued in Notes Of A Son And Brother. The third volume, The Middle Years, appeared posthumously in 1917. The outbreak of World War I was a shock for James and in 1915 he became a British citizen as a declaration of loyalty to his adopted country and in protest against the US's refusal to enter the war. James suffered a stroke on December 2, 1915. He died three months later in Rye on February 28, 1916.

Works

An International Episode
Confidence
Eugene Pickering
Glasses
In The Cage
Nona Vincent
Pandora
Roderick Hudson
Sir Dominick Ferrand
The Altar of the Dead
The Ambassadors
The American
The Aspern Papers
The Awkward Age

The Beast in the Jungle
The Beldonald Holbein
The Bostonians
The Chaperon
The Coxon Fund
The Death of the Lion
The Europeans
The Golden Bowl Volume 1
The Golden Bowl Volume 2
The Lesson of the Master
The Patagonia
The Pension Beaurepas
The Portrait of a Lady
The Pupil
The Reverberator
The Tragic Muse
The Turn of the Screw
The Wings of the Dove
Washington Square
What Maisie Knew
Non-Fiction
A Little Tour In France
Hawthorne
Italian Hours
Short Stories
Daisy Miller
The Author of Beltraffio
A Bundle of Letters
The Diary of a Man of Fifty
The Figure in the Carpet
Julia Bride
Greville Fane
The Jolly Corner
Louisa Pallant
Madame de Mauves
The Madonna of the Future
The Marriages
A Passionate Pilgrim

The Point of View
The Real Thing
Brooksmith
The Story of It
Flickerbridge
Mrs. Medwin
A Light Man
The Tree of Knowledge

Chapter 5

Historical Context

Although the period known as the Enlightenment took place a century before The Portrait of a Lady was written, the Enlightenment is the historical period that most influences the novel's characters and its story. Isabel, especially, is a product of Enlightenment ideas.

The Enlightenment was a philosophical, political, and literary movement that swept Europe and the United States throughout the 1700s. Its major feature was the elevation of reason and scientific observation above the mysticism and superstition of the Middle Ages. All traditions and conventions, from the religious to the political and social, were reevaluated. No idea or authority was to be accepted blindly or merely because it had been accepted in the past; only those ideas that could be supported by reason or proven scientifically were considered valid.

The idea of the superiority of the intellect led to the idea that human beings were essentially good and were capable of improving and even perfecting themselves. People did not need religious dogma or political authorities to tell them how to live; they had the ability, and therefore the right, to make their own decisions. It is easy to see how such thinking led directly to an emphasis on the political and social rights of individuals.

In The Portrait of a Lady, Isabel and the other American characters are products of the Enlightenment whose lives show how completely these ideas were adopted in the United States and how strong their influence still was a century later. It was the big ideas of the Enlightenment that fueled the American

Revolution and forever shaped what it meant to be an American. Hence, Isabel takes for granted that she should be able to make her own decisions in life and to do what she feels is best, regardless of social conventions or other people's opinions.

Enlightenment ideas actually first took shape in Europe, but they never fully took hold in England, which is home to most of the novel's European characters. The French Revolution followed the American war of independence and represented the victory of Enlightenment ideas in France. But the English monarchy, Parliament, and ruling class defended themselves against the rising tide of democracy and individualism around them. England never had a revolution. Old ideas about authority and tradition were never swept cleanly away. In the late 1800s, when The Portrait of a Lady was written and takes place, England was still very much a society based on wealth, class, tradition, and the supremacy of society over the individual; and it was still consolidating its rule over a vast empire of subject peoples. In stark contrast to America, England saw democracy as a radical ideology and a threat.

Characters such as Ralph and Lord Warburton find Isabel's independence and individualism captivating because Isabel is a captivating young woman who clearly is not a threat. These men, although they reflect European ideas in their own lives, find Isabel's ways refreshing — as long as they are expressed by a lovely young woman and not by an angry mob. To the darker personalities of Madame Merle and Gilbert Osmond, on the other hand, Isabel's new and different ideas make her an adversary. She is not one of them — she does not value the same things or follow the same conventions — and therefore their impulse is to set themselves against her in some way, just as their government and their society has long set itself against the ideas she represents.

Compare & Contrast

Late 1800s: England, France, and Italy are the cultural epicenters of the Western world. England produces the best literature and drama; Italy leads in art and architecture; and French style and society are considered the height of sophistication. The United States is viewed as a sort of cultural country cousin to Europe; its arts and culture are considered far inferior to those of the Continent.

Today: The United States is the cultural pace-setter for the world. American movies, television, music, fashions, and lifestyles are in demand and emulated, not only in Europe but around the globe.

Late 1800s: Most wealthy Americans made their money in industry during the Industrial Revolution of the early 1800s. Factory owners and railroad developers are among those who have amassed huge fortunes. Many of the wealth-producing ventures are family-owned and passed down from father to son. The gap between the rich and poor is growing, as the rich get richer and the poor struggle to maintain a decent lifestyle in an economy producing more and more expensive goods.

Today: Many of the new wealthiest Americans made their money in the high-tech boom of the late 1990s and in other businesses, such as finance, that benefited from it. Most wealth-producing companies are publicly owned, and scandal erupts in 2001 when many of these companies suddenly fail, costing stockholders billions, while top executives continue to receive multi-million-dollar salaries.

Late 1800s: Women do not have the right to vote in the United States or in England. In England, voting rights have long been limited to wealthy men, but they are gradually being extended to more men.

Today: In both the United States and Great Britain, all men and women have the right to vote.

Chapter 6

Characters

Isabel Archer

The novel's central character, Isabel is a young American woman who embodies all the best of what James depicts as American qualities, especially vitality, sincerity, and independence. As the novel opens, Isabel is arriving at the English home of her aunt and uncle. Her father has recently died. (Her mother died previously.) Her aunt, who traveled to the United States after Isabel's father's death, feels that Isabel has more potential than her circumstances in America will allow her to fulfill, and so she brings Isabel back to England with her. Isabel wins the admiration of everyone she meets, including her cousin Ralph. Ralph talks his dying father into leaving half his estate to Isabel so that she can be free to do as she pleases. In addition to this benefactor, Isabel also has suitors. Caspar Goodwood travels from America to urge Isabel to marry him. Lord Warburton, a wealthy friend of the Touchett family, also wants to marry Isabel. But Isabel's independent nature leads her to reject both men. She finds Caspar boring and turns down Warburton partly because she is not ready to marry and partly because she fears life with him would be too easy. She longs for some adventure — even for some difficulty that will test her resourcefulness and mettle.

Isabel's independent spirit is the driving force in her personality, and it is what propels her into an unhappy marriage. When she falls in love with Gilbert Osmond, her friends and relatives almost unanimously warn her against him. But she refuses to take anyone's counsel but her own and learns too late that she completely misjudged her husband. Her failure to accurately judge Gilbert's character springs from an innocence that is characteristic of youth and also, in James's view, of Americans. Isabel's direct, trusting nature is contrasted to thatof the book's European characters, who have secret pasts and ulterior motives for everything they do. Although she makes a bad marriage, Isabel is not a tragic character. Once she realizes that she made a mistake in marrying Gilbert, she resolves to bring her strength of character to bear upon the circumstances that she has created by her own free choice. By refusing to leave her marriage, Isabel refuses to adopt the corrupt ways of her European circle. Instead, Isabel intends to graciously and courageously accept the consequences of her unwise decision and to make the best life she can.

Mr. Bantling

An old acquaintance of Ralph, Mr. Bantling meets Henrietta when she is in London with Ralph and Isabel. He becomes Henrietta's companion and guide as she travels around Europe as a journalist.

Countess Gemini

Countess Gemini is Gilbert Osmond's sister. She is well aware of Gilbert's true character and thus has no affection for him, but the two have a familial relationship in spite of this. The Countess catches on quickly to Madame Merle's scheme to get Isabel to marry Gilbert and voices her objection to it, but she doesn't actually do anything to prevent it. Four years after the marriage, at a time when Isabel is distraught over Gilbert's controlling nature, the Countess, out of sympathy, finally tells Isabel the truth about Gilbert's past.

Caspar Goodwood

Caspar is Isabel's American suitor. Having fallen in love with Isabel in the United States, he follows her to England to try to get her to agree to marry him. Isabel sees his persistence as aggression and is only irritated by it. However, the novel's one moment of passion takes place between Caspar and Isabel, when Caspar goes to see Isabel at Gardencourt one last time after Ralph's death. The couple's passionate kiss can be seen as Isabel's belated appreciation of the honesty and simplicity of character that Caspar personifies.

Madame Merle

Madame Merle is a friend of Mrs. Touchett. Isabel first meets her when both women are guests at Mrs. Touchett's home in England just before Mr. Touchett's death. Madame Merle is older than Isabel and very accomplished socially. She is charming and congenial and, as becomes clear only later, adept at manipulating people and events to serve her interests. Isabel is dazzled by Madame Merle's apparent refinement.

Gilbert Osmond

Gilbert Osmond was born in the United States but has lived virtually his entire life in Europe. He has the same qualities as Madame Merle, and Isabel is attracted to both of them for the same reason. Gilbert is an art collector, and he has an air of charm, sophistication, and refinement that greatly impresses Isabel. While all of her friends and relatives see Gilbert for the self-centered dilettante he is, Isabel is completely taken in and falls in love with him. More than any other character, Gilbert is not what he appears to be. Although he has expensive tastes, he does not have money. Although he is charming and seductive, he does not really care about Isabel. And although he pretends that his daughter is the child of his deceased first wife, she is actually the product of an affair with Madame Merle.

Pansy Osmond

Pansy is Gilbert's daughter, and she is fifteen years old when Isabel meets Gilbert. Gilbert has always said that Pansy is the child of his first wife, who died giving birth to her, and Pansy was brought up in a convent. The nuns have reared her to be a completely obedient child, which pleases Gilbert.

Readers, along with Isabel, learn the truth about Pansy years after Isabel's marriage to Gilbert. Pansy is actually the product of a long affair between Madame Merle and Gilbert, whose first wife did die, but not in childbirth. Pansy does not know that Madame Merle is her mother but has an obvious dislike for the woman. Pansy likes Isabel and is very happy when she learns that Isabel is going to marry her father. Isabel's love for Pansy may be one reason why she returns to Gilbert at the end of the novel.

Henrietta Stackpole

Henrietta is an American journalist and a friend of Isabel. She is the quintessential "ugly American": loud, brassy, and boorish. Although Isabel sees Henrietta's faults, she is loyal to her friend, as Henrietta is to her. And, although Henrietta does not have Isabel's refinement, she is a better judge of people, and she warns Isabel not to marry Gilbert.

Mr. Touchett

Mr. Touchett is Isabel's wealthy uncle. Like most of the novel's characters, he was born in the United States, but at the time of the story, he has lived for many years in England. He comes to care deeply for Isabel and, when he hesitates to leave her half his fortune, it is only because he is afraid that the money will bring her harm rather than good. Mr. Touchett dies early in the novel after letting Ralph persuade him to leave Isabel a fortune.

Mrs. Touchett

Isabel's aunt, Mrs. Touchett, goes to New York after the death of her brother, from whom she was estranged, and decides to bring Isabel back to Europe with her. Mrs. Touchett is a well-meaning woman who shares some of Isabel's independence and, more surprisingly considering her age and her long time in Europe, her naiveté. Her independence is clear from the fact that she long ago set up her own home in Florence while her husband remained in England, since the two did not enjoy the same kind of life. The two crafted an amicable marriage out of visits to each other's homes. Mrs. Touchett's naiveté is clear in her unwarranted trust of Madame Merle.

Like Isabel, Mrs. Touchett is impressed with Madame Merle's mastery of the social graces and fails to see that she is corrupt until it is too late to save Isabel from her scheme. Mrs. Touchett does realize the truth before Isabel does, however.

Ralph Touchett

Ralph is Isabel's cousin. He becomes her admirer, friend, and confidant. Like Isabel, he is intelligent and good-hearted. Unlike her, though, he is physically frail. He is also much less naive than his cousin. He understands and condemns the conniving of Madame Merle and others like her. Because Ralph cares for Isabel and sees her potential to blossom into a sophisticated woman, he wants to do what he can to give her an advantage in life. Ralph is ill and knows that he will not live long, and therefore he persuades his dying father to leave half his estate to Isabel. Throughout the novel, until his death at the end of the story, Ralph remains Isabel's supporter, although Isabel's insistence on marrying Gilbert causes tension and even a brief rupture in their relationship. It is significant that when Ralph is near death and asks Isabel to travel to England to see him, she does so even over her husband's objections. Isabel also admits to Ralph that she made a terrible mistake when she married Gilbert. These two actions show the closeness and loyalty that Isabel feels toward Ralph. For his part, Ralph dies feeling that, while he hoped to benefit Isabel by securing a fortune for her, he actually brought about her ruin.

Lord Warburton

Lord Warburton is a friend of the Touchetts who falls in love with Isabel almost as soon as he meets her. He proposes to Isabel, and when she rejects him, he asks for an explanation but then accepts her decision graciously. Since Warburton is not only extremely wealthy but also considerate and kind, Isabel's rejection of him stuns everyone. Isabel's choice of Gilbert over Warburton is a clear sign of her lack of judgment. Like Caspar Goodwood, Warburton comes to see Isabel at Gardencourt at the end of the novel and, like Goodwood, he is rejected one final time.

Chapter 7

Themes

American Versus European Character

The contrast between the American character and the European character is a theme that appears throughout James's work. This is not surprising, since it is a contrast he observed throughout his life as an American who spent most of his adulthood in Europe. According to James, Americans tend to be naive, energetic, practical, sincere, direct, and spontaneous, and they value the individual above society. Conversely, Europeans are sophisticated, lethargic, formal, insincere, obtuse, and scheming, and they value society above the individual. This theme is especially interesting in The Portrait of a Lady because most of its characters are Americans who have been living in Europe for varying periods of time.

In general, the longer an American-born character has been in Europe, the more European traits he or she has. Gilbert has lived nearly his whole life on the Continent and is completely European in character. James uses him to personify the worst manifestations of European traits. At the other end of the spectrum is Isabel, who is just arriving in Europe as the novel opens. The things that make her distinctively American, such as her energy and independent attitude, are fresh and interesting to the European characters. They are also, however, the things that lead to her downfall. By refusing to take the counsel of those who care about her, Isabel falls prey to the more sophisticated Europeans who manipulate her for their own purposes.

James does make a moral judgment about which culture

produces better people; he clearly portrays the Americans as having more integrity. But he also shows that, taken as individuals, most Americans and Europeans alike have both good and bad qualities. While Isabel is almost wholly admirable and Gilbert is almost wholly despicable, the other characters are drawn in shades of gray. Henrietta is an example of an American whom James portrays less positively. Her American qualities are exaggerated so that her directness is actually rudeness. Her lack of regard for society and convention is so extreme that she offends as routinely as Isabel enchants. Lord Warburton, on the other hand, exemplifies European qualities in their most positive form. He is sophisticated and conventional, but he is also courteous, sensitive, and gracious even in defeat. Ralph is also a positive European character, a physically weak man who is nevertheless morally strong.

Social and Emotional Maturation

Isabel's social and emotional development is thrown into high relief by James's contrast of American and European natures. Yet Isabel's experiences and the wisdom she gains from them are certainly not unique to American women coming of age in European society. Isabel's naiveté is common among young women in all cultures, which is one reason why the novel remains popular. It is almost a rule that young women make poor romantic choices. In fact, they often make exactly the mistake that Isabel makes: they choose a man who is charming and seductive, yet self-centered, over one who is less worldly but more substantial and caring.

This oft-repeated error of youth has been the subject of many works of literature. Perhaps the best-known is Jane Austen's Sense and Sensibility, which contrasts the naive Marianne and her wiser sister, Elinor. In The Portrait of a Lady, James uses one theme, the contrasts between Americans and Europeans, to intensify another, more universal theme of a woman's development from naive youth to mature wisdom as she suffers the consequences of a poor romantic choice.

Chapter 8

Style

Psychological Realism

James is considered the foremost author of psychological realism, a subcategory of American realism.

The Realist period in American literature followed Romanticism, a movement that produced stories of idealized love and that elevated emotion above reason. The harsh realities of the Civil War suddenly made Romanticism irrelevant. The year of the war's end, 1865, marks the end of the Romantic period and the beginning of American realism.

Realism got its name from the fact that its stories depicted realistic characters in believable, lifelike situations. Heroes and heroines were not larger than life; they were often "just plain folks" that readers could identify with. And these characters faced problems similar to those that real people faced — neither melodramatic and overblown nor magically solved by some unexpected and incredible twist of the plot. These stories were told in straightforward, objective prose that sought to engage readers' minds more than their emotions.

James was one of the leading authors of American realism, along with Mark Twain (who is sometimes classified as a regionalist) and William Dean Howells. Some critics complained that there was nothing realistic about James's stories, in which everyone was wealthy and refined. The simple answer is that James never pretended to write about all elements of human society. He wrote about the wealthy because it was the wealthy and their problems that he was familiar with and interested in.

In addition to limiting his subject matter to the lives of the wealthy, James also built his stories on the psychology of his characters. The stories are about what goes on inside characters' minds, how they experience and think about the things that happen to them, and how these inner experiences change them as people.

The events that happen in James's stories are included not primarily for their own importance but because they shed light on the minds and personalities of the characters. The Portrait of a Lady is the story of Isabel's mind and how it shapes her destiny and her character. For this and other masterful tales of human psychology, James is considered the father of psychological realism.

Point of View

Modern readers are unlikely to take special notice of point of view in The Portrait of a Lady, but James's contemporaries did. While the point of view that James uses is common today, it was an innovation in James's time. In fact, it was an innovation to which James was an important contributor.

In most novels published before this one, the author was a prominent narrator — almost a character. In addition to telling the story, the author-narrator often inserted asides directly addressing the reader, commenting on the characters' actions, and so on.

This gives fiction an artificial quality; the reader never forgets that he or she is being told a story that has been invented and shaped by the author. To put it another way, the author is always "visible" as an intermediary between the characters and the reader.

This technique of storytelling was not suitable to realism, which strove to make the story seem lifelike rather than artificial. James wanted readers to observe his characters directly and to interpret characters' actions themselves, just as they would observe people around them in life.

This meant that he had to get himself as author out of the picture. So, while The Portrait of a Lady does have a third-person narrator, that narrator is not James and does not intrude into the story. Instead of readers learning about Isabel through a narrator's comments and interpretations, readers learn about Isabel directly by observing Isabel's actions. James was influenced by George Eliot, who was a pioneer in minimizing the author's role in the story, but he developed the new point of view into the form that is common today.

Chapter 9

Critical Overview

When The Portrait of a Lady was published, James was a well-known and respected author whose story Daisy Miller was enjoying great popularity. The Portrait of a Lady was widely reviewed, and most reviews, including those in the leading American publications, were positive.

Horace E. Scudder reviewed The Portrait of a Lady for Atlantic, in which the novel was serialized before its book publication. Scudder's review focuses almost exclusively on what he calls the story's "consistency," by which he means that the novel's "characters, the situations, the incidents, are all true to the law of their own being." Scudder's single complaint is that he does not like the novel's ending. Simply put, he objects to James's sending Isabel back to Gilbert. Isabel deserves better than this, Scudder insists, and when one reads of her return to the dastardly Gilbert, "one's indignation is moved."

An anonymous review for Harper's, the other leading American literary magazine of the day, calls The Portrait of a Lady a "long and fragmentary but profoundly interesting tale." In the Nation, W. C. Brownell calls the novel "an important work, the most important Mr. James has thus far written" and "his masterpiece." Brownell, too, has one complaint, though he voices it hesitantly: he thinks the story lacks excitement. He writes:

The Portrait of a Lady is not only outside of the category of the old romance of which Tom Jones, for example, may stand as the type, but also dispenses with the dramatic movement and passionate interest upon which the later novelists, from

Thackeray to Thomas Hardy, have relied. In a sense, and to a certain extent, Turgeneff may be said to be Mr. James's master, but even a sketch or a study by Turgeneff is turbulence itself beside the elaborate placidity of these 519 pages.

Brownell then calls his complaint "ungracious" and "hypercritical," and concludes that The Portrait of a Lady is the best piece of realistic fiction published to date.

A long, unhappy review in the British magazine Blackwood's, by Margaret Oliphant, is fascinating for its litany of political and cultural objections and its paucity of comment on the book's literary merit or lack thereof. Two brief excerpts from Oliphant's review sum up her attitude. Of James, she writes:

This gentleman's work in the world seems to be a peculiar one. It is to record and set fully before us the predominance of the great American race, and the manner in which it has overrun and conquered the Old World.

This is an interesting view of an American who chose to live his life in Europe. But Oliphant is certain in it, and describes Isabel Archer as

the young lady who suddenly appears in the doorway of an old English country-house, inhabited like most other desirable places by American tenants fresh from her native country, prepared to take instant possession of her birthright as explorer, discoverer, and conqueror of the old country, — and, in fact, reducing the gentlemen who meet her into instant subjection in the course of half an hour.

The Portrait of a Lady has grown in stature in the century and a quarter since its publication. It continues to be included among James's best novels, among the greatest novels written in English, and even among the greatest works in all of world literature. George Perkins writes in his Reference Guide to American Literature article on James, "In The Portrait of a Lady, The Wings of the Dove, The Ambassadors, and The Golden Bowl, the theme of partial perspectives (which involves often the theme of too late awareness) merges with the international theme to provide the substance of James's most lasting achievement."

The chapter on The Portrait of a Lady in the Twayne's United States Authors Series volume Henry James: The Early Novels pays high tribute to the novel while acknowledging its impact on literature to come:

The Portrait of a Lady shows James in the fullness of his powers. The sheer beauty, grace, and assurance of the writing, almost startling in the opening description of Gardencourt, and sustained for five-hundred pages, reveal James at a new level of achievement as a prose stylist; and the richness of his character portraits and intensity of his engagement with his subject are of a kind that belong to history-making novels. The Portrait of a Lady is history-making literally. The opening account of Gardencourt, in which a densely solid actuality has begun to dissolve into psychological atmosphere, shows literary impressionism at a high stage of development. And Isabel's chapter-length meditative vigil, projected in a long, dramatic interior monologue, lays the foundations of the stream-of-consciousness novel of Joyce, Dorothy Richardson, and Virginia Woolf.

Criticism

Norvell is an independent educational writer who specializes in English and literature. In this essay, Norvell discusses James's descriptions of the various houses in The Portrait of a Lady and how these descriptions function in the story.

Every novel can be said to have an architecture in the sense of having a structure. But The Portrait of a Lady has an entire neighborhood of architectures. It has a minutely planned, carefully executed structure that reflects the sensibilities of its designer every bit as clearly as a great building reflects those of its architect. But, in addition, James uses houses throughout the novel to create his settings, to establish moods, to illuminate the characters who occupy them, and to foreshadow what kinds of things will happen to his main character during the time she spends in each house.

Since the novel opens in England, Isabel's childhood home in Albany, New York, is described only as a memory — a dull memory to show that Isabel's life and her prospects were dull compared to what Europe offers her. The house is described in minimalist terms as "the old house at Albany, a large, square, double house." The room in which Isabel met Mrs. Touchett on the latter's visit is pointedly described as "the most depressed" area of the house. The place is so shabby that, at least for Isabel, it cast a shadow even over the coming of spring. The narrator describes her sitting alone in the house on a rainy afternoon after her father's death and feeling that the promise of spring is only a "cosmic treachery."

In short, every piece of information that James gives about the house in Albany is designed to portray Isabel's life in the United States as little better than a prison that she was fortunate to escape.

The contrast between this and her aunt and uncle's English country house could not be greater — starting with the latter's name, Gardencourt. This beautiful old estate is where Isabel makes her first appearance in the novel, and to set the stage for his heroine's entry, James describes the estate at length. The first words about the place depict perfection: "the shadows on the perfect lawn were straight and angular." James continues that the house stood upon a low hill, above the river — the river being the Thames some forty miles from London. A long gabled front of red brick, with the complexion of which time and weather had played all sorts of pictorial tricks, only, however, to improve and refine it, presented to the lawn its patches of ivy, its clustered chimneys, its windows smothered in creepers. Privacy here reigned supreme, and the wide carpet of turf that covered the level hilltop seemed but the extension of a luxurious interior. The great still oaks and beeches flung down a shade as dense as that of velvet curtains.

When Isabel makes her entrance into this scene a few pages later, James paints her as a pretty, gracious, enchanting young woman who belongs in just this kind of setting. The reader understands immediately that Gardencourt will be like a home to her; that this is a place where her fine qualities will be appreciated and where she will be loved and protected.

The next house Isabel visits belongs to the wealthy and

noble Lord Warburton. James describes his house in just the way that Isabel will come to think of its owner; it has qualities that make it seem both chivalric and staid: "as they saw it from the gardens, a stout grey pile, of the softest, deepest, most weather-fretted hue, rising from a broad, still moat, it affected the young visitor as a castle in a legend." Warburton himself is the novel's most noble character, not only in title but in character, as gallant and strong as an old castle. But a moat is a symbol of isolation, and isolation is the last thing Isabel wants. Though she likes Warburton, Isabel sees him as "a stout grey pile" who would bore her at best and imprison her at worst, even if he did so with only the purest and best motives — those of protecting and providing for her.

The next house that James describes in detail is the villa in Florence, Italy, that belongs to Gilbert Osmond. As with Gardencourt, James describes it thoroughly before Isabel visits, so that once again he is setting the scene into which the heroine will step and planting clues about what will befall her there. If Isabel could have read James's description of the villa, it might have dissuaded her in a way that all of her friends and relatives could not:

The villa was a long, rather blank-looking structure, with the far-projecting roof which Tuscany loves and which, on the hills that encircle Florence make so harmonious a rectangle with the straight, dark, definite cypresses that usually rise in groups of three or four beside it. The house had a front upon a little grassy, empty, rural piazza which occupied a part of the hilltop; and this front had a somewhat incommunicative character. It was the mask, not the face of the house. It had heavy lids, but no eyes. The windows seemed less to offer communication with the world than to defy the world to look in. They were massively cross-barred.

The house's occupant, of course, also wears a mask that prevents anyone from seeing what is really inside. Four years later, Isabel has become Gilbert's wife, and the couple are living in a house in Rome. James describes it in much more explicit and forceful terms than he does Gilbert's house in Florence, signifying that Isabel's entrapment and ruin are complete. She lives with Gilbert in a dark and massive structure a palace by Roman measure, but a dungeon to [an onlooker's] apprehensive mind a kind of domestic fortress, a pile which bore a stern old Roman name, which smelt of historic deeds, of crime and craft and violence which had a row of mutilated statues and dusty urns in the wide, nobly-arched loggia overhanging the damp court where a fountain gushed out of a mossy niche. Having fled a moat, Isabel has been imprisoned in a fortress.

Though Isabel's fate is sealed in this house, her story does not end there. When the dying Ralph calls her to come to Gardencourt to see him, she temporarily flees her Roman prison and returns to the peaceful sanctuary on the Thames. It is her true home — the place where she is loved and safe. Ralph knows this and invites her to live there permanently. Her former suitors, Caspar Goodwood and Lord Warburton, return to her there as well, each offering her a second chance at real love.

Isabel refuses them both, though, and returns to the grotesque husband in the grotesque house in Rome. But it is significant that readers do not actually see her there again. Isabel's last appearance is at green, friendly Gardencourt, which confirms what James has already conveyed about Isabel: that she will not allow the tragic mistake she has made to destroy her good nature. Though it may seem on the surface that Isabel has traded a dingy house in Albany for a fabulous dungeon in Rome, it is clear that she will find some way to transplant a measure of Gardencourt's brightness to her home and her life in Rome. It may be only a small measure, but it will be enough to sustain her, as a single candle flickering in a dark window can enliven an entire house on a foreboding night. "Having fled a moat, Isabel has been imprisoned in a fortress."

Chapter 10

Brief Summary

Context

Henry James was born in New York City in 1843 and was raised in Manhattan. James's father, a prominent intellectual and social theorist, traveled a great deal to Geneva, Paris, and London, so Henry and his brother, William, accompanied him and virtually grew up in those locations as well. As a child, James was shy, delicate, and had a difficult time mixing with other boys—his brother, who was much more active, called him a sissy. William James, of course, went on to become a great American philosopher, while Henry became one of the nation's preeminent novelists.

The James family moved to Boston when Henry was a teenager, and Henry briefly attended Harvard Law School. But he soon dropped out in order to concentrate on his writing. He found success early and often: William Dean Howells, the editor of the Atlantic Monthly, befriended the young writer, and by his mid- twenties James was considered one of the most skilled writers in America. In novels such as The American,The Europeans, and Daisy Miller, James perfected a unique brand of psychological realism, taking as his primary subject the social maneuverings of the upper classes, particularly the situation of Americans living in Europe. For James, America represented optimism and innocence, while Europe represented decadence and social sophistication; James himself moved to Europe early on in his professional career and was naturalized as a British citizen in 1915 to protest America's failure to enter World War I.

Throughout his career, James earned criticism for the slow pacing and uneventful plotting of his novels, as well as for his elliptical technique, in which many of a work's important scenes are not narrated, but only implied by later scenes. But as a stylist James earned consistent admiration; he is often considered to be a "writer's writer," and his prose is remarkable for its elegance of balance, clarity, and precision.

First written in the 1880s and extensively revised in 1908, The Portrait of a Lady is often considered to be James's greatest achievement. In it, he explored many of his most characteristic themes, including the conflict between American individualism and European social custom and the situation of Americans in Europe. It also includes many of his most memorable characters, including the lady of the novel's title, Isabel Archer, the indomitable Mrs. Touchett, the wise and funny Ralph Touchett, the fast-talking Henrietta Stackpole, and the sinister villains, Gilbert Osmond and Madame Merle.

While he was a dedicated observer of human beings in society, James was a socially distant man who formed few close friendships. He never married and openly claimed to practice celibacy. Perhaps this gave him time to write: in four decades of his writing career, he produced nearly 100 books, including such classics as The Golden Bowl,The Wings of the Dove, and the immortal ghost story "The Turn of the Screw." He died on February 28, 1916, shortly after receiving the English Order of Merit for his dedication to the British cause in World War I.

Plot Overview

Isabel Archer is a woman in her early twenties who comes from a genteel family in Albany, New York, in the late 1860s. Her mother died when she was a young girl, and her father raised her in a haphazard manner, allowing her to educate herself and encouraging her independence. As a result, the adult Isabel is widely read, imaginative, confident in her own mind, and slightly narcissistic; she has the reputation in Albany for being a formidable intellect, and as a result she often seems intimidating to men. She has had few suitors, but one of them is Caspar Goodwood, the powerful, charismatic son of a wealthy Boston mill owner. Isabel is drawn to Caspar, but her commitment to her independence makes her fear him as well, for she feels that to marry him would be to sacrifice her freedom. Shortly after Isabel's father dies, she receives a visit from her indomitable aunt, Mrs. Touchett, an American who lives in Europe. Mrs. Touchett offers to take Isabel on a trip to Europe, and Isabel eagerly agrees, telling Caspar that she cannot tell him whether she wishes to marry him until she has had at least a year to travel in Europe with her aunt. Isabel and Mrs. Touchett leave for England, where Mrs. Touchett's estranged husband is a powerful banker. Isabel makes a strong impression on everyone at Mr. Touchett's county manor of Gardencourt: her cousin Ralph, slowly dying of a lung disorder, becomes deeply devoted to her, and the Touchetts' aristocratic neighbor Lord Warburton falls in love with her. Warburton proposes, but Isabel declines; though she fears that she is passing up a great social opportunity by not marrying Warburton, she still believes that marriage would damage her treasured independence. As a result, she pledges to accomplish something wonderful with her life, something that will justify her decision to reject Warburton.

Isabel's friend Henrietta Stackpole, an American journalist, believes that Europe is changing Isabel, slowly eroding her American values and replacing them with romantic idealism. Henrietta comes to Gardencourt and secretly arranges for Caspar Goodwood to meet Isabel in London. Goodwood again presses Isabel to marry him; this time, she tells him she needs at least two years before she can answer him, and she promises him nothing. She is thrilled to have exercised her independence so forcefully. Mr. Touchett's health declines, and Ralph convinces him that when he dies, he should leave half his wealth to Isabel: this will protect her independence and ensure that she will never have to marry for money. Mr. Touchett agrees shortly before he dies. Isabel is left with a large fortune for the first time in her life. Her inheritance piques the interest of Madame Merle, Mrs. Touchett's polished, elegant friend; Madame Merle begins to lavish attention on Isabel, and the two women become close friends. Isabel travels to Florence with Mrs. Touchett and Madame Merle; Merle introduces Isabel to a man named Gilbert Osmond, a man of no social standing or wealth, but whom Merle describes as one of the finest gentlemen in Europe, wholly devoted to art and aesthetics. Osmond's daughter Pansy is being brought up in a convent; his wife is dead. In secret, Osmond and Merle have a mysterious relationship; Merle is attempting to manipulate Isabel into marrying Osmond so that he will have access to her fortune. Osmond is pleased to marry Isabel, not only for her money, but also because she makes a fine addition to his collection of art objects. Everyone in Isabel's world disapproves of Osmond, especially Ralph, but Isabel chooses to marry him anyway.

She has a child the year after they are married, but the boy dies six months after he is born. Three years into their marriage, Isabel and Osmond have come to despise one another; they live with Pansy in a palazzo in Rome, where Osmond treats Isabel as barely a member of the family: to him, she is a social hostess and a source of wealth, and he is annoyed by her independence and her insistence on having her own opinions. Isabel chafes against Osmond's arrogance, his selfishness, and his sinister desire to crush her individuality, but she does not consider leaving him. For all her commitment to her independence, Isabel is also committed to her social duty, and when she married Osmond, she did so with the intention of transforming herself into a good wife.

A young American art collector who lives in Paris, Edward Rosier, comes to Rome and falls in love with Pansy; Pansy returns his feelings. But Osmond is insistent that Pansy should marry a nobleman, and he says that Rosier is neither rich nor highborn enough. Matters grow complicated when Lord Warburton arrives on the scene and begins to court Pansy. Warburton is still in love with Isabel and wants to marry Pansy solely to get closer to her. But Osmond desperately wants to see Pansy married to Warburton. Isabel is torn about whether to fulfill her duty to her husband and help him arrange the match between Warburton and Pansy, or to fulfill the impulse of her conscience and discourage

Warburton, while helping Pansy find a way to marry Rosier. At a ball one night, Isabel shows Warburton the dejected-looking Rosier and explains that this is the man who is in love with Pansy. Guiltily, Warburton admits that he is not in love with Pansy; he quietly arranges to leave Rome. Osmond is furious with Isabel, convinced that she is plotting intentionally to humiliate him. Madame Merle is also furious with her, confronting her with shocking impropriety and demanding brazenly to know what she did to Warburton. Isabel has realized that there is something mysterious about Madame Merle's relationship with her husband; now, she suddenly realizes that Merle is his lover.

At this time, Ralph is rapidly deteriorating, and Isabel receives word that he is dying. She longs to travel to England to be with him, but Osmond forbids it. Now Isabel must struggle to decide whether to obey his command and remain true to her marriage vows or to disregard him and hurry to her cousin's bedside. Encouraging her to go, Osmond's sister, the Countess Gemini, tells her that there is still more to Merle and Osmond's relationship. Merle is Pansy's mother; Pansy was born out of wedlock. Osmond's wife died at about the same time, so Merle and Osmond spread the story that she died in childbirth. Pansy was placed in a convent to be raised, and she does not know that Merle is her real mother. Isabel is shocked and disgusted by her husband's atrocious behavior—she even feels sorry for Merle for falling under his spell—so she decides to follow her heart and travel to England.

After Ralph's death, Isabel struggles to decide whether to return to her husband or not. She promised Pansy that she would return to Rome, and her commitment to social propriety impels her to go back and honor her marriage. But her independent spirit urges her to flee from Osmond and find happiness elsewhere. Caspar Goodwood appears at the funeral, and afterwards, he asks Isabel to run away with him and forget about her husband. The next day, unable to find her, Goodwood asks Henrietta where she has gone. Henrietta quietly tells him that Isabel has returned to Rome, unable to break away from her marriage to Gilbert Osmond.

Chapter 11

Chapterwise Summary and Analysis

Chapters 1–3

Summary

It is teatime at Gardencourt, an old English country manor built during the reign of Edward VI and now owned by an old American banker. The old man now sits on the lawn holding a large teacup; his sickly son and a young Englishman stroll nearby, stopping occasionally to make sure that he is comfortable. The old man tells them lightly that he has always been comfortable. The young Englishman, Lord Warburton, drolly replies that comfort is boring. The old man's son, Ralph, counters by saying that Lord Warburton only pretends to be bored by everything. Lord Warburton replies that the old man's son always seems cynical, but that he is really a fairly cheerful person. The old man says that Warburton would find life more interesting if he found himself an interesting woman to marry; the young men politely keep quiet about the fact that the old man's own marriage is unhappy. Lord Warburton wonders what sort of woman he might find "interesting."

The old man says that his wife, Mrs. Touchett, will soon be returning from her visit to America and that she plans to bring their niece with her for a stay in England. He jokingly tells Warburton not to fall in love with his niece. Mr. Touchett and Ralph joke about the telegram they received from Mrs.

Touchett informing them of her intention to bring this niece back to England with her. The telegram is nearly incomprehensible ("sister's girl, died last year, go to Europe"), but it mentions that the girl is "quite independent." Mr. Touchett says that American girls today are all engaged but that they continue to behave however they like regardless. He jokes again that Warburton must not fall in love with his niece.

Ralph strolls away from his father and Lord Warburton. He hears his dog barking near the door of the house and sees that a young woman has just emerged; she picks up the eager little dog, and Ralph notices that she is beautiful. He approaches her, and she introduces herself as his cousin Isabel, saying that she has just arrived with his mother. She compliments the house, and when Ralph points out his father and Lord Warburton on the lawn, she happily declares that having a real lord about the place makes it seem just like a novel.

Ralph introduces this strange young girl to his father, who kisses her and asks where his wife has gone. Isabel says that Mrs. Touchett has retired to her room; Mr. Touchett observes wryly that they will not see her for a week. But Isabel predicts that she will make an appearance at dinner. Looking about her, Isabel says that the old manor is the most beautiful thing that she has ever seen. Lord Warburton offers to show her his own Tudor manor, and he and Mr. Touchett joke with one another about who has the better house. Ralph asks Isabel if she likes dogs and offers to give her his own dog. She agrees to keep it while she is at the house.

Ralph asks how long she will stay, and she says that Mrs. Touchett will have to decide that, as they are to travel to Florence after leaving England. Ralph notes that Isabel does not seem like the kind of woman who lets people decide things for her. Isabel agrees that she is very independent. He asks why they have never met, and she says that after her mother died, her father had a quarrel with Mrs. Touchett. Mr. Touchett asks Isabel how his wife is—she has been traveling in America for a long time. Isabel begins to tell him, and Warburton says quietly to Ralph that he has found his idea of a very interesting woman, and it is Isabel. Mrs. Touchett has been traveling in America for a year, and has only stopped in England on her way home to Florence—she has been separated from Mr. Touchett since the first year of their marriage, though she spends one month with him each year. When Mrs. Touchett went to visit Isabel, she found her reading in the library of her grandmother's house, which she had been given unrestricted access to as a young girl and which formed the basis of her education. Mrs. Touchett invited Isabel to come to Florence, and Isabel agreed, though she warned her aunt that she was not always obedient.

Analysis

The opening sentence of Portrait of a Lady may not be the most exciting in all of literature ("Under certain circumstances there are few hours in life more agreeable than the hour dedicated to the ceremony known as afternoon tea"), but the novel's opening perfectly prepares the reader for the development of the novel's main themes.

The main theme of Portrait of a Lady is the conflict between individualism (represented here by Isabel Archer's "independence") and social custom. The novel begins with the ultimate social custom, the English tea ceremony, set amid a genteel landscape populated by good-natured, affectionate members of the high upper classes. This well-ordered and familiar scene, which has obviously been acted out by the three men involved a hundred times before, is then disturbed by the appearance of Isabel, who arrives amid a chaos of barking dogs and ruffled expectations. At once, Isabel is at odds with the calm traditions of social convention, and the novel's thematic exploration is off to a strong start.

To say that Isabel's individualism is at odds with social convention is not to say that she is at odds with the conventional people around her; on the contrary, all of the men on the lawn seem very taken with her, especially Ralph, who impulsively gives her his dog, and Lord Warburton, who declares that she is his idea of an "interesting woman." It is important to note that we do not learn a great deal about Isabel herself in this section, virtually nothing of her past, and very little of her personality beyond what we see through the eyes of the other characters. All we are told is that she is an "independent woman," a very vague description that nevertheless piques the interest of Lord Warburton and the Touchetts—in the late 1860s in upper-class English country houses, we can infer, independent women of any sort are in very short supply.

Throughout Portrait of a Lady, James will alternate between showing us Isabel's life from Isabel's perspective and showing it through the perspective of peripheral characters such as Ralph. The use of peripheral points of view casts a great deal of light on Isabel's actions—here, for instance, James uses Ralph's perspective to show us what kind of impression Isabel makes on those around her, giving us the sense that she is different and special, a sense that would have been difficult to impart had we viewed the same scene through Isabel's eyes.

It is also important to note that Portrait of a Lady is set almost entirely among a group of Americans who live in Europe, and the novel's most significant secondary theme is the contrast between the idea of Europe and the idea of America, and how those ideas are negotiated in the minds of the expatriated Americans. In a very general sense, James uses the idea of America to represent innocence, individualism, optimism, and action, while Europe tends to represent sophistication, social convention, decadence, and tradition.

In these early chapters, we are given very little sense of those distinctions; here, Europe is simply a familiar home to the American Touchetts, and an exciting place to visit for Isabel Archer. But as the novel progresses, and Isabel travels deeper into continental Europe, the contrasts will be made very clear, and Gardencourt will emerge as a kind of ideal combining the best of Europe with the best of America.

Chapters 4–7

Summary

Of Isabel's three sisters, she was always considered the

intellectual. Edith was the prettiest, and Lillian was the most sensible. Lillian is now married to a lawyer in New York and considers it her duty to look after Isabel. Her husband, Edmund, disapproves of Isabel—when Lillian says that her trip to Europe will give her the chance to develop, Edmund replies that she is already too original and should stop developing at once.

The night before leaving for Europe, Isabel sits in her room thinking about her life; she has felt restless for a long time and longs for a change of scene. This longing has grown increasingly acute since she learned that she would be traveling to Europe. Isabel thinks that she has been lucky in life: she has never experienced anything unpleasant and wonders whether misfortune would be interesting. She remembers her father, whom she loved very dearly. Other people considered her father's handling of his daughters' education to be scandalous, but Isabel is fiercely proud of her independent mind. She thinks about marriage, and reflects that she has few suitors because she is known to spend so much time reading; this frightens many men away. A maid enters to announce the arrival of Caspar Goodwood, Isabel's favorite suitor. Isabel goes down to talk to him, and he soon leaves the house, disappointed.

Ralph Touchett goes to see his mother in her room. Ralph first came to England as a boy, when his father moved there to work in a bank. His father decided to remain in England, but he sent Ralph to be educated in America. After Harvard, Ralph attended Oxford so that he would learn how to be English enough to take over Mr. Touchett's bank. Ralph would have done anything his father asked—he considered his father to be his best friend and admired him very much. Ralph spent two years traveling after Oxford and then began work in the bank. But a worsening lung condition soon forced him to give up work and live as an invalid. Ralph, who has a great appreciation for life, hates his fragility—he says that it is like reading a bad translation of a good book, when he had hoped to master the language. Ralph is quite taken with his cousin Isabel and asks his mother where she plans to take her for her

European tour. Mrs. Touchett says that Isabel will decide for herself but that she does hope to take her to Paris for a wardrobe and eventually to Florence for the autumn. Mrs. Touchett says that she and Isabel both speak their minds, which makes them very compatible. The only problem is that Isabel insists on paying her own way through Europe—Isabel does not know anything about money and cannot afford to pay her own way, so Mrs. Touchett is forced to fool her into thinking that she is doing so, when in fact Mrs. Touchett is funding most of the trip. Ralph wonders what Isabel excels at, and Mrs. Touchett says that Warburton seems to think it is flirting. She says that Warburton will never understand the girl. Ralph asks his mother if she plans to find a husband for Isabel, but Mrs. Touchett denies it.

After dinner that night, Ralph shows Isabel his paintings—he has a passion for art—and notes that she has a good eye. She asks him to show her the manor's ghost, but Ralph says that only people who have suffered can see it. He says that he has seen the ghost, but that Isabel is too young and innocent to see it. Isabel replies that she is not afraid of suffering.

Isabel spends a great deal of time thinking about herself and generally accepts the idea that she is smarter than everyone around her. She has a powerful self- assurance and an extraordinary faith in her own goodness. She often wishes for hardship, so that she could demonstrate her ability to overcome it without losing her moral essence. Isabel often compares herself to her friend Henrietta Stackpole, who is even more independent than Isabel—she is a journalist for the New York Interviewer and professes not to believe in marriage. Isabel loves her time in England. She often visits with Mr. Touchett on the lawn, arguing about the merits of the English—from her reading of novels, Isabel asserts that they are terribly conventional and obsessed with class, but Mr. Touchett replies that being an American in England means that one does not have any particular class affiliation.

Isabel also spends a great deal of time talking to Ralph about English politics. Isabel is very critical of England, but she is fiercely defensive of America. She wonders about Ralph—she realizes that he uses his quick wit to turn everything into a joke while hiding his deeper thoughts and feelings. For his part, Ralph thinks of Isabel constantly and even wonders if he is in love with her. He decides that he is not, thinking that she is like a beautiful building that he can look at but never enter. But he admires her personality: while most women allow men to define their lives, Isabel has her own ideas and plans.

Lord Warburton visits one day; Isabel finds that she is very fond of him, thinking that he seems like the romantic hero of a story. After dinner, the young people sit and talk with Mrs. Touchett, who at last declares to Isabel that they should go to bed. Isabel says that she wishes to stay downstairs and talk to Ralph and Warburton. Mrs. Touchett insists that it is not proper for a young woman to sit alone with young men late at night. Isabel submits and goes upstairs with her aunt. She tells her that she did not know her behavior was improper and says that she would like Mrs. Touchett to tell her whenever her behavior violates social convention. If she knows what the social conventions are, she says, she will be able to tell whether she wishes to follow them or not.

Analysis

The flashback that opens Chapter 4 is the first time in the novel that Isabel's perspective becomes the center of the novel. Isabel's long rumination about her life and her desire to travel seems fairly natural—these are the things an intelligent girl in her situation would be likely to consider before leaving on a long voyage to Europe—but James also very cleverly uses it to bring out some of the elements of Isabel's character that will define her conflict in Europe later in the novel. He shows, for instance, that Isabel has a very high opinion of her own moral stature and shows her longing for hardship so that she might prove to herself that she could suffer and still remain a good person. We also see Isabel's uncertainty about marriage and about her suitor, Caspar Goodwood, a very stiff but very imposing figure whose apparent power Isabel finds threatening.

Isabel's conversation with Caspar is not recorded in the book, but it is clear to the reader that he has asked her to marry him and that she has rejected him. James uses this technique of skipping over important incidents throughout the novel; many of the most crucial events in the plot are only implied or hinted at in the aftermath of their occurrence. In a narrative, this technique is known as ellipses—literally, the incident that is left out is like a "…" in the middle of a sentence. James is a master of elliptical narrative, and will employ it throughout the book.

The narration of Ralph's personal history in Chapter 5 brings us closer to his character, which is one of the most important in the novel. As Lord Warburton noted in the opening scene of the book, Ralph often seems to be skeptical or cynical, and his quick wit causes him to make a joke out of everything, but he is also a deeply loving and well-adjusted young man who forms, in many ways, the moral center of the novel. Where other characters often complain about boredom and suffering, Ralph is in the ultimate position of boredom and suffering—his lung illness essentially forces him to sit on the sidelines of life and watch those around him have experiences he will never have. But instead of complaining, Ralph loves life, and when he meets Isabel, he seems to decide to live vicariously through her. Throughout the book, Ralph will be fascinated by every choice Isabel makes, and he will never pressure her, even though, in the overall scheme of the book, his opinions about her actions and about other people are always right.

Isabel and Ralph develop a very close relationship, which begins in this section as they walk through the portrait gallery and talk about politics and art. Though Isabel is educated and intelligent, she also has a deep-seated, naïve romanticism in her character, which we first saw when she first arrived at Gardencourt and thought that it was like "a novel." In this section, her romantic streak leads to a moment of foreshadowing, as Isabel asks Ralph to show her the ghost of Gardencourt—in every novel, she says, old English manors always have a ghost. Ralph tells her that one must suffer before one can see Gardencourt's ghost and that Isabel has never suffered. At the very end of the novel, Isabel will return to Gardencourt for Ralph's death, and she will see the ghost.

The main thematic conflict of the novel, the struggle between social convention and independence in the life of Isabel Archer, comes to a miniature climax in Chapter 7, when Isabel and Mrs. Touchett argue about whether Isabel should stay up talking to Ralph and Warburton without a chaperone. Isabel rebelliously wants to disregard custom and stay downstairs, but to Ralph's surprise, she docilely obeys Mrs. Touchett.

The implication is that for all that Isabel considers herself independent and seems independent to those around her, she also has a desire to fit in and will not routinely thwart social convention even when it grates her. In fact, Mrs. Touchett, who enforces social convention in this scene, is in many ways far more independent and rebellious than Isabel—after all, she is separated from her husband and lives alone in Florence, making her own decisions and forming her own opinions. Isabel is a charismatic and individualistic character, but she will never really achieve this level of autonomy.

Chapters 8–11

Summary

Lord Warburton is quite taken with Isabel, and he convinces Mrs. Touchett to grant her permission for the young woman to pay a visit to Lockleigh, his manor house. Here, he tells Isabel something of his family history, and they discuss English and American politics. Isabel realizes that Warburton does not think much of her understanding of political situations, but she is impressed nevertheless with his commitment to social progress and reform, unusual for a British nobleman. When she asks Ralph about him later, he says that he feels sorry for him, observing that Warburton likes being an aristocrat but disapproves of the idea of aristocracy. Mr. Touchett thinks much the same thing: like the other liberals in the House of Lords, he says, Warburton wants to change society without losing his own position in it. In Mr. Touchett's opinion, that sort of politics is merely a luxury with which the wealthy amuse themselves. He advises Isabel not to fall in love with Warburton, joking that the lord has a craving to become a martyr. Isabel replies that she would never make anyone a martyr, and Touchett says that he hopes she will never become one, either.

Lord Warburton's two unmarried sisters, the Misses Molyneux, pay a call on Isabel at Gardencourt. Though they are somewhat simple, leading a life of thoughtless luxury as daughters of the aristocracy, Isabel finds them sweet and even envies their uncomplicated lives. Ralph teases her for liking them so much, saying that Isabel could never be happy in such a routine existence. Isabel visits the young women at Lockleigh and tries to discuss politics and other serious subjects to learn more about them; she discovers that they tend to echo their brother's ideas, telling her sincerely that their family has been liberal for years.

She goes for a walk with Lord Warburton along the grounds of Locksleigh; here, he asks her if he might come to visit her more often. Isabel reminds him that the matter is really up to her aunt but says that she would like to get to know him better. He tells her that she has "charmed" him; Isabel notices that his tone is very serious, even romantic, and she reminds him lightly that she intends to leave soon to travel through Europe with Mrs. Touchett. Dispirited, Warburton blurts out that he thinks Isabel spends too much time judging people, saying that he always feels scrutinized by her. Isabel is shocked by his emotional intensity and slightly frightened by it; when he says that he will come to see her next week, she replies coldly, "Just as you wish."

Isabel receives a note from Henrietta Stackpole, telling her that she has arrived in England and would like to see her and to talk to her about the English aristocracy, which she is covering for the Interviewer. Thinking that Henrietta's modern attitudes might not mesh well with the more traditional life at Gardencourt, Isabel feels slightly uneasy about the prospect of inviting her there, but nevertheless, she speaks to Mr.

Touchett and obtains his permission for Henrietta to visit. Ralph takes her to the train station to wait for Henrietta and asks what she is like. Isabel tells him that she is unconcerned with the opinions of men; Ralph assumes that she will be ugly. But when she steps off the train, Ralph is surprised to see that Henrietta is actually quite attractive. Henrietta surprises Ralph by asking extremely pointed questions, wondering whether he considers himself English or American. Ralph laughingly evades her examination.

After she has been in England for some time, Henrietta begins an article about life at Gardencourt. But Isabel asks her to keep the Touchetts out of her writing, saying that Henrietta should develop a stronger sense of privacy. She says that Henrietta should be modest about other people as well as about herself; Henrietta simply writes this down as a quote to include in an article. Henrietta feels slightly uneasy about Ralph; she is put off by his sickliness and his idle existence. She tells him pointedly that he should marry, and he, misunderstanding, thinks that she means he should marry her. When he declines, Henrietta storms away angrily. Isabel reveals to Ralph that Henrietta does not mean to be offensive; she simply asks personal questions without personally involving herself in the answer. Ralph and Isabel agree that Henrietta embodies the democratic attitude of America.

From that point on, Ralph cautiously reminds himself not to misunderstand Henrietta's interest in him. Mrs. Touchett, on the other hand, finds her extremely dull and annoying; the two women argue about hotels and servants, with Mrs. Touchett criticizing American attitudes and Henrietta defending them. Henrietta, who seems to disapprove of the Touchetts and England generally, criticizes Isabel for having been taken in by the conservative English environment. She chastises Isabel for not even having asked about Caspar Goodwood. Henrietta shocks Isabel by saying that Caspar Goodwood traveled to England on the same ship as Henrietta and that he talked incessantly about Isabel the entire time. Eventually, Isabel receives a letter from Caspar, telling her that he has traveled to England to see her and that he hopes she will change her mind about her earlier rejection of him. Isabel hears footsteps as she finishes the letter; she looks up and sees Lord Warburton coming toward her.

Analysis

The first part of this section focuses on Isabel's developing relationship with Lord Warburton, the aristocratic lord who uses his power to advocate anti- aristocratic political reform. Warburton's political leanings lead to one of the novel's brief, secondary explorations of the theme of social class, as Warburton advocates class equality, and the irascible Mr. Touchett declares that Warburton's radical stance is really just a kind of pleasing vanity—after all, he still goes home to Lockleigh every night.

Isabel has speculated that there must be "fifty" different social classes in England; Mr. Touchett replies that being an American in Europe means that one is free from the constraints of social class. While this may seem ironic coming from a man who lives in a mansion and has essentially limitless wealth, it is an important clue to understanding how James's europeanized Americans think of themselves—along with their displacement comes a greater amount of mobility and liberty. At least Isabel, who is in love with the idea of mobility and liberty, certainly hopes so.

Lockleigh provides Isabel with her first glimpse of an upper-class European existence, and though she is frightened by Warburton's obvious romantic attraction to her (Isabel is always frightened by romance, since its end result—marriage—would curtail her independence), she is strangely attracted to the sedate and conventional life at the manor house. Warburton's sisters, the Misses Molyneux, are not even individual enough to obtain first names in the novel; they are simply the height of conformity and convention, seeming placid, submissive, and thoughtless—exactly the opposite of what Isabel seems to want out of life. And yet Isabel likes them and even envies their lives.

While she is independent in her own mind, something in Isabel's character seems to crave stability, safety, and order—

after all, the source of her independence is her disorganized childhood, when she was given the run of her father's library but was largely neglected by any authority figure. This may have been a mixed blessing for Isabel: it made her intellectually independent, but also made her yearn to be cared for and protected. In a sense, the conflict Isabel experiences between independence and social convention is really an outward manifestation of this inner conflict between the freedom of self-confidence and the desire for security. Social independence is a manifestation of Isabel's self-confidence, but her general tendency to accept social convention is a manifestation of her desire for security.

The second half of this section is largely made up of humorous scenes involving Henrietta Stackpole, who seems to represent the conservative Henry James's idea of a feminist. Henrietta is used broadly in the novel to represent the spirit of American liberty and democratic optimism—she is pugnacious, entirely without subtlety, and determined to get things done and make a mark on the world. Henrietta and Caspar Goodwood are the most important symbols of America in the novel, and they each tend to bring out the European qualities of those around them. Compared to Henrietta, for instance, Isabel often seems impractical, romantic, and sensual, which are important qualities in her personality that she rarely considers as important. As in the case of Ralph, Henrietta is an important peripheral character who is used to draw out a side of Isabel that we might otherwise miss.

Chapters 12–15

Summary

Lord Warburton approaches, and Isabel can tell at once that he has come to declare his feelings for her. She is deeply confused by this, as she has always considered men solely for their moral qualities and never for their positions of power and influence; she has never met a man as aristocratic as Warburton and worries that if she decides to reject him, she will be turning away a great social opportunity. Warburton asks her to stroll with him, and he quickly declares that he has fallen in love with her; he asks her to marry him. Isabel is deeply moved by his obvious sincerity, but she asks for some time before she gives him an answer. She feels that they do not know each other well and tells Warburton that she has not decided whether or not she ever wants to marry. Warburton leaves, and Isabel swiftly realizes that she does not want to marry him. She hopes she will be able to convince him that the marriage would be a bad idea, because she does not want to hurt him. She worries again that she is giving up a great opportunity by refusing the proposal and tells herself that she will have to do great things with her life to justify her decision. As she goes back into the house, Isabel feels strangely frightened of her own mind.

Isabel talks to Mr. Touchett about her decision; surprisingly, he has known of Warburton's intentions for three days, since he received a long letter from the lord asking his permission to marry Isabel. Isabel thinks about her other suitor, Caspar Goodwood; Goodwood is the son of a Boston cotton mill owner, who invented a device to improve the operation of the mill. He is a powerful person and a forceful manager of the mill, but he is possessive about Isabel and makes her feel confined. Isabel decides not to respond to Goodwood's letter; instead, she writes to Warburton, rejecting his proposal.

Henrietta tells Ralph that she is worried about the ways in which Isabel has changed since she came to Europe; Henrietta hopes that Isabel will marry Caspar Goodwood to prove her commitment to her old American attitudes. Complying with Henrietta's wishes, Ralph invites Goodwood to Gardencourt, but Goodwood declines the invitation. Henrietta decides to take Isabel on an excursion to London; when Ralph hears about this plan, he offers to go with them, implying that it would not be suitable for two women to take a trip to London unaccompanied by a man.

Lord Warburton comes to visit a few days later, accompanied by the elder Miss Molyneux. Isabel is again struck with the quiet contentment and simplicity with which Miss Molyneux goes about her life. After dinner, Isabel walks with Lord Warburton in the picture gallery. He is desperate to learn why she has rejected his proposal, and she replies that she cannot tell him until she can back up her thinking with evidence. He presses her, and eventually she tells him that she feels that to marry him would be to turn away from life and that she is committed to facing life directly. Henrietta, Ralph, and Miss Molyneux enter the gallery; Henrietta is badgering Miss Molyneux for information about the life of an aristocrat, just as she badgered Lord Warburton all through dinner. Henrietta wrangles an invitation to Lockleigh from Warburton.

That night, Mrs. Touchett comes to Isabel's room and asks her why she did not tell her about Warburton's proposal. Isabel replies that Mr. Touchett is better acquainted with Warburton. Mrs. Touchett says that she knows Isabel better, but Isabel says lightly that she is not sure. Mrs. Touchett later tells Isabel that she would have liked Isabel to marry Warburton, but when Isabel declares that she does not love him, Mrs. Touchett agrees that she did the right thing.

Isabel, Henrietta, and Ralph leave for a long trip to London, where Ralph finds Isabel more appealing than ever; she is bright and inquisitive and fascinated by everything she sees. One day, the three young people dine at the Touchetts' London home with Mr. Bantling, a friend of Ralph's. Mr. Bantling is taken with Henrietta and promises to obtain an invitation for her to visit the home of his sister, the Lady Pensil. Henrietta leaves to meet two of her friends from America, and Mr. Bantling decides to escort her.

Alone in the garden, Ralph and Isabel talk about Lord Warburton, whom Ralph praises highly. He understands that Isabel has rejected Lord Warburton out of a desire to remain free and independent. He says that he will be fascinated to watch Isabel's life unfold, because it is so surprising that a young woman would have thought her life more interesting without Lord Warburton in it. Isabel says that she merely wants to observe life. She takes her leave; Ralph wants to escort her back to the hotel room she shares with Henrietta, but Isabel says that he is clearly too exhausted. As Ralph helps her into her carriage, he thinks that his life is often troubled by people forgetting that he is an invalid but that it is much worse when people remember it.

Analysis

Twelve chapters into the novel, Isabel has already faced two marriage proposals, one from the quintessentially American Caspar Goodwood, and one from the quintessentially English Lord Warburton. As Henrietta points out to Ralph, Isabel's romantic crisis with Warburton signifies the extent to which her American ideas and values have been affected by her time in Europe.

For all her life, Isabel has thought of men not as social opportunities, but as moral creatures, whom she admired or disliked based strictly on their personal qualities. With Lord Warburton, however, after having been attracted by the lives of the Misses Molyneux, Isabel suddenly has a powerful awareness that to marry into the English nobility would represent an extraordinary social opportunity. Of course Isabel eventually rejects this thought and then rejects Lord Warburton, but she is surprised that she has it in the first place—clearly, as Henrietta says, Europe has begun to change her. Henrietta's solution to this problem is that Isabel should marry Caspar Goodwood, the symbol of the American character. For all her commitment to independence, Isabel cannot seem to escape the tendency of those around her to conceive of her destiny in terms of marriage and romance: who Isabel is, even to the fiercely democratic Henrietta, is to some extent a question to be answered based on whom she chooses to marry. This trend is further exemplified by Mr. Touchett, who is glad that Isabel did not marry Warburton, and Mrs. Touchett, who wishes that she had decided to marry him.

Only Ralph, the moral center of Portrait to a Lady, can see beyond this pitfall and conceive of a truly independent life for Isabel, where she will be able to think, act, and be exactly as she pleases. Ralph conveys all this to Isabel in their conversation at the end of Chapter 15, by which time another development should be obvious to the reader: though he denies it even to himself, Ralph is clearly in love with Isabel.

Chapters 16–19

Summary

Isabel's decision to forbid Ralph from accompanying her to the hotel was not due to a desire to humiliate him, but rather to a realization that she has been taxing his strength by taking up so much of his time since they left for London. She also realizes that she has had very little time to herself, and she looks forward to an evening alone. Shortly after she reaches her room, however, a servant informs her that Caspar Goodwood is waiting for her downstairs. Isabel is surprised and annoyed to realize that Henrietta has set her up to be alone with Caspar.

In the parlor, Caspar says that even though Isabel has asked him to spend a year apart from her, he is too miserable without her to stay away. As always, Isabel is struck by his intimidating physical presence and his aggressive demeanor. She tells him resolutely that she cannot marry him now, that she has no place for him in her life now, and that she will need at least two years to travel in Europe before she will know whether she could even consider marriage. She insists on preserving her independence, and even though Caspar says he will not threaten her independence—he even says that a married woman is more independent than a sheltered girl—she cannot quite believe him. Caspar is visibly hurt and worries that Isabel will fall in love with another man. But he reluctantly agrees to give her two years, even though she says that she does not promise to marry him even then. Caspar strides away; Isabel goes upstairs, collapses next to her bed, and buries her face in her hands.

Isabel is overcome with a curious emotion: she is nearly ecstatic with excitement at having demonstrated her independence by warding off Caspar. She thinks that it is a visible sign of her commitment to her independence. When Henrietta returns, Isabel confronts her and says that she was wrong to arrange the meeting with Caspar. Henrietta disregards Isabel's anger, saying that Isabel is acting ridiculous by allowing her romantic notions of Europe to make her forget her practical American values—she says that if Isabel marries one of her European acquaintances, Henrietta will cease to be her friend. But Henrietta says that she was motivated to arrange the meeting with Caspar by her love for Isabel.

The next morning, Henrietta says that she plans to stay in London and wait for her invitation to Lady Pensil's house—she hopes to use her experience there to gain more insight on the English aristocracy, so that her articles will be a great success in America. Ralph arrives and tells Isabel that Mr. Touchett's health is in decline. He and Isabel agree to visit a great doctor named Sir Matthew Hope that afternoon. While he waits for Isabel before their visit, Ralph talks to Henrietta, who admits to him that she arranged for Caspar to show up at the hotel without Isabel's knowledge. She says that if she really believed that Isabel would never marry Caspar, she would break off their friendship.

Isabel and Ralph arrange for Matthew Hope to go to Gardencourt and then hastily return there themselves. In the parlor, Isabel finds a middle-aged woman playing piano very beautifully. This is Madame Merle, an acquaintance of Mrs. Touchett; she seems very charming and charismatic. Isabel has tea with Madame Merle and Mrs. Touchett and learns that Madame Merle is an American, whose father was a naval officer in Europe. Matthew Hope arrives, and Mrs. Touchett excuses herself to speak to him. The news about Mr. Touchett's health is good, and Ralph is cheered enough to talk to Isabel about Madame Merle, whom he describes as a very clever, accomplished, and popular woman. He also reveals that Madame Merle's husband has been dead for many years and that she has no children.

Despite the promising news about his health, Mr. Touchett declines rapidly, and, fearing that he will soon die, asks to speak to Ralph. Mr. Touchett tells Ralph that he wants Ralph to find more direction in his life and urges him to marry Isabel. Ralph acknowledges that if he were not ill, he would be in love with Isabel but says that he could never marry her as things are. Instead, he urges his father to divide his inheritance equally with Isabel, leaving her with the vast fortune of sixty thousand pounds. This notion perplexes Mr. Touchett, who cannot fathom why Ralph would want to give up half his fortune. Ralph explains that Isabel does not understand that she does not have very much money, and he wants to protect her and to enable her to make her own life without ever having to marry for money. Mr. Touchett agrees.

Over the coming days, Isabel grows quite close to Madame Merle, who seems to be almost perfect to her—she is graceful, talented, and interesting, and her only fault seems to be that she is so much a social being that she seems to have no inner self. Madame Merle tells Isabel that Americans who live in Europe are displaced—she compares Ralph, whose illness essentially functions as a career and a lifestyle, with a man she knows in Florence, Gilbert Osmond. Osmond, she says, devotes his life to painting and raising his daughter. Isabel asks why Madame Merle seems to dislike Ralph, but Madame Merle replies that Ralph is the one to dislike her—she herself feels nothing about Ralph. Madame Merle confides in Isabel that she feels as though her life has been a failure, because she has no family and no fortune. She says that a person is defined by what she possesses. Isabel disagrees, but when Madame Merle departs Gardencourt, she and Isabel bid farewell as close friends.

Isabel continues corresponding with Henrietta, whose promised invitation to Lady Pensil's manor never materializes. Henrietta now hopes to travel to Paris with Mr. Bantling. Not long after Madame Merle leaves, Isabel is reading in the library, when Ralph enters with an unhappy piece of news: Mr. Touchett has died.

Analysis

This section involves three important narrative events: Isabel's second rejection of Caspar Goodwood, the introduction of Madame Merle, and the death of Mr. Touchett, which unexpectedly brings Isabel a fortune. The scene with Caspar is interesting for two reasons. First, it reveals what happened in the conversation Isabel had with Caspar before she left for Europe, which James chose to skip over in the opening chapters of the book. Isabel asked Caspar to give her a year in Europe before deciding whether or not to marry him. Now, though it has not been a year since Isabel left Albany, Caspar is impatient for an answer and desperate to be with her. As intimidatingly masculine as Isabel seems to find Caspar, he is also extremely devoted to her and seems to need her presence in order to be happy. Ironically, his rash decision to follow her to Europe rather than waiting a year to see her is rewarded by her forcing him to agree to wait two years before she will even consider the question of whether or not to marry him.

The second interesting feature of the Caspar scene in Chapter 16 is that it provides Isabel another opportunity to defend her independence from a suitor's desire to marry her. She has already rejected Caspar once and then rejected Lord Warburton, but where those past experiences left her feeling confused or sad, this one leaves her feeling exultant and powerful, as though a weight has been lifted from her shoulders. Though Isabel is never entirely clear about what "independence" means to her exactly, clearly it implies a kind of personal autonomy that would be incompatible with a conventional marriage, in which the wife is expected to be submissive to her husband. By warding off three successive proposals, Isabel has demonstrated her commitment to her personal autonomy, even if she has only a vague idea of what she wants to do with her life.

Madame Merle will soon become an important and sinister character in Portrait of a Lady, and will play an enormous role in Isabel's life by manipulating her into marrying Gilbert Osmond and thereby losing her treasured independence. But in this section, Madame Merle is more an enigma than a villain. Isabel likes her very much, and the redoubtable Mrs. Touchett thinks the world of her. But Ralph, whose opinions the reader instinctively values, does not like her, and this makes it natural to look for her flaws. If the novel explores the opposition between personal independence and social propriety, Madame Merle seems to exist uneasily between the two polarities.

On the one hand, she is an independent woman,

accomplished in every grace and extremely popular; she clearly makes her own decisions. But on the other hand, her commitment to popularity means that she seems to observe every social convention; Isabel thinks that she even seems to lack an inner self. In this regard, Merle is Isabel's first introduction to continental Europe—throughout the novel, America represents individualism, Europe represents social convention, and England seems halfway in between. Isabel has moved from America to England, and now has a taste of what she will find in Europe. In a sense, at this stage of the novel, Madame Merle represents the complete sacrifice of individualism to society: no one has taken her independence from her, but she has chosen not to exercise it in any meaningful way. Though Isabel is very attached to her by the time she leaves Gardencourt, the reader rightly looks upon their new friendship with a sense of suspicion and disapproval.

The death of the admirable Mr. Touchett changes Isabel's life by bringing her a vast fortune. True to his desire to live vicariously through Isabel, Ralph has arranged with his father to split the money that would have otherwise all gone to Ralph between Ralph and Isabel. At this stage of the novel, this would appear to be a wonderful development for Isabel: as Ralph observes, it will preserve her independence and protect her from having to marry for money. She will be able to lead her own life, which is what Ralph most dearly wants her to do.

As the book progresses, however, the consequences of Isabel's inheritance become worse and worse, and Ralph's decision becomes more and more tragically ironic. In effect, it is Ralph's desire for Isabel to be independent that leads to Isabel's inheriting a fortune, and Isabel's wealth that prompts Madame Merle to scheme to marry Isabel to Gilbert Osmond, ruining any hope of independence that Isabel might have had.

Chapters 20–24

Summary

Not long after Mr. Touchett's death, Madame Merle arrives at the Touchetts' London home and discovers that the family is preparing to sell it. Mrs. Touchett tells Madame Merle how happy she is that her husband has left her financially secure; Merle is extremely jealous, though she keeps her feelings guarded. When she learns that Isabel has also inherited a fortune, she says that Isabel is very clever and hurries in to see her. Since Mr. Touchett's death, Isabel has spent a great deal of time thinking about her wealth and what it means; she has decided to be grateful for the freedom her money will afford her.

Isabel soon travels to Paris with Mrs. Touchett, but she finds her aunt's American friends there to be depressingly American. She encounters Henrietta, who is traveling happily with Mr. Bantling. Henrietta says that she disapproves of Isabel's new fortune—she thinks that it will allow Isabel to continue living in a world of dreams and ideals. Henrietta insists that Isabel should worry less about pleasing others and concentrate on facing hard truths about the world.

Mrs. Touchett offers Isabel the choice about whether to travel with her to Italy for the autumn, saying that, now that Isabel is rich, she may do as she pleases. Isabel, out of respect for social conventions, chooses to go to Italy with her aunt. On the way to Florence, they stop in San Remo, where Ralph is staying. Isabel and Ralph discuss her new fortune; Ralph admits that he knew about his father's decision to change his will before he died. Isabel worries that Henrietta is right and that the fortune will be bad for her. Ralph encourages her to embrace the things that happen to her and enjoy her new wealth. His advice reassures Isabel, and she begins to look forward to her trip to Italy, which seems like a great adventure. Thinking of Warburton and Caspar, she wonders if either of them will marry; she thinks that she would feel hurt if Caspar fell in love with another woman but that she would be glad if Warburton did.

Six months after Mr. Touchett's death, Gilbert Osmond meets his daughter Pansy and a group of nuns at his home near Florence; he discusses with the nuns the possibility that he might take Pansy away from their convent and bring her to live with him. He is joined by Madame Merle, who tells him about a beautiful twenty-three-year-old girl named Isabel Archer, who has inherited half the Touchett fortune. She promises to bring Isabel into Gilbert's orbit and says that she wants him to marry her. Gilbert says that Merle is a remarkable woman, but he has no interest in marrying. Merle insists, reminding him that he has no money of his own, and Isabel's fortune could provide a dowry for Pansy. As she watches Pansy playing outside, Merle notes dryly that the girl does not like her.

Not long thereafter, Merle arrives for a month-long visit at the Palazzo Crescentini, Mrs. Touchett's home in Florence. She fills Isabel's ears with flattering descriptions of Gilbert Osmond; eventually, Osmond pays a visit and invites Isabel to visit him at home and meet his daughter. During the visit, Isabel is strangely withdrawn; she is impressed with Osmond's refined manner, and he seems to catch her imagination. Isabel talks to Ralph about Osmond; Ralph says that he is indeed very refined but seems to have no other qualities. But he reminds her that she should judge people for herself.

They discuss Madame Merle, and Ralph tells Isabel that he dislikes the older woman's apparent perfection—she is too devoted to maintaining the impression that she has no flaws. Inwardly, he thinks that Isabel's friendship with Merle will not harm Isabel; one day, he thinks, Isabel will see through Merle and, in all likelihood, will lose interest in her.

Not long after this conversation, Merle takes Isabel to visit Gilbert Osmond's house; looking at the imposing villa from the outside, Isabel has the impression that once you were inside, it would be very difficult to get out. Inside, she meets the Countess Gemini, Osmond's annoying sister; she talks incessantly, and eventually Osmond draws Isabel aside while Merle keeps the Countess entertained. He tells Isabel that his sister is unhappily married and that she covers up her pain by acting foolish.

As Osmond describes his life—he says that he has sacrificed everything but his devotion to art and good taste—Isabel is again impressed with his refinement and his obvious taste. In fact, as he shows her his paintings, she works very hard to say the right things about them; like no one she has ever met, he makes her feel a need to measure up. He tells her that, though he has lived a life of renunciation, he will soon need to find a source of income, because he must provide for his daughter.

Analysis

This section initiates a new phase of the novel, which centers on Isabel's wealth and Merle's scheme to marry her to Gilbert Osmond. This scheme becomes more and more obvious to the reader throughout this section, just as it remains entirely opaque to Isabel, who believes that Merle is her friend and that Osmond is the wonderful and brilliant man Merle says he is. To virtually every other character in the book, Osmond is unremarkable, pretentious, and selfish; Ralph dislikes him very strongly. But Merle presents Osmond to Isabel as one of the finest gentlemen in Europe, who has cast off the bonds of society and chosen to live for his art. Because Osmond also seems cleverer than Isabel, her romantic side is deeply drawn to him.

James uses a number of literary techniques to make certain that the reader will find Osmond and Merle increasingly sinister throughout these chapters. One technique is a character's unconscious exclamation: in Chapter 20, for instance, when Merle learns that Isabel has inherited her fortune, she unintentionally blurts out that Isabel is "clever." She immediately covers up her mistake, but this exclamation indicates to the reader that Merle assumes that Isabel has manipulated her way into inheriting Mr. Touchett's wealth—hardly a flattering thing to think about someone who is supposed to be your close friend. This seems to indicate that Merle considers manipulation the most likely path to wealth and also that she herself is capable of such manipulation. It follows that she will attempt to manipulate Isabel into gaining access to her newfound wealth.

Another literary technique James uses to make Osmond seem unsavory is to make his surroundings seem ominous: Isabel finds Osmond extremely attractive, but she is unsettled by the sight of his house, which seems prison-like to her, as though, once in, it would require a force of will for a person to get out. (Prison imagery is associated with Osmond throughout Portrait of a Lady, especially as regards his treatment of Pansy.) Throughout the novel, James implies a strong correlation between a person's character and the environment of their home: Gardencourt is a loving, beautiful place, and is a symbol of the Touchetts, while Isabel's ramshackle home in Albany perfectly matches her disorganized upbringing and education. Because Isabel finds Osmond's home ominous, the reader finds Osmond himself ominous.

The Portrait of a Lady is a very sedate novel in terms of action: narrative developments occur slowly, and when they do occur, they are rarely exciting in the conventional sense. The novel is given the pace of the upper- class drawing rooms it portrays, and as a result, it is lacking in visceral excitement. One of the ways in which James sustains the reader's interest as his slow-paced story develops is to propose questions and mysteries and then to delay the answers for a great many chapters.

Will Isabel marry? What will she do with her independence? Characters are often introduced and then dismissed, and we are left wondering: what will become of Lord Warburton? Of Caspar Goodwood? Of Henrietta? In this way, James keeps the reader reading, even when his plot seems to lack some of the other elements that normally draw people into a work of fiction.

In this section, James introduces the most lasting and most compelling unsolved mystery that occurs in Portrait of a Lady and one that is not explicitly solved until the end of the book: what is the relationship between Madame Merle and Gilbert Osmond? They seem to be very close, to have a long history together, and to work together in certain ways, but their history is not elaborated and their relationship seems very mysterious. What kind of relationship, particularly in sedate nineteenth-century Europe, features a woman manipulating another woman into marrying a man to which she is very close?

Chapters 25–27

Summary

As Osmond talks to Isabel, the Countess Gemini tells Madame Merle in hushed tones that she does not agree with her scheme to manipulate Isabel into marrying her brother. She threatens to disrupt the plan, but Merle intimidates her by noting that she, Isabel, and Osmond all have stronger wills than the Countess. But the Countess says that it is not fair to trick a remarkable woman such as Isabel. Pansy enters and asks whether her father would like her to make tea; Merle replies that she should make tea, because her father would think it the daughterly thing to do. The Countess comments that if Osmond's standards are so high, she is frightened for Isabel's future.

Over the next weeks, Gilbert Osmond begins to visit the Palazzo Crescentini so often that Mrs. Touchett realizes that he must be interested in Isabel. Merle pretends not to have noticed but promises to try to find out by asking Osmond. Ralph tells his mother that Isabel would never let herself be taken in by Osmond, but in her own heart Isabel has formed a deeply romantic picture of Osmond and even tries to like the Countess Gemini. When the Countess visits the Palazzo, Mrs. Touchett is annoyed, as the Countess is an unwelcome guest. Madame Merle tells Isabel about the Osmonds' family: their mother was a poet who moved to Italy after their father died.

Henrietta arrives in Florence, still accompanied by the game Mr. Bantling. They have finished a tour of France and are now traveling through Italy. Mr. Bantling tells Ralph that he intends to follow Henrietta as long as she will let him; Henrietta proposes that the group should make an excursion to Rome. Henrietta, Bantling, Ralph, and Isabel all set off on the trip.

In a whispered conversation held in secret at a party, Osmond and Madame Merle discuss Isabel and plan for Osmond to follow her to Rome. Osmond says that he finds Isabel acceptable, and Merle replies that she worries about what she will have done to Isabel's life by causing her to marry

Osmond. Osmond says that Merle has taken his interest in Isabel well, and Merle replies that the better he likes Isabel, the better it is for her. She promises to look after Pansy while he is in Rome.

Isabel greatly enjoys touring Rome with her friends. After they have been there for some time, Isabel is shocked to encounter Lord Warburton on the street. He has been traveling in the east and is now on his way back to England. He tells Isabel that he has been unable to forget her and that he has even written her a number of letters which he has not sent. Isabel is happy to see Warburton, though she fears it will be inconvenient for him to be in Rome. And she is right: one day, she and Lord Warburton are touring Saint Peter's, when she suddenly comes face-to-face with Gilbert Osmond, who says that he has come to Rome because of Isabel. Isabel worries that Warburton will have heard about Osmond. Warburton walks away with Ralph, and the men speculate about whether Isabel is in love with Gilbert Osmond. Ralph assures Warburton that Isabel is looking for something entirely different.

Analysis

The very confusing conversation between Merle and Osmond at the party in Chapter 26 underscores the very mysterious connection between them; at this point, the reader is left to flounder, assuming that all will be explained as the novel progresses. The answer, of course, is that Merle and Osmond have been lovers, and Merle is still devoted to Osmond even though his romantic interest in her has subsided.

Because Osmond treats people as objects, he allows Merle to remain in his life because she is so useful—manipulating Isabel into marrying him, for example. This is why Merle worries about what she will have done to Isabel's life by causing her to marry Osmond: she is not entirely without conscience, and she recognizes Osmond's cruelty to others better than anyone. But she is still subject to her feelings for Osmond and is willing to endure guilt to help him acquire a fortune. (Her other reason, not even hinted at in this section of the novel, is that Pansy is really her daughter, a fact kept secret from everyone in the world but Osmond, Merle, and the Countess Gemini.) The extent to which Merle is willing to go to control her social schemes is evident throughout this section, especially by the deft way in which Merle manipulates her friend and patroness, Mrs. Touchett. Mrs. Touchett would protect Isabel from Osmond if she could, but because Merle, whom she trusts, promises to dissuade Osmond from pursuing Isabel, Mrs. Touchett does nothing. As a result, Merle is able to keep Mrs. Touchett from disrupting her scheme while making Mrs. Touchett believe that Merle is doing her a favor. The sinister nature of Merle and Osmond is no longer implied through subtle literary devices in this section—it is out in the open and obvious to the reader.

Isabel's trip to Rome brings about a moment of romantic entanglement, as she encounters Osmond, the man she is falling in love with, while sightseeing with Warburton, the man who loves her. This entanglement has no direct consequence, but serves the larger purpose of keeping Warburton in Isabel's life and allowing the reader to see that he still loves her. This will be important later in the novel, when Warburton attempts to marry Pansy solely to be closer to Isabel.

Chapters 28–31

Summary

Lord Warburton still loves Isabel, and Isabel is just as obviously taken with Gilbert Osmond. It hurts Warburton to see them together; one night at the opera, he hurries away after seeing them seated next to one another. On his way out, he sees Ralph, who also seems miserable. The next day, Warburton tells Isabel that he is leaving Rome, because he is unable to stand being near Isabel in these circumstances. Isabel does not know whether to turn him away coldly or to treat him with kindness. She tells Osmond that she likes Lord Warburton but has no real interest in him. Osmond, who longs to be an aristocrat, thinks smugly to himself that it will be a feather in his cap to win a woman who turned down an English nobleman.

During his time in Rome, Osmond is so charming that almost everyone in Isabel's life is taken in by him. Osmond is thrilled with his success; he likes everything about Isabel, except that she is too eager to praise things and to enjoy things in which he sees flaws. Isabel prepares to leave on a trip to Bellaggio with Mrs. Touchett and wonders to herself whether she will ever see Gilbert Osmond again. Before she leaves, Osmond tells her that he loves her. Isabel is overcome with emotion, but she is also confused, and she asks him not to say such things to her; she says that she does not know him. Osmond says that he does not want anything from her, as he has nothing to offer her; he merely wants to enjoy the feeling of being in love with her. He tells her that he is glad she is going on the trip with her aunt, as it is the perfectly conventional thing to do. And he asks her to look in on Pansy on her way.

Alone, Isabel ponders this new development. She has been fantasizing about being in love with Osmond, but now that he has confessed his love, she feels strangely oppressed. She feels as though there is a space inside her that she is unable to cross, but that if she could cross it, she could return Gilbert's love. Ralph escorts Isabel back to Florence, where she pays the promised visit to Pansy.

She finds the pretty girl practicing the piano. She is amazed at how natural and simple Pansy seems, despite the extraordinary regimen of her education and upbringing. Pansy seems to live to please her father; she repeats to Isabel all the instructions he has given her about how to spend her time, and Isabel agrees that Pansy must do all she can to please him and obey him. Pansy concurs, noting that her father is inwardly a sad man. Isabel longs to ask Pansy what she means, but Isabel feels that it would be unfair of her.

When Isabel kisses Pansy good-bye, she feels a strange pang of envy about the girl; she longs again to ask Pansy for insight into Osmond's character.

A year passes, during which Isabel spends five months vacationing with Lily, her sister, and Lily's family, and she chooses not to tell her sister about all the romantic developments in her life, such as Warburton's proposal. She thinks of Osmond almost constantly but feels that to tell Lily about him would drain the romance from her situation. Lily, for her part, finds Isabel vaguely disappointing; she had expected that Isabel would be a popular socialite, but instead she seems to be her same old introverted self. When Lily leaves to return to America, Isabel feels a powerful sense of relief. She hurries back to Rome to take a trip through the east with Madame Merle. Watching events from afar, Mrs. Touchett is pleased that Isabel has not returned to Florence to be with Gilbert Osmond.

After a three-month journey—Isabel pays Madame Merle's way across Greece and Turkey—Isabel feels as though she has learned a great deal about Madame Merle. She was married to a Frenchman who treated her cruelly, and Isabel notices a slight cruel streak in Madame Merle as well; she sometimes even finds her ominous or depressing. But she admires Merle for retaining her interest in life despite her unpleasant experience with her husband.

At last they return to Rome. Gilbert Osmond hurries there from Florence and begins to lavish attention on Isabel, but in the spring, Isabel travels to Florence. Ralph is on his way to visit his mother, and Isabel has not seen him for nearly a year. She looks forward eagerly to his arrival.

Analysis

With this section, James begins Volume II of Portrait of a Lady. By the time Warburton sees Isabel and Osmond together at the opera, Osmond's seduction of Isabel is nearly complete. Though Madame Merle is the primary agent enabling Isabel to fall in love with Osmond, Osmond is also forced to play his role, and he does so perfectly. Where Isabel's past suitors have always left her with a feeling of panic and fear—Caspar Goodwood seems to inhibit her independence, while Warburton's life seemed like a "gilded cage" to Isabel—Osmond only leaves her with a slight feeling of oppression, one that she wants desperately to learn how to overcome.

As befits the thematic exploration of Portrait of a Lady,

Isabel's primary romantic hangup has been her desire to protect her independence from the social constraints of a marriage. Both Goodwood and Warburton have wanted something very specific from her—marriage—which has left her terrified. But Osmond cleverly declares his love to Isabel without proposing to her.

He tells her that he does not want anything from her; he simply wants to tell her how he feels to relieve the pressure of keeping his passion a secret. By presenting his love for Isabel in such a way as to leave her freedom unthreatened, Osmond circumvents Isabel's usual defensive reaction against any man attempting to win her heart. Though she feels slightly troubled after their conversation, and though she cannot immediately fathom giving herself to Osmond, Isabel does begin to conceive of that as an end goal, thinking that if only she could cross the difficult country before her, she could love him. Isabel has been defined by her love of independence throughout the novel; this section marks the turning point when she begins to imagine sacrificing her independence for the sake of love.

Interestingly, Ralph is one of Isabel's staunchest defenders during her courtship with Osmond, during which every other character worries that Isabel will fall in love with him. Ralph always insists that Isabel is too intelligent to be taken in by Osmond's arrogance and narcissistic charm. Though he is always right when judging other characters, the great love Ralph feels for Isabel gives him something of a blind spot with regard to her; he simply has too much faith in her at this stage of the book.

Ralph's great hope is for Isabel to remain independent, and he believes that that is her primary goal as well. But Ralph has overlooked Isabel's latent romantic streak, which has been apparent to the reader throughout the novel—she tends to imagine her life as though it is a story, and she loves to imbue the people and places around her with the qualities of a novel or a play. As a result of this overactive imagination, she is able to construct a façade of Osmond in her own mind that she comes to believe in, essentially ignoring Osmond's real character. Ralph thinks too highly of Isabel to imagine her indulging such naïveté, and as a result he commits one of his only significant lapses in judgment in the novel, refusing to speak to Isabel about his suspicions of Osmond and Madame Merle. When Isabel was being courted by Lord Warburton, we saw that she was attracted to the life of his sisters, even though it seemed to contradict everything she claimed to want. The Misses Molyneux were docile, thoughtless, and passive, where Isabel wanted to be independent, intelligent, and active, and yet she admired them and even envied them. Here, she has exactly the same response to Pansy, Gilbert Osmond's stifled daughter.

Because she thinks the best of Osmond, she is unable to see what is extremely apparent to the reader: that Osmond has monstrously limited his daughter's education, squelched her independence, and essentially imprisoned her in a convent for many years solely to make her the person he wanted her to be—someone who was slavishly loyal to him and whose first thought was to his comfort and happiness. Pansy is a sweet-natured, passive, and tragic figure who is barely able to conceive of life outside her father's opinions and desires. But Isabel is drawn to Pansy, and though she will later come to pity and protect her, in this section she is basically attracted to the security and apparent normalcy of her life. Again, we see that Isabel's scattered upbringing, her patchy relationship with her own father, and her haphazard education, while they may have contributed to her desire for independence, also left her with a repressed inner yearning for the kind of security and comfort she sees in the lives of Pansy and the Misses Molyneux.

After Osmond declares his love for Isabel, the narrative begins to break up slightly, skipping over sections of the plot and jumping ahead through short intervals in time. Because Isabel's relationship with Osmond seems to cause a kind of disintegration in her own life, this narrative disintegration is appropriate to its subject matter. It also finds James beginning to employ the elliptical method he demonstrated in Isabel's first conversation with Caspar Goodwood, skipping over certain events and periods of development in Isabel's life.

Chapters 32–36

Summary

Some time passes; when we rejoin Isabel's life, she is waiting anxiously for Caspar Goodwood to arrive, dreading the scene she believes will ensue. Goodwood enters and tells Isabel that he has received her letter informing him of her decision to marry Gilbert Osmond. Isabel says that she has told no one but him and Madame Merle. Goodwood is obviously hurt, but he is his usual aggressive self: he presses Isabel to tell him about Osmond's attitudes, opinions, and personality, particularly his feeling for America. Isabel angrily insists that Osmond does nothing, thinks nothing, and has no opinions. Brokenly confessing his selfishness, Goodwood tells Isabel that he would rather she never marry than to marry another man. He storms away, and Isabel begins to cry.

After a short time, Isabel collects herself; she goes to tell Mrs. Touchett about her engagement. Mrs. Touchett is furious, realizing that Merle has tricked her, having convinced her not to interfere in Isabel and Gilbert's romance by promising to end it herself. Mrs. Touchett implies that Merle and Osmond have tricked her into the engagement, and in any case she cannot understand why Isabel would be interested in a man as insubstantial as Gilbert Osmond. Isabel says that if he has no substance, he cannot hurt her. Ralph arrives in Florence two days later, looking grim and ill. To Isabel's surprise, he says nothing about the engagement; she assumes that he disapproves, and Mrs. Touchett tells her as much, but she chalks up his disapproval to their family relationship—she thinks that all cousins must disapprove of one another's marriages. While coming to terms with her family's disapproval, Isabel continues to meet with Osmond every day.

After three days, Ralph encounters Isabel in the garden at the Palazzo, and tells her that he is ready to speak to her about her engagement. He says that he worries that she is putting herself into a cage, forfeiting her chance to travel and to observe a wide array of life and allowing herself to be taken adavantage of by a narrow, dry, selfish man; he says that

Osmond's only quality is his aesthetic taste, and Isabel deserves to do more in her life than protect the aesthetic taste of such an insignificant man.

Isabel defends Osmond, implying that he has inner qualities that only she appreciates. She says that she is eternally grateful to Mr. Touchett for giving her the means to marry a man such as Osmond, who has no money and little social position. Ralph says that he worries that her love of Osmond is based on an illusion that she has convinced herself to believe. Ralph also confesses to Isabel that he loves her, but he says he has no hope of ever acting on his love or having it returned.

Isabel does not tell Osmond that her family disapproves of the engagement, but he guesses it; one day he tells Isabel that he has never worried about money, and he hopes her family does not believe that he would marry her for her money. Inwardly, Osmond is very pleased with Isabel; he thinks that she reflects all his ideas like a perfect silver dish. Pansy is also pleased that Isabel will be her stepmother. When she encounters Pansy at a party thrown by the Countess Gemini, she has a brief sense of fear, thinking that she may one day have to protect Pansy from her father. But she puts the thought out of her head without fully understanding it. At the party, the Countess also tells Isabel that she is pleased with the engagement. She asks Pansy to leave them for a time, as she has some advice for Isabel about marriage. Isabel asks Pansy to stay, saying that she does not wish to hear anything that is unfit for Pansy.

Three years pass. A young man named Edward Rosier, who was friendly with Isabel and Madame Merle in Paris, calls on Madame Merle in Rome. He asks her for help with his suit to marry Pansy; he and Pansy love one another, but he suspects that Pansy's father will oppose their marriage. He wants to speak to Isabel about it, but Madame Merle warns him that Isabel has no standing in her marriage—she is barely treated as part of the family. Instead, she and Gilbert disagree about everything and seem to despise one another. She also reveals that Isabel gave birth to a son two years ago, but he died when he was only six months old.

Rosier leaves Madame Merle's house chastising himself for bringing his problem to her—he realizes that she has no intention of helping him convince Gilbert Osmond that he should marry Pansy. Every Thursday night, Isabel holds a social gathering at her house in Rome, the Palazzo Roccanero. Rosier attends, thinking that the building is a prison in which Pansy is an inmate. Though he is impressed with the opulent collection of art and furniture the Osmonds have acquired, Rosier tells himself that he has more important things to do than look at art: he must find a way to convince Pansy's father to allow him to marry her.

Analysis

This section begins with the news of Isabel's engagement to Osmond, an event that James chooses not to narrate. It ends after Isabel has been married for three years—years James also skips over, after skipping over the wedding and the birth and death of Isabel's son.

James's elliptical technique is in full swing throughout this section; almost all of the scenes that are narrated are conversations that are peripheral to Isabel's life—and even they are almost always shown through the perspective of someone else. The important events are left out altogether, and only implied by the peripheral conversations. The reader loses touch with Isabel almost completely, and in this way James creates the sense that, by giving herself to Osmond, Isabel has been lost.

The question arises: if James leaves so much out, what can we ascertain from that which he leaves in? First, in Isabel's conversation with Mrs. Touchett, we receive a brief glimpse of what Isabel sees in Gilbert Osmond. We have already seen that she has superimposed her own romantic idea of a refined, artistic genius over Osmond's arrogance and selflishness; now, she tells Mrs. Touchett something of her feeling for the real Osmond. Mrs. Touchett says that Osmond is a "nothing," that he has no qualities; Isabel replies that if he is so insubstantial, he cannot hurt her.

In the conflict between independence and social

convention as it applies to Isabel's romantic life, it seems that the idea of "substance" in a man is what threatens Isabel's notion of her own independence. Though she is drawn to Caspar Goodwood, he is such a powerful physical presence that he seems to overwhelm Isabel's own independence. Osmond is in many ways Goodwood's opposite, a man with no presence—he is simply a graceful nothing in Isabel's mind. Where Goodwood is forceful, Osmond is charming; where Goodwood is a symbol of American capability, Osmond is a symbol of European decadence. Ironically, of course, as Henrietta perceives, it is Osmond and not Goodwood who represents the real threat to Isabel's freedom.

Ralph's conversation with Isabel in the garden is a watershed moment in the novel. To this point, Ralph has been an unfailing source of strength for Isabel; he has provided her with support, sympathy, and understanding since their first meeting at Gardencourt, and he has consistently advocated the very independence that Isabel claims to want for herself. In the last several chapters, he refused to believe that Isabel would fall in love with Osmond, claiming that she was far too intelligent not to see the threat that he would represent.

Now, however, Isabel has announced her engagement to Osmond, and Ralph can no longer deny that his beloved cousin is in jeopardy of throwing her independence away. He tells her how he feels, and she becomes self-righteous and emphatic, insisting that her imaginary picture of Osmond is the real thing: that he is kind and devoted to higher things. Ralph is far too good a judge of character to be fooled by Isabel's naïve portrayal of her fiancé, and he tells her that he worries she is fooling herself. She angrily rejects his advice, and from this moment until the end of the novel, Ralph and Isabel's relationship becomes distant and strained.

Though nothing of special narrative importance happens in this moment, it is still extremely important in the novel. The issues are placed very clearly before Isabel: she is shown that she can either rely on herself and choose independence or that she can rely on Osmond and give up her independence in favor of safety and social convention. Rather than exercising her intelligence and choosing to remain independent, Isabel follows her immature, romantic imagination and chooses to sacrifice her independence for safety and social convention. Nothing will be the same for Isabel again.

After the three years of Isabel's marriage, we are taken into a new subplot, involving the drab art collector Edward Rosier's desire to marry the placid and submissive Pansy. James utilizes this subplot to take us gradually back into Isabel's life, allowing us to feel out the changes that have befallen her since her marriage to Osmond. Rosier's conversation with Madame Merle lets us slowly back into the situation: Merle is still present in Osmond's life and apparently still quite important in it; Merle is still manipulative and still tries to control social situations.

Isabel, we learn, has fallen into a miserable sham of a marriage, as the reader might have predicted; Merle says that she is barely given any status in her marriage, treated as though she is barely even part of the family. Osmond married Isabel for two reasons: her money, and because she is an object he can add to his collection, drawing admiration and envy from his acquaintances and acting as a hostess for his parties. Beyond these roles he has no interest in her. The reader has long realized that this would be the case; Isabel has just learned it and has learned it the hard way.

Chapters 37–40

Summary

Rosier wanders through the Osmonds' palazzo, searching for Pansy. He encounters Gilbert Osmond, who insultingly refuses to shake his hand, instead offering him only two fingers to grasp. They discuss Osmond's art collection, and when Rosier asks whether he would like to sell anything, Osmond replies that there is nothing he wishes to match. The subtle implication, Rosier realizes, is that Madame Merle has revealed to Osmond Rosier's desire to marry Pansy, and Osmond has no intention of allowing the marriage to take place. Hastily excusing himself, Rosier encounters Isabel, who asks him to speak to a young woman who has shyly kept to herself throughout the party. Rosier asks Isabel why Osmond does not speak to her, and she replies that her husband does not do her such favors. Rosier finds the young woman and discovers that Pansy is with her. Moved by Pansy's beauty and by her innocence, he asks her to show him something in another room. Here, he confesses to Pansy that he has come to the party solely because she is there. She replies somewhat passively that she likes him as well.

Elsewhere in the palazzo, Madame Merle and Gilbert Osmond discuss the problem of Rosier: Osmond says that he is tired of Rosier, but Madame Merle advises him to keep Rosier around, as he might find a use for him. Merle says that Pansy has been thinking about Rosier, but Gilbert insists that he has no interest in what Pansy thinks, only what Pansy does. Rosier and Pansy enter the room; Merle says to Osmond that Rosier is coming to declare his feelings for Pansy. Osmond glares at Pansy and then strides away. Merle tells Rosier to pay her a visit the following afternoon. Rosier finds Isabel, who admits to him that Osmond thinks he is not wealthy enough to marry Pansy. She says that there is nothing she can do to change her husband's mind.

The next day, Madame Merle advises Rosier that if he has any desire to marry Pansy, he must stay away from her except at Mrs. Osmond's weekly gatherings on Thursday nights. Rosier agrees. The next Thursday, Gilbert Osmond tells him that he is glad to see that Rosier has been staying away from his daughter, who will never marry him. Lord Warburton approaches and greets Osmond, and Rosier excuses himself to speak to Isabel. She assures him that Pansy still hopes to marry him, despite Osmond's claims. As Rosier leaves to find Pansy, Warburton approaches Isabel and says that she seems changed. He tells her that Ralph Touchett is very ill and that he has planned to spend the winter in Sicily against the advice of his doctors. Alarmed, Isabel agrees to see Ralph the next morning. Isabel offers to introduce Warburton to her guests, but he says that he has come only to speak to her. When he notices Pansy, however, he says that he would like to meet her. He mentions to Isabel that he is interested in finding a wife. Pansy is deep in conversation with Rosier, telling him not to listen to her father—she has not lost interest in him. She says that she plans to turn to her stepmother for help. Rosier tells her that Isabel will be useless, because she is obviously afraid of her husband. Pansy replies that Isabel is not afraid.

Ralph thinks about the recent past in his friendship with Isabel. He has scarcely seen her since her marriage and feels that he alienated her by telling her how he felt about her engagement. Isabel has distanced herself from all her old friends, including Henrietta, whom Osmond despises, and Mrs. Touchett, whose friendship with Madame Merle has been destroyed by Merle's deceitful role in helping Osmond win Isabel. Ralph is disgusted by Osmond, whose entire life seems to him nothing more than a pose—he pretends to be above the world, but what he really wants is for the world to notice that he is above it. Now Ralph worries that Osmond has transformed Isabel into a mere acquisition, a piece of his collection designed to make the right impression on the world.

After the last time he saw Isabel, Ralph worried that Osmond would disapprove of their friendship, so he left Rome; now, he has decided to stay in Rome instead of going to Sicily, to be near Isabel and to help her if he can. He is also keenly interested to see how she will handle life with her husband—especially now that a new complication has entered her life, the arrival of Lord Warburton and his obvious interest in marrying Pansy. Warburton has even confessed his intentions to Ralph, though he denies that, as Ralph suggests, he only wants to marry Pansy to make himself a part of Isabel's life.

In the time since her marriage to Osmond, Isabel has lost her fascination with Madame Merle; she has even recognized part of Merle's role in arranging her marriage with Osmond, though she believes that she herself must finally bear the responsibility for it. Merle even warns Isabel not to become jealous of her relationship with Osmond, a remark that perplexes Isabel. One day, however, Isabel returns from a walk with Pansy to find Osmond and Merle alone in the drawing room, gazing silently into one another's eyes; Merle is standing, and Osmond is sitting. Watching them in this pose gives Isabel a shock of insight, and she realizes that their relationship is far more intimate than they pretend. Osmond hastily excuses himself, while Merle stays behind to talk to Isabel about Rosier. She says that she is tired of dealing with him and that she does not want him to marry Pansy. Isabel coldly refuses to intervene and refuses again when Merle tries to convince her to have Warburton speak to Pansy. Isabel says only that she would be glad if Lord Warburton married Pansy and asks Madame Merle to be gentle with Rosier if she decides to snub him.

Analysis

A great deal of this section is devoted to the exploration of subtle social maneuvering in the parlors and drawing rooms of upper-class parties. This is a subtle, sophisticated world in which seemingly insignificant glances, gestures, and comments can take on a world of significance—when Rosier speaks to Osmond in Chapter 37, for instance, Osmond first snubs him by shaking his hand with only two fingers. This may seem like a minor insult, but it is such a departure from the elaborate rules of courtesy that govern these characters lives that it continues to infuriate Ralph when he thinks of much later in the chapter.

Additionally, when Rosier, who is also an art collector, asks Osmond if he would be interested in selling anything, Osmond replies that he has nothing he wishes to match—this is a highly coded way of telling Rosier that he knows about his desire to marry Pansy and that he intends to oppose the romance. Though the reader may miss the exchange altogether, Rosier understands it immediately and realizes that he is in for a struggle if he hopes to marry Pansy.

Though we are still kept relatively distant from Isabel at this point, and though much of the action is relatively insignificant to the main plotline, this section does serve an important purpose in that it brings us more fully into the world in which Isabel now finds herself. In America, communication is frank and expressive, represented by the to-the-point statements of Caspar Goodwood and by Henrietta's unselfconscious way of saying whatever crosses her mind. In England, communication is frank and often jovial, governed by a mixture of forthrightness and manners—Mrs. Touchett, Isabel, and Ralph can all tell each other what they think without speaking in code, though they are not so blunt as Henrietta.

Now Isabel is deep in continental Europe, a decadent world in which social proprieties are rigidly enforced, even if they are often used to pervert or circumvent the moral proprieties that seem natural to Isabel and the Touchetts. In this world, Osmond cannot simply tell Rosier that he does not want him to marry Pansy; instead he must express his opposition in a kind of sinister hieroglyphic. James emphasizes the insincerity of these exchanges in order to give Isabel's new environment a very dark and ominous undertone—looking back on the early chapters, places such as Gardencourt seem extremely bright and uncomplicated compared to the vicious and hypocritical world of the expatriate society in Rome.

This section also finds some of Isabel's old friends returning to her side—Lord Warburton appears, as does Ralph, who is still motivated by his love of Isabel even though their relationship has grown distant. The appearance of Lord Warburton, though its significance is not commented upon in these chapters, foreshadows a troubling new development. Warburton, as we saw in his last trip to Rome, seems still to love Isabel, but he tells her that he is looking for a wife. He also asks to meet Pansy, who is the only person at the party besides Isabel in whom he is interested. Further, we know that Osmond is deeply interested in the English nobility—he thought once that since his life thwarted him by not making him a lord, he would have the satisfaction of knowing that his wife had once rejected a lord. And we know that Pansy is of marrying age.

The entanglement, then, seems clear: Pansy wishes to marry Rosier, but her father forbids it; Warburton will seek to marry Pansy solely to move closer to Isabel, and Osmond will support the marriage. Isabel will be forced to choose between

Pansy's wishes and her marital duty to Osmond, which she takes very seriously even though he makes her miserable. This will become the most direct conflict in the book between Isabel's inner desire and her commitment to social propriety.

Complicating everything is the mystery that resurfaces in Chapter 40, which is the question of the exact nature of the relationship between Osmond and Merle. It should be clear by now to the reader that they either are lovers or have been lovers; Isabel has not yet arrived at that conclusion, but she does realizes that their relationship is more intimate and more complicated than she had previously assumed.

Chapters 41–44

Summary

Isabel sits in the drawing room listening to Pansy and Lord Warburton converse; she is pleased by the way Warburton treats her daughter- in-law, noting that he speaks to her as an equal. She wonders briefly what Pansy will think about her father and Madame Merle's dismissal of Rosier, but she decides that Pansy is so passive that she will probably not be terribly hurt by it. After Pansy and Warburton leave, Osmond enters and asks Isabel about Warburton's visit and his intentions toward Pansy.

Their conversation is strained; though Isabel is honestly trying to be a dutiful wife, he is angry that she failed to tell him about Warburton's interest in his daughter. Isabel insists that because their relationship is distant, she has not had an opportunity to tell him. He acknowledges that he wishes to see Pansy married to this powerful English lord and tells Isabel that he will expect her help in bringing the marriage about. He says that because she rejected Warburton when he loved her, she will now be able to influence his feelings.

Left alone, Isabel thinks about her relationship with Osmond. She wants to be a good wife and had planned to help him effect the match between Pansy and Warburton—but as soon as he pressed her to do so, she felt disgusted by the entire proposition. She is miserable in her marriage, though she was full of confidence at the outset. After a year with him, Isabel realized that Osmond despised her, and she understood that because she had tried during their courtship to seem exactly the way he wanted her to be, he believed that she would become that ideal person in their marriage. She realizes further that it was her imagination that enabled her to love Osmond, because it constructed such a powerful, romantic illusion of him that she was able to believe. She realizes that Osmond's life is defined by his arrogant notion of himself as a superior gentleman and his deep desire to have the world acknowledge him as such; where she thought that their life together would be one of intellect and liberty, he intended it to be one of social conventions and poses.

She realizes that her husband is ashamed of the fact that she has her own mind and that she disagrees with many of his ideas—for instance, his assertion that all women are dishonest and unfaithful to their husbands. Osmond wanted to own her like an object in his collection, and he is irritated and threatened by the fact that his acquisition has her own ideas and her own way of looking at life. Isabel suffers greatly when she thinks about her marriage. She is also sad to think about Ralph, who is growing weaker and sicker, and whose goodness Isabel only now appreciates fully. At four o'clock in the morning, Isabel rises and readies herself for bed; she is suddenly struck by a memory of that she saw earlier that day: Osmond and Merle, gazing silently into one another's eyes.

Isabel escorts Pansy to a ball, where she acts as her stepdaughter's chaperone. As she holds Pansy's flowers and watches her dance, Rosier approaches her, looking sorrowful, and asks to take one of Pansy's flowers. Isabel allows him to take a flower, but as Pansy leaves the dance floor to approach them, Isabel asks Rosier to leave; Osmond has forbidden Pansy to dance with him. Warburton arrives and stays to talk to Isabel when Pansy rejoins the dance. Isabel is surprised that Warburton has not asked Pansy to dance the cotillion, a very long and intimate dance but instead has asked for the quadrille, a dance that involves a large group. Warburton says that he hopes to talk to Isabel during the cotillion.

Isabel realizes that Warburton is still in love with her and is pursuing Pansy only to be closer to her. When Warburton sees Rosier looking dejected, Isabel tells him that the man is his rival for Pansy's affections and that he is in love with her. Looking guilty, Warburton acknowledges that he is not in love with Pansy and tells Isabel that he can no longer pretend; he goes to write a note to Osmond. Isabel finds Rosier and promises that she will try to help him. As the ball ends, she finds Warburton and tells him to send the note to Osmond.

Henrietta visits the Countess Gemini in Florence and tells her that she is worried that Isabel is unhappy and that she is going to Rome. The Countess is also going to Rome to visit her brother and surprises Henrietta by telling her that Lord Warburton is also in Rome and apparently still in love with Isabel. Henrietta then goes to speak to Caspar Goodwood, whom she encourages to come to Rome as well, for Isabel's sake. With difficulty, Goodwood agrees. He would prefer to travel alone, but when Henrietta tells him that she is leaving the next day, courtesy compels him to offer to escort her. Henrietta agrees, and they set out to see what they can do for Isabel.

Analysis

After having been suspended for four years and a great many chapters, Isabel's perspective finally makes a complete return in Chapter 41. In Chapters 41 and forty-two, as Isabel talks to Osmond about Warburton's interest in Pansy and then thinks deeply about her strained relationship with Osmond, we finally see Isabel's painful marriage through her own eyes. Essentially, Isabel has realized what Ralph, Henrietta, and the reader realized from the beginning, that Osmond would force her to conform to social convention at the expense of her independent spirit; she has at last seen through the romantic façade of Osmond that she created for herself and realized that his life is defined by social posing, a desire for other people to confirm his high opinion of himself and a desire to extract servitude and pleasure from everyone he can with no regard for their feelings. Despite this realization, Isabel remains committed to her marriage and to the idea of being a good and dutiful wife. This may be hard for many readers to understand; having already seen the positive example of Mrs. Touchett, readers may be inclined to think that Isabel should just leave Osmond and live happily. There are essentially three reasons why the circumstance is not so simple.

First, despite the example of Mrs. Touchett, the idea and ideal of marriage in 1873 was far more rigid and powerful than it is today; divorce was looked upon as a scandalous disgrace, and marriage vows were treated as sacred oaths to be taken literally. Isabel entered into her marriage with this understanding of it; she did not consider, as most people do today, that if her marriage went poorly, she would end it. Second, Isabel has always prided herself on her moral strength—remember that earlier in the novel, she wished that she would encounter hardship in her life, so that she could prove to herself that she could overcome suffering without losing her moral identity. Now she has found hardship, and her pride insists that she confront it and not shrink from it. To leave Osmond would represent a kind of moral capitulation to Isabel, and she cannot imagine making such an admission of defeat. Thirdly, Isabel legitimately loves and pities Pansy and considers it her duty to remain with the Osmonds to try to help Pansy in whatever way she can.

The difficulty of her current entanglement, then, is that her desire to help Pansy is directly at odds with her commitment to become a dutiful wife for Osmond, no matter how much she hates him. In a sense, Isabel's moral identity has fractured into two competing sides. One side says that Warburton wants to marry Pansy for the wrong reasons and that Pansy and Rosier love each other; therefore, Isabel should discourage Warburton and help Pansy and Rosier. The other side says that her duty is to do whatever her husband desires, and therefore she should help Osmond marry Pansy to Warburton, regardless of Pansy's feelings and Warburton's motives.

Marriage is a social contract, and this conflict represents

a severe recurrence of the struggle within Isabel between individual desire and social convention: Isabel's personal conscience tells her to help Pansy, but her social conscience tells her to help her husband. As a result, we see Isabel oscillate throughout this section, first promising Osmond that she will help him and then discouraging Warburton and promising Rosier that she will help him. At the end of this section, Isabel seems to be acting based on her personal feelings at the expense of her perceived social duty; whether this state of affairs will hold, however, remains to be seen.

Chapters 45–48

Summary

Osmond is angry with Isabel for spending so much time with Ralph; Isabel knows that Osmond wants to deny her any freedom of thought, and he knows that Ralph encourages her freedom. Isabel continues to see Ralph, who is clearly dying; but she tries to limit the time she spends with him to avoid conflict with her husband. Isabel meets Ralph and asks him about Lord Warburton's feelings for her. After some joking evasion, Ralph acknowledges to Isabel that Warburton is not in love with Pansy—he is in love with Isabel. As Ralph chuckles about the situation, Isabel breaks down and tells Ralph that he is "no help."

With this emotional outburst, Ralph feels as though Isabel has reached out to him at last. He offers to listen to her problems and to try to help her, but Isabel closes herself off and tries to end the conversation. She tells Ralph that Warburton will simply drop the matter of his relationship with Pansy, which, since he has never proposed to her, will be acceptable. But Ralph tells her that Osmond will blame Isabel for Warburton's disappearance. Embarrassed, Isabel tells Ralph that he is cruel to her; Ralph offers again to listen to her problems and prove that he is kind. But Isabel hastily leaves.

Isabel goes to speak to Pansy, who tells her that her only desire in life is to marry Rosier. Trying once more to be a dutiful wife, Isabel tells Pansy that her father does not wish her to marry Rosier and that she must do as her father wishes. Pansy agrees that she will not violate her father's orders and will remain single. But Isabel tells her that her father wishes her to marry Warburton. Relieved, Pansy says that Warburton will never propose to her; but she hopes that Osmond will not realize this, as having Warburton around will keep her father from finding another suitor for her. Isabel warns Pansy that her father is determined to see her married to a nobleman, and Pansy says that in her eyes, Rosier is noble.

Warburton does not call at the Osmonds' palazzo for four days. At last Osmond angrily accuses Isabel of having betrayed him and encouraged Warburton not to marry Pansy. At that moment, Warburton arrives at the palazzo. He tells Osmond and Isabel that he is returning to England and has come to say good-bye to Pansy. Osmond leaves, and Warburton says farewell briefly to Isabel and Pansy, who seems untroubled by his departure. After Pansy goes to bed, Osmond furiously accuses Isabel of trying deliberately to thwart him; he thinks that she intentionally convinced him to seek Warburton as a suitor for Pansy and then intentionally ruined the possibility of an engagement. Isabel is dismayed to discover the extent of his paranoia. Contemptuously, Isabel tells Osmond that he is wrong and leaves the room, feeling intensely sorry for Pansy.

Caspar Goodwood and Henrietta arrive in Rome just as Madame Merle and Rosier leave it—Rosier on a somewhat mysterious errand that no one can explain. Isabel thinks again of Merle's mysterious relationship with her husband, realizing that there is something extremely ominous about Merle. Henrietta asks Isabel whether she is miserable with Osmond, and Isabel admits that she is.

But she says that she can never leave him, because she is too ashamed. Henrietta and Caspar befriend Ralph, and the three of them grow to like one another a great deal. But Osmond is deeply irritated to find that so many of Isabel's old friends have reentered her life. Still, he is bolstered by the arrival of Countess Gemini and the return of Madame Merle, who asks Isabel haughtily what she did to ruin Pansy's chances of marrying Warburton. Finally, Rosier returns to Rome; no one seems to know where he has been. Ralph, who is in good cheer despite his increasingly frail health, eventually decides that he must return to Gardencourt. Henrietta and Caspar insist on going with him, the latter at Isabel's insistence. (Isabel hopes that Caspar can look after Ralph; Caspar believes that Isabel is bored with him.) Before they leave, Countess Gemini foolishly tells Henrietta that Isabel and Warburton had been having an affair. Annoyed, Henrietta contradicts her, but the Countess is quite sure of herself. When Henrietta tells Isabel that she is leaving for England, Isabel says that she is pleased—she feels that Henrietta and Ralph have been observers of her life; now she will be left alone with those who are actually involved in the sad little plot. Henrietta asks Isabel to vow that if things with Osmond get much worse, she will leave him. Isabel refuses; she says that she has failed in her marriage vows, and she will not make vows again.

Isabel and Ralph bid one another farewell. Isabel tells Ralph that she would go with him to England but that she cannot because of Osmond. But she says that if he sends for her, she will find a way to come to him. Isabel tells Ralph that he has been her dearest friend; Ralph says that Isabel is the sole reason he has struggled to stay alive.

Caspar Goodwood comes to the palazzo to say goodbye to Isabel as well. Before he sees her, Osmond arrives and treats him mockingly, saying that Goodwood has helped him resign himself to the future. Perplexed and annoyed, Caspar does not know what he means but realizes that Osmond is more sinister than he had thought—before, he always felt that Osmond was an insignificant, dilettantish man with a quick wit; now, he has an inkling that he has a darker side. Osmond tells him again and again that his marriage to Isabel is blissful, which confuses Goodwood to no end.

Goodwood at last speaks to Isabel, and with a pang in his heart he tells her that she has changed and no longer reveals to him how she feels. He says that he loves her ana that he knows she is unhappy with Osmond. He asks her if he may devote his life to feeling pity for her. Nearly weeping, Isabel tells him that he must not devote his life to it but that he may think of her every now and then. Isabel hastily excuses herself; Goodwood leaves, having at last received a glimpse of Isabel's inner self.

Analysis

In this section, all of the people who love Isabel the most—Caspar, Ralph, and Henrietta—have come to Rome and reentered her life, and as a result, this section is dominated by a new kind of tension in Isabel's life. On the one hand, she is happy to have her friends close at hand; on the other, being around people who know her well makes it much more difficult for Isabel to sacrifice her happiness for the sake of social propriety and her marriage. She is cold to Ralph, evasive with Goodwood, and fatalistic with Henrietta. When they leave for England, Isabel is at the same time sad (after all, Ralph is going home to die) and relieved. With her friends gone, Isabel will be able to devote herself to working for her marriage. She has discouraged Warburton from marrying Pansy, as her conscience seemed to require, but her duty to Osmond stops her short of helping Pansy marry Rosier. Instead, she tells Pansy that she must do as her father wishes.

In previous chapters, Osmond has emerged as a sinister, even monstrous character, treating other people as objects, stifling his wife, shamelessly using Madame Merle for his own benefit, and even basing his daughter's upbringing on his desire for her to be devoted and obedient only to him. He has exhibited bizarre and unsavory ideas, such as his claim to Isabel that married women all lie and cheat on their husbands, as his sister does.

In this section, Osmond's self-absorption and ominous quality of mind come out in a new way: his increasing paranoia. Deeply threatened that his wife, rather than being a reflection of him, seems to have ideas of her own—and possibly recognizing that Isabel is more intelligent and charismatic than he is, and furthermore that his social status is based on his access to money that belongs to her—he begins to harbor dark fantasies that she is consciously working against him and that her goal in life is to thwart his desires.

In a sense, this paranoia is the flipside of Osmond's desire for other people to admire him; he assumes that other people are as obsessed with him as he is obsessed with himself, so that when they do not adore him, he suspects that they are working against him. Isabel's love for Pansy comes to the fore when, at the height of Gilbert's paranoid rage, she walks coolly out of the room, not feeling sorry for herself, but feeling deeply sorry for her stepdaughter.

Chapters 49–51

Summary

When Madame Merle confronts Isabel about her role in Lord Warburton's departure from Rome, Isabel is shocked by Merle's presumptuousness—she sounds as though she is speaking as Osmond's representative, and not merely as a distant acquaintance of the family. Propriety would dictate that the entire incident is none of Madame Merle's business, but Merle brazenly questions Isabel about it as though she, and not Isabel, was Osmond's wife. Isabel feels again that Madame Merle plays a powerful and sinister role in her life. Upset, Isabel asks Merle what role she is playing and what her relationship to Osmond is; Merle replies that it is "everything." Isabel gasps and covers her face in her hands; Merle sardonically congratulates her for taking the news so well. She realizes that Mrs. Touchett was right: Merle did orchestrate her marriage to Osmond so that the two of them could have access to her money. Merle leaves, and Isabel goes for a long drive, alone, thinking about what she has learned. She recognizes that Osmond married her only for her money. After some time, she comes to pity Madame Merle for having fallen under Osmond's sway.

Osmond sits in Madame Merle's parlor, listening to his former lover tell him what has happened with Isabel. Merle is deeply upset by the way she acted, and she tells Osmond that he has caused her soul to wither—she is unable even to cry. Osmond argues that the soul cannot be harmed, and she says that, on the contrary, it can. He tells her that all women have monstrous imaginations, as if they were all bad novelists. He says that he really only wanted Isabel to adore him, and since she does not, he is content with the adoration of Pansy. Merle says longingly that she wishes she had a child, and Osmond cuttingly replies that she can live vicariously through people who do have children. Merle says that after all that has happened, something still holds them together. Osmond thinks that it is the harm he could do her. Merle says that he is wrong: it is the good that she can do him. Osmond leaves. Merle thinks to herself that she has made herself a monster, all for nothing.

The Countess Gemini is obsessed with gossiping about the extramarital affairs of women in Florence, even though she is now in Rome. To give her something else to think about, Isabel often takes her driving through the streets of Rome. One day, she and the Countess are on an excursion with Pansy when Isabel sees Edward Rosier, back from his mysterious trip. Isabel speaks to him alone, and he tells her that he has been away to sell his collection of art objects; he has raised fifty thousand dollars and hopes he will now be allowed to marry Pansy. Isabel tells him that Osmond intends to marry Pansy to a nobleman. Pansy approaches, and Isabel moves to intercept her. The Countess goes to speak to Rosier, and after some time, Isabel sends the coachman to retrieve her. But the Countess sends him back, saying that she prefers to speak to Mr. Rosier and will return home in a cab.

A week later, Pansy shocks Isabel by saying that her father is sending her back to the convent; the nuns will arrive for her that very evening. Osmond tells Isabel that there is something he wants to give Pansy the space to think about "in the right way." Isabel is not sure what Osmond is trying to accomplish, but she is stunned that he would go so far, simply to have his own way. At dinner that night, the Countess says to her brother that she believes he has banished his daughter to remove her from the Countess's influence, for the Countess admits that she has taken the part of Edward Rosier. Osmond replies harshly that if that were the case, he would simply have banished the Countess and allowed Pansy to stay.

Mrs. Touchett writes Isabel that Ralph is near death and

asks Isabel to come at once. When Isabel tells Osmond this news, he forbids her to leave Rome, saying that if she does so, it would simply be an act of revenge against him. Isabel realizes that he sees the entire situation as merely an elaborate game, and in his paranoia, he believes that all her actions are calculated either to help him or hurt him. She asks what would happen if she defied him. He refuses to discuss it. Isabel tells the Countess what has happened; the Countess urges her to defy Osmond and leave Rome. But Isabel is haunted by the memory of her wedding vows, which she does not wish to break. The Countess tells Isabel that Osmond has lied to her: his first wife did not die during childbirth, because she was never pregnant. Pansy's mother is Madame Merle. Madame Merle and Osmond have been lovers for years; Osmond's first wife died around the time Pansy was born, so they simply claimed that she had died in childbirth and put Pansy in a convent. Merle chose Isabel to marry Osmond both because Pansy needed a mother—she dislikes Merle, her real mother—and because Isabel has money for Pansy's dowry. Isabel realizes that this explains why Merle was so upset when she thought Isabel had encouraged Warburton not to marry Pansy.

Isabel asks why Merle and Osmond never married. The Countess says that Merle always hoped to marry above Osmond and worried that if she married Osmond, people would realize that she had a child out of wedlock. Isabel feels intense pity for Madame Merle. Isabel says sadly that she must see Ralph and prepares to leave for England.

Analysis

These chapters largely suspend the great problem at hand in Isabel's life—how to handle the conflict between Pansy's desire to marry Rosier and Osmond's resistance to that idea—and focus instead on unraveling the long mystery of the relationship between Madame Merle and Osmond. The reader has long understood that Merle and Osmond were or had been lovers, but when the realization strikes Isabel in Chapter 49, it is still quite a shock to her. The knowledge arrives after a slow buildup of tension in which Merle becomes more and more presuptuous and begins to treat Isabel more and more insolently about her role in discouraging Warburton to marry Pansy. At last, as if solely to hurt Isabel, Merle implies her intimacy with Osmond strongly enough for Isabel to make the connection.

But the mystery is still not complete until Chapter 51, when the Countess Gemini reveals that Madame Merle is Pansy's mother. This is likely to come as a shock to the reader as well as to Isabel, but it clears up a number of confusing points, such as why Merle was so dedicated to the idea of having Pansy marry Lord Warburton. It also clarifies the baffling exchange between Merle and Osmond in Merle's parlor, when Merle comments bitterly that she has no children of her own, and Osmond replies cruelly that she can still enjoy the children of others—he is taunting her for the fact that she is forever cut off from her relationship to Pansy. This exchange also brings out Merle's human side for the first time in the novel, and she emerges as a victim of Osmond's rather than as a pure villain in her own right. Isabel is able to pity Merle, and James seems to intend for the reader to share the feeling.

Edward Rosier's pathetic last gasp as a suitor is to sell his art collection, raise fifty thousand dollars, and appeal to Osmond's sister for help. He does not realize that without social status, his money is meaningless to Osmond and that Osmond holds his sister in complete contempt. Osmond's sudden, ruthless decision to return Pansy to the convent, essentially imprisoning her until she agrees to forget about Rosier, ends any possibility of a marriage.

But the scene in which Rosier speaks to the Countess among the Roman statues is still important in a way, because, by emphasizing the physical presence of the city of Rome, it underscores the moral geography of Portrait of a Lady. Though the novel is set entirely among Americans who live in Europe (Warburton is the only important character who is not of American ancestry), the expatriates certainly tend to take on the qualities of their surroundings, and the environments of different parts of Europe are extremely important to the novel. In fact, they take on symbolic meanings of their own, as we have seen. America represents innocence, capability, and optimism; England represents a natural mix of individuality and social convention; and continental Europe represents an extreme of human decadence combined with rigid social forms.

In a sense, the deeper thatIsabel goes into the continent, the more noticeable this trend becomes. Rome—the most ancient and historically important city in Europe, the center of both the Roman Empire and of the Catholic Church—is the most sinister city in the novel. It is very possible, in fact, to trace a moral trajectory from Albany to London, London to Florence, and Florence to Rome, with each new city representing a new degree of social rigidity and human cruelty in Isabel's life. In this way, James ties the moral themes of Portrait of a Lady to the physical locales of his characters and creates a trajectory of moral disintegration based specifically on the Isabel's physical travel throughout the novel.

Chapters 52–55

Summary

Isabel visits Pansy at the convent shortly before leaving for England. Here, she is surprised to encounter Madame Merle. Merle seems uncharacteristically awkward around her, even fumbling over her words, and Isabel realizes that Merle has guessed that she knows Pansy is Merle's daughter. Pansy seems slightly dejected, as though she has been confined in a prison; she says that she is now willing to do whatever her father asks of her but that she hopes Isabel will be with her to make things seem easier. Isabel promises to return from England to be with Pansy.

After she says good-bye to Pansy, Isabel is confronted by Merle, who announces that she has just realized something about Isabel's fortune: she says that it must have been Ralph who convinced Mr. Touchett to leave it to her. Isabel icily replies that she thought it was Merle's doing. Merle whimpers that she is miserably unhappy and reveals that she plans to travel to America, perhaps permanently, very soon.

Isabel makes the long journey to England. When she arrives, Henrietta and Mr. Bantling meet her at the station near Gardencourt. Mr. Bantling tells her that he has received a telegraph from the Touchetts, saying that Ralph's health is holding steady. Henrietta tells Isabel that she and Mr. Bantling are going to be married. Isabel feels somewhat let down by this news; it seems a very conventional thing for Henrietta to do, and Isabel had thought that Henrietta valued her liberty. But Mr. Bantling is a comforting presence, and Isabel congratulates him sincerely.

Isabel wanders through the portrait gallery at Gardencourt, which she has not seen for many years. She thinks about her past and wonders what would have happened if Mrs. Touchett had not brought her to Europe: she might have married Caspar Goodwood; she would never have known Gilbert Osmond; everything would have been different. Mrs. Touchett comes downstairs, and Isabel talks to her about their family and the neighbors at Gardencourt. Lord Warburton is planning to marry an English lady. Mrs. Touchett wonders whether Isabel regrets not marrying Warburton when she had the chance. Isabel replies that she does not, but Mrs. Touchett says that she will be hard to get along with if she is dishonest. Isabel opens up and admits that she is very unhappy with Osmond. She also admits to Mrs. Touchett that she dislikes Madame Merle; when she tells Mrs. Touchett that Merle is leaving for America, Mrs. Touchett is surprised and thinks that she must have done something very unpleasant to feel that she had to leave Europe. Isabel says that Merle treated her as a mere convenience; Mrs. Touchett replies that that is how Merle treats everyone.

Isabel sits at Ralph's bedside; he is too weak to talk. On the third night, he manages to speak to her and tells her that she is his angel. Isabel weeps, and Ralph tells her that he feels responsible for her problems: the money he secured for her is what drew Osmond to her in the first place and helped to punish her for her desire to see the world. Isabel says that she has been punished, but she does not think Ralph is to blame. Ralph asks if she will return to Rome, and she says that she does not know. Ralph urges her to remember that there has been love in her life and that she is still loved; no matter how bad things are for her, she is still loved.

That night, Isabel lies in bed, fully clothed in case Ralph should die. She remembers Ralph telling her about the ghost of the manor, which one cannot see unless one has suffered. Isabel suddenly sees Ralph standing next to her bed. She hurries to his room and finds Mrs. Touchett kneeling over him. He is dead. Mrs. Touchett tells Isabel to leave her and to be grateful that she has no children of her own.

Caspar Goodwood arrives in order to attend Ralph's funeral. Miserably, Isabel wonders whether she can bring herself to go back to Rome. She tries not to think about the problem. Mrs. Touchett tells her about Ralph's will: he has left his house to his mother and his library to Henrietta but nothing to Isabel. Isabel has an awkward meeting with Lord Warburton; she congratulates him on his marriage, and he invites her to call on the Misses Molyneux. She finds him strangely lifeless. When everyone is gone, Isabel sits on the garden bench—the same bench where Warburton proposed to her six years ago. Suddenly, Caspar Goodwood approaches her. He says that Ralph has asked him to help her, and he urges her not to return to Rome, but instead to leave with him. He kisses her deeply; Isabel feels as though she is drowning in the intensity of her emotion. She pulls herself away and runs into the house.

The next day, Goodwood finds Henrietta and asks her where Isabel has gone. Henrietta says that Isabel has returned to her husband in Rome. Goodwood is stunned; Henrietta takes him by the arm and leads him away.

Analysis

And so, in the end, social convention seems to win out over American individualism and independence: Isabel returns to her agonizing marriage with Osmond, and even Henrietta decides to marry Mr. Bantling. Isabel's decision to return to Rome and to her husband is based on a variety of factors, each of which has been set up by the preceding chapters: her devotion to Pansy, her pride, her moral commitment to doing her duty even in times of suffering, her fear of the emotionally overwhleming Caspar Goodwood. Apart from Goodwood's obvious opposition, the principal resistance to Isabel's return to Rome seems to dissipate in this section. Ralph and Henrietta have been the staunchest champions of her independence and her freedom, and they each lose their voices—Ralph because he dies and Henrietta because she decides to give up her own independence in order to marry Bantling.

But just as James chose not to show us Isabel's engagement to Osmond or their wedding, he skips over her decision to return to Rome as well. We learn of it after the fact, and only second-hand, when Henrietta explains to Goodwood in Chapter 55 where Isabel has gone. James tends to use the elliptical technique whenever Isabel makes a decision that favors social custom over her independence, as though these moments are either intensely private or impossible to explain. In any case, the effect at the end of the novel is that Isabel simply dissipates, vanishing into the memory of her marriage; we are given no explanation of her thought process, and, for the first time, no hint as to what will become of her.

The novel solves its driving mysteries, then definitively answers its main conflict—social convention defeats individual freedom in a way that is not quite tragic and not quite morally inspiring—and then puts its story to rest. James's remarkable portrait of Isabel Archer has shown her development from an innocent, independent, optimistic young girl to a mature woman who has suffered and learned to commit herself to social propriety. After that lesson—which is not characterized by the novel as either right or wrong, and which is hard for the reader to accept as it is hard for Isabel herself—James seems to imply that there is nothing more to say.

Analytical Overview

The Portrait of a Lady explores the conflict between the individual and society by examining the life of Isabel Archer, a young American woman who must choose between her independent spirit and the demands of social convention. After professing and longing to be an independent woman, autonomous and answerable only to herself, Isabel falls in love with and marries the sinister Gilbert Osmond, who wants her only for her money and who treats her as an object, almost as part of his art collection. Isabel must then decide whether to honor her marriage vows and preserve social propriety or to leave her miserable marriage and escape to a happier, more independent life, possibly with her American suitor Caspar Goodwood. In the end, after the death of her cousin Ralph, the staunchest advocate of her independence, Isabel chooses to return to Osmond and maintain her marriage. She is motivated partly by a sense of social duty, partly by a sense of pride, and partly by the love of her stepdaughter, Pansy, the daughter of Osmond and his manipulative lover Madame Merle.

As the title of the novel indicates, Isabel is the principal character of the book, and the main focus of the novel is on presenting, explaining, and developing her character. James is one of America's great psychological realists, and he uses all his creative powers to ensure that Isabel's conflict is the natural product of a believable mind, and not merely an abstract philosophical consideration. In brief, Isabel's independence of spirit is largely a result of her childhood, when she was generally neglected by her father and allowed to read any book in her grandmother's library; in this way, she supervised her own haphazard education and allowed her mind to develop without discipline or order. Her natural intelligence has always ensured that she is at least as quick as anyone around her, and in Albany, New York, she has the reputation of being a formidable intellect.

After she travels to England with her aunt, Mrs. Touchett, however, it becomes clear that Isabel has a woefully unstructured imagination, as well as a romantic streak that suits her position as an optimistic, innocent American. (For James, throughout Portrait of a Lady, America is a place of individualism and naïveté, while Europe is a place of sophistication, convention, and decadence.) Isabel often considers her life as though it were a novel. She also has a tendency to think about herself obsessively and has a vast faith in her own moral strength—in fact, recognizing that she has never faced hardship, Isabel actually wishes that she might be made to suffer, so that she could prove her ability to overcome suffering without betraying her principles.

When Isabel moves to England, her cousin Ralph is so taken with her spirit of independence that he convinces his dying father to leave half his fortune to Isabel. This is intended to prevent her from ever having to marry for money, but ironically it attracts the treachery of the novel's villains, Madame Merle and Gilbert Osmond. They conspire to convince Isabel to marry Osmond in order to gain access to her wealth. Her marriage to Osmond effectively stifles Isabel's independent spirit, as her husband treats her as an object and tries to force her to share his opinions and abandon her own.

This is the thematic background of Portrait of a Lady, and James skillfully intertwines the novel's psychological and thematic elements. Isabel's downfall with Osmond, for instance, enables the book's most trenchant exploration of the conflict between her desire to conform to social convention and her fiercely independent mind. It is also perfectly explained by the elements of Isabel's character: her haphazard upbringing has led her to long for stability and safety, even if they mean a loss of independence, and her active imagination enables her to create an illusory picture of Osmond, which she believes in more than the real thing, at least until she is married to him. Once she marries Osmond, Isabel's pride in her moral strength makes it impossible for her to consider leaving him: she once longed for hardship, and now that she has found it, it would be hypocritical for her to surrender to it by violating social custom and abandoning her husband.

In the same way that James unites his psychological and thematic subjects, he also intertwines the novel's settings with its themes. Set almost entirely among a group of American expatriates living in Europe in the 1860s and 70s, the book relies on a kind of moral geography, in which America represents innocence, individualism, and capability; Europe represents decadence, sophistication, and social convention; and England represents the best mix of the two. Isabel moves from America to England to continental Europe, and at each stage she comes to mirror her surroundings, gradually losing a bit of independence with each move. Eventually she lives in Rome, the historic heart of continental Europe, and it is here that she endures her greatest hardship with Gilbert Osmond.

Narratively, James uses many of his most characteristic techniques in Portrait of a Lady. In addition to his polished, elegant prose and his sedate, slow pacing, he utilizes a favorite technique of skipping over some of the novel's main events in telling the story. Instead of narrating moments such as Isabel's wedding with Osmond, James skips over them, relating that they have happened only after the fact, in peripheral conversations. This literary technique is known as ellipses. In the novel, James most often uses his elliptical technique in scenes when Isabel chooses to value social custom over her independence—her acceptance of Gilbert's proposal, their wedding, her decision to return to Rome after briefly leaving for Ralph's funeral at the end of the novel. James uses this method to create the sense that, in these moments, Isabel is no longer accessible to the reader; in a sense, by choosing to be with Gilbert Osmond, Isabel is lost.

Chapter 12

Complete Text

The Portrait of a Lady by Henry James
VOLUME I
PREFACE

"The Portrait of a Lady" was, like "Roderick Hudson," begun in Florence, during three months spent there in the spring of 1879.Like "Roderick" and like "The American," it had beendesigned for publication in "The Atlantic Monthly," where itbegan to appear in 1880. It differed from its two predecessors,however, in finding a course also open to it, from month tomonth, in "Macmillan's Magazine"; which was to be for me one ofthe last occasions of simultaneous "serialisation" in the twocountries that the changing conditions of literary intercoursebetween England and the United States had up to then leftunaltered. It is a long novel, and I was long in writing it; Iremember being again much occupied with it, the following year,during a stay of several weeks made in Venice.

I had rooms onRiva Schiavoni, at the top of a house near the passage leadingoff to San Zaccaria; the waterside life, the wondrous lagoonspread before me, and the ceaseless human chatter of Venice camein at my windows, to which I seem to myself to have beenconstantly driven, in the fruitless fidget of composition, as ifto see whether, out in the blue channel, the ship of some rightsuggestion, of some better phrase, of the next happy twist of mysubject, the next true touch for my canvas, mightn't come intosight. But I recall vividly enough that the response mostelicited, in general, to these restless appeals was the rathergrim admonition that romantic and historic sites, such as theland of Italy abounds in, offer the artist a questionable aid toconcentration when they themselves are not to be the subject ofit. They are too rich in their own life and too charged withtheir own meanings merely to help him out with a lame phrase;they draw him away from his small question to their own greaterones; so that, after a little, he feels, while thus yearningtoward them in his difficulty, as if he were asking an army ofglorious veterans to help him to arrest a peddler who has givenhim the wrong change.

There are pages of the book which, in the reading over, haveseemed to make me see again the bristling curve of the wide Riva,the large colour-spots of the balconied houses and the repeatedundulation of the little hunchbacked bridges, marked by the riseand drop again, with the wave, of foreshortened clickingpedestrians. The Venetian footfall and the Venetian cry—alltalk there, wherever uttered, having the pitch of a call acrossthe water—come in once more at the window, renewing one's oldimpression of the delighted senses and the divided, frustratedmind. How can places that speak IN GENERAL so to the imaginationnot give it, at the moment, the particular thing it wants? Irecollect again and again, in beautiful places, dropping intothat wonderment.

The real truth is, I think, that they express,under this appeal, only too much—more than, in the given case,one has use for; so that one finds one's self working lesscongruously, after all, so far as the surrounding picture isconcerned, than in presence of the moderate and the neutral, towhich we may lend something of the light of our vision. Such aplace as Venice is too proud for such charities; Venice doesn'tborrow, she but all magnificently gives. We profit by thatenormously, but to do so we must either be quite off duty or beon it in her service alone. Such, and so rueful, are thesereminiscences; though on the whole, no doubt, one's book, andone's "literary effort" at large, were to be the better forthem. Strangely fertilising, in the long run, does a wastedeffort of attention often prove. It all depends on HOW theattention has been cheated, has been squandered. There arehigh-handed insolent frauds, and there are insidious sneakingones. And there is, I fear, even on the most designing artist'spart, always witless enough good faith, always anxious enoughdesire, to fail to guard him against their deceits. Trying to recover here, for recognition, the germ of my idea, Isee that it must have consisted not at all in any conceit of a"plot," nefarious name, in any flash, upon the fancy, of a set ofrelations, or in any one of those situations that, by a logic oftheir own, immediately fall, for the fabulist, into movement,into a march or a rush, a patter of quick steps; but altogether inthe sense of a single character, the character and aspect of aparticular engaging young woman, to which all the usual elementsof a "subject," certainly of a setting, were to need to be superadded. Quite as interesting as the young woman herself at herbest, do I find, I must again repeat, this projection of memoryupon the whole matter of the growth, in one's imagination, ofsome such apology for a motive.

These are the fascinations of thefabulist's art, these lurking forces of expansion, thesenecessities of upspringing in the seed, these beautifuldeterminations, on the part of the idea entertained, to grow astall as possible, to push into the light and the air and thicklyflower there; and, quite as much, these fine possibilities ofrecovering, from some good standpoint on the ground gained, theintimate history of the business—of retracing and reconstructingits steps and stages. I have always fondly remembered a remarkthat I heard fall years ago from the lips of Ivan Turgenieff inregard to his own experience of the usual origin of the fictivepicture.

It began for him almost always with the vision of someperson or persons, who hovered before him, soliciting him, as theactive or passive figure, interesting him and appealing to himjust as they were and by what they were. He saw them, in thatfashion, as disponibles, saw them subject to the chances, thecomplications of existence, and saw them vividly, but then had tofind for them the right relations, those that would most bringthem out; to imagine, to invent and select and piece together thesituations most useful and favourable to the sense of thecreatures themselves, the complications they would be most likelyto produce and to feel.

"To arrive at these things is to arrive at my story," hesaid, "and that's the way I look for it. The result is that I'moften accused of not having 'story' enough. I seem to myself tohave as much as I need—to show my people, to exhibit theirrelations with each other; for that is all my measure. If I watchthem long enough I see them come together, I see them PLACED, Isee them engaged in this or that act and in this or thatdifficulty. How they look and move and speak and behave, alwaysin the setting I have found for them, is my account of them—ofwhich I dare say, alas, que cela manque souvent d'architecture.But I would rather, I think, have too little architecture thantoo much—when there's danger of its interfering with my measureof the truth.

The French of course like more of it than I give—having by their own genius such a hand for it; and indeed onemust give all one can. As for the origin of one's wind-blowngerms themselves, who shall say, as you ask, where THEY comefrom? We have to go too far back, too far behind, to say. Isn'tit all we can say that they come from every quarter of heaven,that they are THERE at almost any turn of the road? Theyaccumulate, and we are always picking them over, selecting amongthem. They are the breath of life—by which I mean that life, inits own way, breathes them upon us. They are so, in a mannerprescribed and imposed—floated into our minds by the current oflife. That reduces to imbecility the vain critic's quarrel, sooften, with one's subject, when he hasn't the wit to accept it.Will he point out then which other it should properly have been?—his office being, essentially to point out. Il en serait bienembarrasse. Ah, when he points out what I've done or failed to dowith it, that's another matter: there he's on his ground. I givehim up my 'sarchitecture,'" my distinguished friend concluded,"as much as he will."

So this beautiful genius, and I recall with comfort the gratitudeI drew from his reference to the intensity of suggestion that mayreside in the stray figure, the unattached character, the imageen disponibilite. It gave me higher warrant than I seemed then tohave met for just that blest habit of one's own imagination, thetrick of investing some conceived or encountered individual, somebrace or group of individuals, with the germinal property andauthority. I was myself so much more antecedently conscious of myfigures than of their setting—a too preliminary, a preferentialinterest in which struck me as in general such a putting of thecart before the horse. I might envy, though I couldn't emulate,the imaginative writer so constituted as to see his fable firstand to make out its agents afterwards.

I could think so little ofany fable that didn't need its agents positively to launch it; Icould think so little of any situation that didn't depend for itsinterest on the nature of the persons situated, and thereby ontheir way of taking it. There are methods of so-calledpresentation, I believe among novelists who have appeared toflourish—that offer the situation as indifferent to thatsupport; but I have not lost the sense of the value for me, atthe time, of the admirable Russian's testimony to my not needing,all superstitiously, to try and perform any such gymnastic. Otherechoes from the same source linger with me, I confess, asunfadingly—if it be not all indeed one much-embracing echo. Itwas impossible after that not to read, for one's uses, highlucidity into the tormented and disfigured and bemuddled questionof the objective value, and even quite into that of the criticalappreciation, of "subject" in the novel.

One had had from an early time, for that matter, the instinct ofthe right estimate of such values and of its reducing to theinane the dull dispute over the "immoral" subject and the moral.Recognising so promptly the one measure of the worth of a givensubject, the question about it that, rightly answered, disposesof all others—is it valid, in a word, is it genuine, is itsincere, the result of some direct impression or perception oflife?—I had found small edification, mostly, in a criticalpretension that had neglected from the first all delimitation ofground and all definition of terms. The air of my earlier timeshows, to memory, as darkened, all round, with that vanity—unless the difference to-day be just in one's own finalimpatience, the lapse of one's attention.

There is, I think, nomore nutritive or suggestive truth in this connexion than that ofthe perfect dependence of the "moral" sense of a work of art onthe amount of felt life concerned in producing it. The questioncomes back thus, obviously, to the kind and the degree of theartist's prime sensibility, which is the soil out of which hissubject springs. The quality and capacity of that soil, itsability to "grow" with due freshness and straightness any visionof life, represents, strongly or weakly, the projected morality.That element is but another name for the more or less closeconnexion of the subject with some mark made on the intelligence,with some sincere experience.

By which, at the same time, ofcourse, one is far from contending that this enveloping air ofthe artist's humanity—which gives the last touch to the worth ofthe work—is not a widely and wondrously varying element; beingon one occasion a rich and magnificent medium and on another acomparatively poor and ungenerous one. Here we get exactly thehigh price of the novel as a literary form—its power not only,while preserving that form with closeness, to range through allthe differences of the individual relation to its generalsubject-matter, all the varieties of outlook on life, ofdisposition to reflect and project, created by conditions thatare never the same from man to man (or, so far as that goes, fromman to woman), but positively to appear more true to itscharacter in proportion as it strains, or tends to burst, with alatent extravagance, its mould.

The house of fiction has in short not one window, but a million—a number of possible windows not to be reckoned, rather; everyone of which has been pierced, or is still pierceable, in itsvast front, by the need of the individual vision and by thepressure of the individual will. These apertures, of dissimilarshape and size, hang so, all together, over the human scene thatwe might have expected of them a greater sameness of report thanwe find. They are but windows at the best, mere holes in a deadwall, disconnected, perched aloft; they are not hinged doorsopening straight upon life. But they have this mark of their ownthat at each of them stands a figure with a pair of eyes, or atleast with a field-glass, which forms, again and again, forobservation, a unique instrument, insuring to the person makinguse of it an impression distinct from every other. He and hisneighbours are watching the same show, but one seeing more wherethe other sees less, one seeing black where the other sees white,one seeing big where the other sees small, one seeing coarsewhere the other sees fine. And so on, and so on; there isfortunately no saying on what, for the particular pair of eyes,the window may NOT open; "fortunately" by reason, precisely, ofthis incalculability of range. The spreading field, the humanscene, is the "choice of subject"; the pierced aperture, eitherbroad or balconied or slit-like and low-browed, is the "literaryform"; but they are, singly or together, as nothing without theposted presence of the watcher—without, in other words, theconsciousness of the artist. Tell me what the artist is, and Iwill tell you of what he has BEEN conscious. Thereby I shallexpress to you at once his boundless freedom and his "moral"reference.

All this is a long way round, however, for my word about my dimfirst move toward "The Portrait," which was exactly my grasp of asingle character—an acquisition I had made, moreover, after afashion not here to be retraced. Enough that I was, as seemed tome, in complete possession of it, that I had been so for a longtime, that this had made it familiar and yet had not blurred itscharm, and that, all urgently, all tormentingly, I saw it inmotion and, so to speak, in transit. This amounts to saying thatI saw it as bent upon its fate—some fate or other; which, amongthe possibilities, being precisely the question. Thus I had myvivid individual—vivid, so strangely, in spite of being still atlarge, not confined by the conditions, not engaged in the tangle,to which we look for much of the impress that constitutes anidentity.

If the apparition was still all to be placed how cameit to be vivid?—since we puzzle such quantities out, mostly,just by the business of placing them. One could answer such aquestion beautifully, doubtless, if one could do so subtle, ifnot so monstrous, a thing as to write the history of the growthof one's imagination. One would describe then what, at a giventime, had extraordinarily happened to it, and one would so, forinstance, be in a position to tell, with an approach toclearness, how, under favour of occasion, it had been able totake over (take over straight from life) such and such aconstituted, animated figure or form. The figure has to thatextent, as you see, BEEN placed—placed in the imagination thatdetains it, preserves, protects, enjoys it, conscious of itspresence in the dusky, crowded, heterogeneous back-shop of themind very much as a wary dealer in precious odds and ends,competent to make an "advance" on rare objects confided to him,is conscious of the rare little "piece" left in deposit by thereduced, mysterious lady of title or the speculative amateur, andwhich is already there to disclose its merit afresh as soon as akey shall have clicked in a cupboard-door. That may he, I recognise, a somewhat superfine analogy for theparticular "value" I here speak of, the image of the youngfeminine nature that I had had for so considerable a time allcuriously at my disposal; but it appears to fond memory quite tofit the fact—with the recall, in addition, of my pious desire butto place my treasure right.

I quite remind myself thus of thedealer resigned not to "realise," resigned to keeping theprecious object locked up indefinitely rather than commit it, atno matter what price, to vulgar hands. For there ARE dealers inthese forms and figures and treasures capable of that refinement.The point is, however, that this single small corner-stone, theconception of a certain young woman affronting her destiny, hadbegun with being all my outfit for the large building of "ThePortrait of a Lady." It came to be a square and spacious house—or has at least seemed so to me in this going over it again; but,such as it is, it had to be put up round my young woman while shestood there in perfect isolation. That is to me, artisticallyspeaking, the circumstance of interest; for I have lost myselfonce more, I confess, in the curiosity of analysing thestructure.

By what process of logical accretion was this slight"personality," the mere slim shade of an intelligent butpresumptuous girl, to find itself endowed with the highattributes of a Subject?—and indeed by what thinness, at thebest, would such a subject not be vitiated? Millions ofpresumptuous girls, intelligent or not intelligent, daily affronttheir destiny, and what is it open to their destiny to be, at themost, that we should make an ado about it? The novel is of itsvery nature an "ado," an ado about something, and the larger theform it takes the greater of course the ado. Therefore,consciously, that was what one was in for—for positivelyorganising an ado about Isabel Archer.

One looked it well in the face, I seem to remember, thisextravagance; and with the effect precisely of recognising thecharm of the problem. Challenge any such problem with anyintelligence, and you immediately see how full it is ofsubstance; the wonder being, all the while, as we look at theworld, how absolutely, how inordinately, the Isabel Archers, andeven much smaller female fry, insist on mattering. George Eliothas admirably noted it—"In these frail vessels is borne onwardthrough the ages the treasure of human affection." In "Romeo andJuliet" Juliet has to be important, just as, in "Adam Bede" and"The Mill on the Floss" and "Middlemarch" and "DanielDeronda," Hetty Sorrel and Maggie Tulliver and Rosamond Vincy andGwendolen Harleth have to be; with that much of firm ground, thatmuch of bracing air, at the disposal all the while of their feetand their lungs.

They are typical, none the less, of a classdifficult, in the individual case, to make a centre of interest;so difficult in fact that many an expert painter, as for instanceDickens and Walter Scott, as for instance even, in the main, sosubtle a hand as that of R. L. Stevenson, has preferred to leavethe task unattempted. There are in fact writers as to whom wemake out that their refuge from this is to assume it to be notworth their attempting; by which pusillanimity in truth theirhonour is scantly saved. It is never an attestation of a value,or even of our imperfect sense of one, it is never a tribute toany truth at all, that we shall represent that value badly. Itnever makes up, artistically, for an artist's dim feeling about athing that he shall "do" the thing as ill as possible. Thereare better ways than that, the best of all of which is to beginwith less stupidity.

It may be answered meanwhile, in regard to Shakespeare's and toGeorge Eliot's testimony, that their concession to the"importance" of their Juliets and Cleopatras and Portias (evenwith Portia as the very type and model of the young personintelligent and presumptuous) and to that of their

Hettys andMaggies and Rosamonds and Gwendolens, suffers the abatement thatthese slimnesses are, when figuring as the main props of thetheme, never suffered to be sole ministers of its appeal, buthave their inadequacy eked out with comic relief and underplots,as the playwrights say, when not with murders and battles and thegreat mutations of the world. If they are shown as "mattering"as much as they could possibly pretend to, the proof of it is ina hundred other persons, made of much stouter stuff; and eachinvolved moreover in a hundred relations which matter to THEMconcomitantly with that one.

Cleopatra matters, beyond bounds, toAntony, but his colleagues, his antagonists, the state of Romeand the impending battle also prodigiously matter; Portia mattersto Antonio, and to Shylock, and to the Prince of Morocco, to thefifty aspiring princes, but for these gentry there are otherlively concerns; for Antonio, notably, there are Shylock andBassanio and his lost ventures and the extremity of hispredicament. This extremity indeed, by the same token, matters toPortia—though its doing so becomes of interest all by the factthat Portia matters to US.

That she does so, at any rate, andthat almost everything comes round to it again, supports mycontention as to this fine example of the value recognised in themere young thing. (I say "mere" young thing because I guess thateven Shakespeare, preoccupied mainly though he may have been withthe passions of princes, would scarce have pretended to found thebest of his appeal for her on her high social position.) It is anexample exactly of the deep difficulty braved—the difficulty ofmaking George Eliot's "frail vessel," if not the all-in-all forour attention, at least the clearest of the call.

Now to see deep difficulty braved is at any time, for the reallyaddicted artist, to feel almost even as a pang the beautifulincentive, and to feel it verily in such sort as to wish thedanger intensified. The difficulty most worth tackling can onlybe for him, in these conditions, the greatest the case permitsof. So I remember feeling here (in presence, always, that is, ofthe particular uncertainty of my ground), that there would be oneway better than another—oh, ever so much better than any other!—of making it fight out its battle. The frail vessel, that chargedwith George Eliot's "treasure," and thereby of such importanceto those who curiously approach it, has likewise possibilities ofimportance to itself, possibilities which permit of treatment andin fact peculiarly require it from the moment they are consideredat all. There is always the escape from any close account of theweak agent of such spells by using as a bridge for evasion, forretreat and flight, the view of her relation to those surroundingher.

Make it predominantly a view of THEIR relation and the trickis played: you give the general sense of her effect, and yougive it, so far as the raising on it of a superstructure goes,with the maximum of ease. Well, I recall perfectly how little, inmy now quite established connexion, the maximum of ease appealedto me, and how I seemed to get rid of it by an honesttransposition of the weights in the two scales. "Place thecentre of the subject in the young woman's own consciousness," Isaid to myself, "and you get as interesting and as beautiful adifficulty as you could wish. Stick to THAT—for the centre;put the heaviest weight into THAT scale, which will be so largelythe scale of her relation to herself. Make her only interestedenough, at the same time, in the things that are not herself, andthis relation needn't fear to be too limited.

Place meanwhile inthe other scale the lighter weight (which is usually the one thattips the balance of interest): press least hard, in short, onthe consciousness of your heroine's satellites, especially themale; make it an interest contributive only to the greater one.See, at all events, what can be done in this way. What betterfield could there be for a due ingenuity? The girl hovers,inextinguishable, as a charming creature, and the job will be totranslate her into the highest terms of that formula, and asnearly as possible moreover into ALL of them. To depend upon herand her little concerns wholly to see you through willnecessitate, remember, your really 'doing' her."

So far I reasoned, and it took nothing less than that technicalrigour, I now easily see, to inspire me with the right confidencefor erecting on such a plot of ground the neat and careful andproportioned pile of bricks that arches over it and that was thusto form, constructionally speaking, a literary monument. Such isthe aspect that to-day "The Portrait" wears for me: a structurereared with an "architectural" competence, as Turgenieff wouldhave said, that makes it, to the author's own sense, the mostproportioned of his productions after "The Ambassadors" which wasto follow it so many years later and which has, no doubt, asuperior roundness. On one thing I was determined; that, though Ishould clearly have to pile brick upon brick for the creation ofan interest, I would leave no pretext for saying that anything isout of line, scale or perspective.

I would build large—in fineembossed vaults and painted arches, as who should say, and yetnever let it appear that the chequered pavement, the ground underthe reader's feet, fails to stretch at every point to the base ofthe walls. That precautionary spirit, on re-perusal of the book,is the old note that most touches me: it testifies so, for my ownear, to the anxiety of my provision for the reader's amusement. Ifelt, in view of the possible limitations of my subject, that nosuch provision could be excessive, and the development of thelatter was simply the general form of that earnest quest. And Ifind indeed that this is the only account I can give myself ofthe evolution of the fable it is all under the head thus namedthat I conceive the needful accretion as having taken place, theright complications as having started. It was naturally of theessence that the young woman should be herself complex; that wasrudimentary—or was at any rate the light in which Isabel Archerhad originally dawned. It went, however, but a certain way, andother lights, contending, conflicting lights, and of as manydifferent colours, if possible, as the rockets, the Roman candlesand Catherine-wheels of a "pyrotechnic display," would beemployable to attest that she was.

I had, no doubt, a gropinginstinct for the right complications, since I am quite unable totrack the footsteps of those that constitute, as the case stands,the general situation exhibited. They are there, for what theyare worth, and as numerous as might be; but my memory, I confess,is a blank as to how and whence they came.

I seem to myself to have waked up one morning in possession ofthem—of Ralph Touchett and his parents, of Madame Merle, ofGilbert Osmond and his daughter and his sister, of LordWarburton, Caspar Goodwood and Miss Stackpole, the definite arrayof contributions to Isabel Archer's history. I recognised them, Iknew them, they were the numbered pieces of my puzzle, theconcrete terms of my "plot." It was as if they had simply, by animpulse of their own, floated into my ken, and all in response tomy primary question: "Well, what will she DO?" Their answer seemedto be that if I would trust them they would show me; on which,with an urgent appeal to them to make it at least as interestingas they could, I trusted them.

They were like the group ofattendants and entertainers who come down by train when peoplein the country give a party; they represented the contract forcarrying the party on. That was an excellent relation with them—a possible one even with so broken a reed (from her slightnessof cohesion) as Henrietta Stackpole. It is a familiar truth tothe novelist, at the strenuous hour, that, as certain elementsin any work are of the essence, so others are only of the form;that as this or that character, this or that disposition of thematerial, belongs to the subject directly, so to speak, so thisor that other belongs to it but indirectly—belongs intimately tothe treatment. This is a truth, however, of which he rarely getsthe benefit—since it could be assured to him, really, but bycriticism based upon perception, criticism which is too little ofthis world. He must not think of benefits, moreover, I freelyrecognise, for that way dishonour lies: he has, that is, but oneto think of—the benefit, whatever it may be, involved in hishaving cast a spell upon the simpler, the very simplest, forms ofattention.

This is all he is entitled to; he is entitled tonothing, he is bound to admit, that can come to him, from thereader, as a result on the latter's part of any act of reflexionor discrimination. He may ENJOY this finer tribute—that isanother affair, but on condition only of taking it as a gratuity"thrown in," a mere miraculous windfall, the fruit of a tree hemay not pretend to have shaken. Against reflexion, againstdiscrimination, in his interest, all earth and air conspire;wherefore it is that, as I say, he must in many a case haveschooled himself, from the first, to work but for a "livingwage." The living wage is the reader's grant of the leastpossible quantity of attention required for consciousness of a"spell." The occasional charming "tip" is an act of hisintelligence over and beyond this, a golden apple, for thewriter's lap, straight from the wind-stirred tree. The artist mayof course, in wanton moods, dream of some Paradise wherethe direct appeal to the intelligence might be legalised; for tosuch extravagances as these his yearning mind can scarce hopeever completely to close itself. The most he can do is toremember they ARE extravagances.

All of which is perhaps but a gracefully devious way of saying thatHenrietta Stackpole was a good example, in "The Portrait," of thetruth to which I just adverted—as good an example as I could namewere it not that Maria Gostrey, in "The Ambassadors," then in thebosom of time, may be mentioned as a better. Each of these personsis but wheels to the coach; neither belongs to the body of thatvehicle, or is for a moment accommodated with a seat inside. Therethe subject alone is ensconced, in the form of its "hero andheroine," and of the privileged high officials, say, who ride withthe king and queen.

There are reasons why one would have likedthis to be felt, as in general one would like almost anything tobe felt, in one's work, that one has one's self contributively felt.We have seen, however, how idle is that pretension, which I shouldbe sorry to make too much of. Maria Gostrey and Miss Stackpolethen are cases, each, of the light ficelle, not of the trueagent; they may run beside the coach "for all they are worth,"they may cling to it till they are out of breath (as poor MissStackpole all so visibly does), but neither, all the while, somuch as gets her foot on the step, neither ceases for a momentto tread the dusty road. Put it even that they are like thefishwives who helped to bring back to Paris from Versailles, onthat most ominous day of the first half of the French Revolution,the carriage of the royal family. The only thing is that I maywell be asked, I acknowledge, why then, in the present fiction,I have suffered

Henrietta (of whom we have indubitably too much)so officiously, so strangely, so almost inexplicably, to pervade.I will presently say what I can for that anomaly—and in the mostconciliatory fashion.

A point I wish still more to make is that if my relation ofconfidence with the actors in my drama who WERE, unlike MissStackpole, true agents, was an excellent one to have arrived at,there still remained my relation with the reader, which wasanother affair altogether and as to which I felt no one to betrusted but myself. That solicitude was to be accordinglyexpressed in the artful patience with which, as I have said, Ipiled brick upon brick. The bricks, for the whole counting-over—putting for bricks little touches and inventions and enhancementsby the way—affect me in truth as well-nigh innumerable and asever so scrupulously fitted together and packed-in. It is aneffect of detail, of the minutest; though, if one were in thisconnexion to say all, one would express the hope that thegeneral, the ampler air of the modest monument still survives. Ido at least seem to catch the key to a part of this abundance ofsmall anxious, ingenious illustration as I recollect putting myfinger, in my young woman's interest, on the most obvious of herpredicates.

"What will she 'do'? Why, the first thing she'lldo will be to come to Europe; which in fact will form, and allinevitably, no small part of her principal adventure. Coming toEurope is even for the 'frail vessels,' in this wonderful age, amild adventure; but what is truer than that on one side—the sideof their independence of flood and field, of the moving accident,of battle and murder and sudden death—her adventures are to bemild? Without her sense of them, her sense FOR them, as one maysay, they are next to nothing at all; but isn't the beauty andthe difficulty just in showing their mystic conversion by thatsense, conversion into the stuff of drama or, even moredelightful word still, of 'story'?"

It was all as clear, mycontention, as a silver bell. Two very good instances, I think,of this effect of conversion, two cases of the rare chemistry,are the pages in which Isabel, coming into the drawing-room atGardencourt, coming in from a wet walk or whatever, that rainyafternoon, finds Madame Merle in possession of the place, MadameMerle seated, all absorbed but all serene, at the piano, anddeeply recognises, in the striking of such an hour, in thepresence there, among the gathering shades, of this personage, ofwhom a moment before she had never so much as heard, aturning-point in her life. It is dreadful to have too much, forany artistic demonstration, to dot one's i's and insist on one'sintentions, and I am not eager to do it now; but the questionhere was that of producing the maximum of intensity with theminimum of strain.

The interest was to be raised to its pitch and yet the elementsto be kept in their key; so that, should the whole thing dulyimpress, I might show what an "exciting" inward life may do forthe person leading it even while it remains perfectly normal. AndI cannot think of a more consistent application of that idealunless it be in the long statement, just beyond the middle of thebook, of my young woman's extraordinary meditative vigil on theoccasion that was to become for her such a landmark. Reduced toits essence, it is but the vigil of searching criticism; but itthrows the action further forward that twenty "incidents" mighthave done. It was designed to have all the vivacity of incidentsand all the economy of picture.

She sits up, by her dying fire,far into the night, under the spell of recognitions on which shefinds the last sharpness suddenly wait. It is a representationsimply of her motionlessly SEEING, and an attempt withal to makethe mere still lucidity of her act as "interesting" as thesurprise of a caravan or the identification of a pirate. Itrepresents, for that matter, one of the identifications dear tothe novelist, and even indispensable to him; but it all goes onwithout her being approached by another person and without herleaving her chair. It is obviously the best thing in the book,but it is only a supreme illustration of the general plan.

As toHenrietta, my apology for whom I just left incomplete, sheexemplifies, I fear, in her superabundance, not an element of myplan, but only an excess of my zeal. So early was to begin mytendency to OVERTREAT, rather than undertreat (when there waschoice or danger) my subject.

(Many members of my craft, Igather, are far from agreeing with me, but I have always heldovertreating the minor disservice.) "Treating" that of "ThePortrait" amounted to never forgetting, by any lapse, that thething was under a special obligation to be amusing. There was thedanger of the noted "thinness"—which was to be averted, toothand nail, by cultivation of the lively. That is at least how Isee it to-day. Henrietta must have been at that time a part of mywonderful notion of the lively. And then there was anothermatter. I had, within the few preceding years, come to live inLondon, and the "international" light lay, in those days, to mysense, thick and rich upon the scene. It was the light in whichso much of the picture hung. But that IS another matter. There isreally too much to say.

Henry James the Protrait of a Lady

Chapter 1

Under certain circumstances there are few hours in life moreagreeable than the hour dedicated to the ceremony known asafternoon tea. There are circumstances in which, whether youpartake of the tea or not—some people of course never do,—thesituation is in itself delightful. Those that I have in mind inbeginning to unfold this simple history offered an admirablesetting to an innocent pastime. The implements of the littlefeast had been disposed upon the lawn of an old Englishcountry-house, in what I should call the perfect middle of asplendid summer afternoon.

Part of the afternoon had waned, butmuch of it was left, and what was left was of the finest andrarest quality. Real dusk would not arrive for many hours; butthe flood of summer light had begun to ebb, the air had grownmellow, the shadows were long upon the smooth, dense turf. Theylengthened slowly, however, and the scene expressed that sense ofleisure still to come which is perhaps the chief source of one'senjoyment of such a scene at such an hour. From five o'clock toeight is on certain occasions a little eternity; but on such anoccasion as this the interval could be only an eternity ofpleasure. The persons concerned in it were taking their pleasurequietly, and they were not of the sex which is supposed tofurnish the regular votaries of the ceremony I have mentioned. The shadows on the perfect lawn were straight and angular; theywere the shadows of an old man sitting in a deep wicker-chairnear the low table on which the tea had been served, and of twoyounger men strolling to and fro, in desultory talk, in front ofhim. The old man had his cup in his hand; it was an unusuallylarge cup, of a different pattern from the rest of the set andpainted in brilliant colours.

He disposed of its contents withmuch circumspection, holding it for a long time close to hischin, with his face turned to the house. His companions hadeither finished their tea or were indifferent to their privilege;they smoked cigarettes as they continued to stroll. One of them,from time to time, as he passed, looked with a certain attentionat the elder man, who, unconscious of observation, rested hiseyes upon the rich red front of his dwelling. The house that rosebeyond the lawn was a structure to repay such consideration andwas the most characteristic object in the peculiarly Englishpicture I have attempted to sketch.

It stood upon a low hill, above the river—the river being theThames at some forty miles from London. A long gabled front ofred brick, with the complexion of which time and the weather hadplayed all sorts of pictorial tricks, only, however, to improveand refine it, presented to the lawn its patches of ivy, itsclustered chimneys, its windows smothered in creepers. The househad a name and a history; the old gentleman taking his tea wouldhave been delighted to tell you these things: how it had beenbuilt under Edward the Sixth, had offered a night's hospitalityto the great Elizabeth (whose august person had extended itselfupon a huge, magnificent and terribly angular bed which stillformed the principal honour of the sleeping apartments), had beena good deal bruised and defaced in Cromwell's wars, and then,under the Restoration, repaired and much enlarged; and how,finally, after having been remodelled and disfigured in theeighteenth century, it had passed into the careful keeping of ashrewd American banker, who had bought it originally because(owing to circumstances too complicated to set forth) it wasoffered at a great bargain: bought it with much grumbling at itsugliness, its antiquity, its incommodity, and who now, at the endof twenty years, had become conscious of a real aesthetic passionfor it, so that he knew all its points and would tell you justwhere to stand to see them in combination and just the hour whenthe shadows of its various protuberances which fell so softlyupon the warm, weary brickwork—were of the right measure.Besides this, as I have said, he could have counted off most ofthe successive owners and occupants, several of whom were knownto general fame; doing so, however, with an undemonstrativeconviction that the latest phase of its destiny was not the leasthonourable.

The front of the house overlooking that portion ofthe lawn with which we are concerned was not the entrance-front;this was in quite another quarter. Privacy here reigned supreme,and the wide carpet of turf that covered the level hill-topseemed but the extension of a luxurious interior. The great stilloaks and beeches flung down a shade as dense as that of velvetcurtains; and the place was furnished, like a room, withcushioned seats, with rich-coloured rugs, with the books andpapers that lay upon the grass. The river was at some distance;where the ground began to slope the lawn, properly speaking,ceased. But it was none the less a charming walk down to thewater.

The old gentleman at the tea-table, who had come from Americathirty years before, had brought with him, at the top of hisbaggage, his American physiognomy; and he had not only brought itwith him, but he had kept it in the best order, so that, ifnecessary, he might have taken it back to his own country withperfect confidence. At present, obviously, nevertheless, he wasnot likely to displace himself; his journeys were over and he wastaking the rest that precedes the great rest. He had a narrow,clean-shaven face, with features evenly distributed and anexpression of placid acuteness. It was evidently a face in whichthe range of representation was not large, so that the air ofcontented shrewdness was all the more of a merit. It seemed totell that he had been successful in life, yet it seemed to tellalso that his success had not been exclusive and invidious, buthad had much of the inoffensiveness of failure. He had certainlyhad a great experience of men, but there was an almost rusticsimplicity in the faint smile that played upon his lean, spaciouscheek and lighted up his humorous eye as he at last slowly andcarefully deposited his big tea-cup upon the table. He was neatlydressed, in well-brushed black; but a shawl was folded upon hisknees, and his feet were encased in thick, embroidered slippers.A beautiful collie dog lay upon the grass near his chair, watchingthe master's face almost as tenderly as the master took in thestill more magisterial physiognomy of the house; and a littlebristling, bustling terrier bestowed a desultory attendance uponthe other gentlemen.

One of these was a remarkably well-made man of five-and-thirty,with a face as English as that of the old gentleman I have justsketched was something else; a noticeably handsome face, fresh-coloured, fair and frank, with firm, straight features, a livelygrey eye and the rich adornment of a chestnut beard. This personhad a certain fortunate, brilliant exceptional look—the air of ahappy temperament fertilised by a high civilisation—which wouldhave made almost any observer envy him at a venture. He wasbooted and spurred, as if he had dismounted from a long ride; hewore a white hat, which looked too large for him; he held his twohands behind him, and in one of them—a large, white, well-shapedfist—was crumpled a pair of soiled dog-skin gloves.His companion, measuring the length of the lawn beside him, was aperson of quite a different pattern, who, although he might haveexcited grave curiosity, would not, like the other, have provokedyou to wish yourself, almost blindly, in his place.

Tall, lean,loosely and feebly put together, he had an ugly, sickly, witty,charming face, furnished, but by no means decorated, with astraggling moustache and whisker. He looked clever and ill—acombination by no means felicitous; and he wore a brown velvetjacket. He carried his hands in his pockets, and there wassomething in the way he did it that showed the habit wasinveterate. His gait had a shambling, wandering quality; he wasnot very firm on his legs. As I have said, whenever he passed theold man in the chair he rested his eyes upon him; and at thismoment, with their faces brought into relation, you would easilyhave seen they were father and son. The father caught his son'seye at last and gave him a mild, responsive smile."I'm getting on very well," he said."Have you drunk your tea?" asked the son."Yes, and enjoyed it." "Shall I give you some more?" The old man considered, placidly. "Well, I guess I'll wait andsee." He had, in speaking, the American tone. "Are you cold?" the son enquired.

The father slowly rubbed his legs. "Well, I'don't know. I can't tell till I feel."

"Perhaps some one might feel for you," said the younger man, laughing.

"Oh, I hope some one will always feel for me! Don't you feel for me, Lord Warburton?"

"Oh yes, immensely," said the gentleman addressed as Lord Warburton, promptly. "I'm bound to say you look wonderfully comfortable."

"Well, I suppose I am, in most respects." And the old man looked down at his green shawl and smoothed it over his knees. "The fact is I've been comfortable so many years that I suppose I've got so used to it I don't know it."

"Yes, that's the bore of comfort," said Lord Warburton. "We only know when we're uncomfortable."

"It strikes me we're rather particular," his companion remarked.

"Oh yes, there's no doubt we're particular," Lord Warburton murmured. And then the three men remained silent a while; the two younger ones standing looking down at the other, who presently asked for more tea. "I should think you would be very unhappy with that shawl," Lord Warburton resumed while his companion filled the old man's cup again.

"Oh no, he must have the shawl!" cried the gentleman in the velvet coat. "Don't put such ideas as that into his head."

"It belongs to my wife," said the old man simply.

"Oh, if it's for sentimental reasons—" And Lord

Warburton made a gesture of apology. "I suppose I must give it to her when she comes," the old man went on.

"You'll please to do nothing of the kind. You'll keep it to cover your poor old legs."

"Well, you mustn't abuse my legs," said the old man. "I guess they are as good as yours."

"Oh, you're perfectly free to abuse mine," his son replied, giving him his tea.

"Well, we're two lame ducks; I don't think there's much difference."

"I'm much obliged to you for calling me a duck. How's your tea?"

"Well, it's rather hot."

"That's intended to be a merit."

"Ah, there's a great deal of merit," murmured the old man, kindly. "He's a very good nurse, Lord Warburton."

"Isn't he a bit clumsy?" asked his lordship.

"Oh no, he's not clumsy—considering that he's an invalid himself. He's a very good nurse—for a sick-nurse. I call him my sick-nurse because he's sick himself."

"Oh, come, daddy!" the ugly young man exclaimed.

"Well, you are; I wish you weren't. But I suppose you can't help it."

"I might try: that's an idea," said the young man.

"Were you ever sick, Lord Warburton?" his father asked.

Lord Warburton considered a moment. "Yes, sir, once, in the Persian Gulf."

"He's making light of you, daddy," said the other young man.

"That's a sort of joke."

"Well, there seem to be so many sorts now," daddy replied, serenely. "You don't look as if you had been sick, any way, Lord Warburton."

"He's sick of life; he was just telling me so; going on fearfully about it," said Lord Warburton's friend.

"Is that true, sir?" asked the old man gravely.

"If it is, your son gave me no consolation. He's a wretched fellow to talk to—a regular cynic. He doesn't seem to believe in anything." "That's another sort of joke," said the person accused of cynicism.

"It's because his health is so poor," his father explained to Lord Warburton. "It affects his mind and colours his way of looking at things; he seems to feel as if he had never had a chance. But it's almost entirely theoretical, you know; it doesn't seem to affect his spirits. I've hardly ever seen him when he wasn't cheerful—about as he is at present. He often cheers me up."

The young man so described looked at Lord Warburton and laughed.

"Is it a glowing eulogy or an accusation of levity? Should you like me to carry out my theories, daddy?"

"By Jove, we should see some queer things!" cried Lord Warburton.

"I hope you haven't taken up that sort of tone," said the old man.

"Warburton's tone is worse than mine; he pretends to be bored. I'm not in the least bored; I find life only too interesting."

"Ah, too interesting; you shouldn't allow it to be that, you know!"

"I'm never bored when I come here," said Lord Warburton. "One gets such uncommonly good talk."

"Is that another sort of joke?" asked the old man. "You've no excuse for being bored anywhere. When I was your age I had never heard of such a thing."

"You must have developed very late."

"No, I developed very quick; that was just the reason. When I was twenty years old I was very highly developed indeed. I was working tooth and nail. You wouldn't be bored if you had something to do; but all you young men are too idle. You think too much of your pleasure. You're too fastidious, and too indolent, and too rich."

"Oh, I say," cried Lord Warburton, "you're hardly the person to accuse a fellow-creature of being too rich!"

"Do you mean because I'm a banker?" asked the old man.

"Because of that, if you like; and because you have—

haven't you?—such unlimited means." "He isn't very rich," the other young man mercifully pleaded. "He has given away an immense deal of money."

"Well, I suppose it was his own," said Lord Warburton; "and in that case could there be a better proof of wealth? Let not a public benefactor talk of one's being too fond of pleasure."

"Daddy's very fond of pleasure—of other people's."

The old man shook his head. "I don't pretend to have contributed anything to the amusement of my contemporaries."

"My dear father, you're too modest!"

"That's a kind of joke, sir," said Lord Warburton.

"You young men have too many jokes. When there are no jokes you've nothing left."

"Fortunately there are always more jokes," the ugly young man remarked.

"I don't believe it—I believe things are getting more serious.

You young men will find that out."

"The increasing seriousness of things, then that's the great opportunity of jokes."

"They'll have to be grim jokes," said the old man. "I'm convinced there will be great changes, and not all for the better."

"I quite agree with you, sir," Lord Warburton declared. "I'm very sure there will be great changes, and that all sorts of queer things will happen. That's why I find so much difficulty in applying your advice; you know you told me the other day that I ought to 'take hold' of something. One hesitates to take hold of a thing that may the next moment be knocked sky-high."

"You ought to take hold of a pretty woman," said his companion.

"He's trying hard to fall in love," he added, by way of explanation, to his father.

"The pretty women themselves may be sent flying!" Lord Warburton exclaimed.

"No, no, they'll be firm," the old man rejoined; "they'll not be affected by the social and political changes I just referred to." "You mean they won't be abolished? Very well, then, I'll lay hands on one as soon as possible and tie her round my neck as a life-preserver."

"The ladies will save us," said the old man; "that is the best of them will—for I make a difference between them. Make up to a good one and marry her, and your life will become much more interesting."

A momentary silence marked perhaps on the part of his auditors a sense of the magnanimity of this speech, for it was a secret neither for his son nor for his visitor that his own experiment in matrimony had not been a happy one. As he said, however, he made a difference; and these words may have been intended as a confession of personal error; though of course it was not in place for either of his companions to remark that apparently the lady of his choice had not been one of the best.

"If I marry an interesting woman I shall be interested: is that what you say?" Lord Warburton asked. "I'm not at all keen about marrying—your son misrepresented me; but there's no knowing what an interesting woman might do with me."

"I should like to see your idea of an interesting woman," said his friend.

"My dear fellow, you can't see ideas—especially such highly ethereal ones as mine. If I could only see it myself—that would be a great step in advance."

"Well, you may fall in love with whomsoever you please; but you mustn't fall in love with my niece," said the old man.

His son broke into a laugh. "He'll think you mean that as a provocation! My dear father, you've lived with the English for thirty years, and you've picked up a good many of the things they say. But you've never learned the things they don't say!" "I say what I please," the old man returned with all his serenity.

"I haven't the honour of knowing your niece," Lord Warburton said. "I think it's the first time I've heard of her."

"She's a niece of my wife's; Mrs. Touchett brings her to England."

Then young Mr. Touchett explained. "My mother, you know, has been spending the winter in America, and we're expecting her back. She writes that she has discovered a niece and that she has invited her to come out with her."

"I see,—very kind of her," said Lord Warburton. Is the young lady interesting?"

"We hardly know more about her than you; my mother has not gone into details. She chiefly communicates with us by means of telegrams, and her telegrams are rather inscrutable. They say women don't know how to write them, but my mother has thoroughly mastered the art of condensation. 'Tired America, hot weather awful, return England with niece, first steamer decent cabin.'

That's the sort of message we get from her—that was the last that came. But there had been another before, which I think contained the first mention of the niece. 'Changed hotel, very bad, impudent clerk, address here. Taken sister's girl, died last year, go to Europe, two sisters, quite independent.' Over that my father and I have scarcely stopped puzzling; it seems to admit of so many interpretations."

"There's one thing very clear in it," said the old man; "she has given the hotel-clerk a dressing."

"I'm not sure even of that, since he has driven her from the field. We thought at first that the sister mentioned might be the sister of the clerk; but the subsequent mention of a niece seems to prove that the allusion is to one of my aunts. Then there was a question as to whose the two other sisters were; they are probably two of my late aunt's daughters. But who's 'quite independent,' and in what sense is the term used?—that point's not yet settled. Does the expression apply more particularly to the young lady my mother has adopted, or does it characterise her sisters equally?—and is it used in a moral or in a financial sense? Does it mean that they've been left well off, or that they wish to be under no obligations? or does it simply mean that they're fond of their own way?"

"Whatever else it means, it's pretty sure to mean that,"

Mr. Touchett remarked. "You'll see for yourself," said Lord Warburton. "When does Mrs. Touchett arrive?"

"We're quite in the dark; as soon as she can find a decent cabin. She may be waiting for it yet; on the other hand she may already have disembarked in England."

"In that case she would probably have telegraphed to you."

"She never telegraphs when you would expect it—only when you don't," said the old man. "She likes to drop on me suddenly; she thinks she'll find me doing something wrong. She has never done so yet, but she's not discouraged."

"It's her share in the family trait, the independence she speaks of." Her son's appreciation of the matter was more favourable.

"Whatever the high spirit of those young ladies may be, her own is a match for it. She likes to do everything for herself and has no belief in any one's power to help her. She thinks me of no more use than a postage-stamp without gum, and she would never forgive me if I should presume to go to Liverpool to meet her."

"Will you at least let me know when your cousin arrives?" Lord Warburton asked.

"Only on the condition I've mentioned—that you don't fall in love with her!" Mr. Touchett replied.

"That strikes me as hard, don't you think me good enough?"

"I think you too good—because I shouldn't like her to marry you. She hasn't come here to look for a husband, I hope; so many young ladies are doing that, as if there were no good ones at home.

Then she's probably engaged; American girls are usually engaged, I believe. Moreover I'm not sure, after all, that you'd be a remarkable husband."

"Very likely she's engaged; I've known a good many American girls, and they always were; but I could never see that it made any difference, upon my word! As for my being a good husband,"

Mr. Touchett's visitor pursued, "I'm not sure of that

either. One can but try!" "Try as much as you please, but don't try on my niece," smiled the old man, whose opposition to the idea was broadly humorous.

"Ah, well," said Lord Warburton with a humour broader still, "perhaps, after all, she's not worth trying on!"

Chapter 2

While this exchange of pleasantries took place between the twoRalph Touchett wandered away a little, with his usual slouchinggait, his hands in his pockets and his little rowdyish terrier athis heels. His face was turned toward the house, but his eyeswere bent musingly on the lawn; so that he had been an object ofobservation to a person who had just made her appearance in theample doorway for some moments before he perceived her. Hisattention was called to her by the conduct of his dog, who hadsuddenly darted forward with a little volley of shrill barks, inwhich the note of welcome, however, was more sensible than thatof defiance. The person in question was a young lady, who seemedimmediately to interpret the greeting of the small beast.

Headvanced with great rapidity and stood at her feet, looking upand barking hard; whereupon, without hesitation, she stooped andcaught him in her hands, holding him face to face while hecontinued his quick chatter. His master now had had time tofollow and to see that Bunchie's new friend was a tall girl in ablack dress, who at first sight looked pretty. She wasbareheaded, as if she were staying in the house—a fact whichconveyed perplexity to the son of its master, conscious of thatimmunity from visitors which had for some time been renderednecessary by the latter's ill-health. Meantime the two othergentlemen had also taken note of the new-comer."Dear me, who's that strange woman?" Mr. Touchett had asked.

"Perhaps it's Mrs. Touchett's niece—the independent young lady," Lord Warburton suggested. "I think she must be, from the way she handles the dog."

The collie, too, had now allowed his attention to be diverted, and he trotted toward the young lady in the doorway, slowly setting his tail in motion as he went.

"But where's my wife then?" murmured the old man.

"I suppose the young lady has left her somewhere: that's a part of the independence."

The girl spoke to Ralph, smiling, while she still held up the terrier. "Is this your little dog, sir?"

"He was mine a moment ago; but you've suddenly acquired a remarkable air of property in him."

"Couldn't we share him?" asked the girl. "He's such a perfect little darling."

Ralph looked at her a moment; she was unexpectedly pretty. "You may have him altogether," he then replied.

The young lady seemed to have a great deal of confidence, both in herself and in others; but this abrupt generosity made her blush.

"I ought to tell you that I'm probably your cousin," she brought out, putting down the dog. "And here's another!" she added quickly, as the collie came up.

"Probably?" the young man exclaimed, laughing. "I supposed it was quite settled! Have you arrived with my mother?"

"Yes, half an hour ago."

"And has she deposited you and departed again?"

"No, she went straight to her room, and she told me that, if I should see you, I was to say to you that you must come to her there at a quarter to seven."

The young man looked at his watch. "Thank you very much; I shall be punctual." And then he looked at his cousin. "You're very welcome here. I'm delighted to see you."

She was looking at everything, with an eye that denoted clear perception—at her companion, at the two dogs, at the two gentlemen under the trees, at the beautiful scene that surrounded her. "I've never seen anything so lovely as this place. I've been all over the house; it's too enchanting."

"I'm sorry you should have been here so long without our knowing it."

"Your mother told me that in England people arrived very quietly; so I thought it was all right. Is one of those gentlemen your father?"

"Yes, the elder one—the one sitting down," said Ralph.

The girl gave a laugh. "I don't suppose it's the other. Who's the other?"

"He's a friend of ours—Lord Warburton."

"Oh, I hoped there would be a lord; it's just like a novel!" And then, "Oh you adorable creature!" she suddenly cried, stooping down and picking up the small dog again.

She remained standing where they had met, making no offer to advance or to speak to Mr. Touchett, and while she lingered so near the threshold, slim and charming, her interlocutor wondered if she expected the old man to come and pay her his respects.

American girls were used to a great deal of deference, and it had been intimated that this one had a high spirit. Indeed Ralph could see that in her face.

"Won't you come and make acquaintance with my father?" he nevertheless ventured to ask. "He's old and infirm—he doesn't leave his chair."

"Ah, poor man, I'm very sorry!" the girl exclaimed, immediately moving forward. "I got the impression from your mother that he was rather intensely active."

Ralph Touchett was silent a moment. "She hasn't seen him for a year."

"Well, he has a lovely place to sit. Come along, little hound."

"It's a dear old place," said the young man, looking sidewise at his neighbour.

"What's his name?" she asked, her attention having again reverted to the terrier.

"My father's name?"

"Yes," said the young lady with amusement; "but don't tell him I asked you."

They had come by this time to where old Mr. Touchett was sitting, and he slowly got up from his chair to introduce himself. "My mother has arrived," said Ralph, "and this is Miss Archer."

The old man placed his two hands on her shoulders, looked at her a moment with extreme benevolence and then gallantly kissed her. "It's a great pleasure to me to see you here; but I wish you had given us a chance to receive you."

"Oh, we were received," said the girl. "There were about a dozen servants in the hall. And there was an old woman curtseying at the gate."

"We can do better than that—if we have notice!" And the old man stood there smiling, rubbing his hands and slowly shaking his head at her. "But Mrs. Touchett doesn't like receptions."

"She went straight to her room."

"Yes—and locked herself in. She always does that. Well, I suppose I shall see her next week." And Mrs. Touchett's husband slowly resumed his former posture.

"Before that," said Miss Archer. "She's coming down to dinner— at eight o'clock. Don't you forget a quarter to seven," she added, turning with a smile to Ralph.

"What's to happen at a quarter to seven?"

"I'm to see my mother," said Ralph.

"Ah, happy boy!" the old man commented. "You must sit down—you must have some tea," he observed to his wife's niece.

"They gave me some tea in my room the moment I got there," this young lady answered. "I'm sorry you're out of health," she added, resting her eyes upon her venerable host.

"Oh, I'm an old man, my dear; it's time for me to be old. But I shall be the better for having you here."

She had been looking all round her again—at the lawn, the great trees, the reedy, silvery Thames, the beautiful old house; and while engaged in this survey she had made room in it for her companions; a comprehensiveness of observation easily conceivable on the part of a young woman who was evidently both intelligent and excited. She had seated herself and had put away the little dog; her white hands, in her lap, were folded upon her black dress; her head was erect, her eye lighted, her flexible figure turned itself easily this way and that, in sympathy with the alertness with which she evidently caught impressions. Her impressions were numerous, and they were all reflected in a clear, still smile. "I've never seen anything so beautiful as this." "It's looking very well," said Mr. Touchett. "I know the way it strikes you. I've been through all that. But you're very beautiful yourself," he added with a politeness by no means crudely jocular and with the happy consciousness that his advanced age gave him the privilege of saying such things—even to young persons who might possibly take alarm at them.

What degree of alarm this young person took need not be exactly measured; she instantly rose, however, with a blush which was not a refutation. "Oh yes, of course I'm lovely!" she returned with a quick laugh. "How old is your house? Is it Elizabethan?"

"It's early Tudor," said Ralph Touchett.

She turned toward him, watching his face. "Early Tudor? How very delightful! And I suppose there are a great many others."

"There are many much better ones."

"Don't say that, my son!" the old man protested. "There's nothing better than this."

"I've got a very good one; I think in some respects it's rather better," said Lord Warburton, who as yet had not spoken, but who had kept an attentive eye upon Miss Archer. He slightly inclined himself, smiling; he had an excellent manner with women. The girl appreciated it in an instant; she had not forgotten that this was Lord Warburton. "I should like very much to show it to you," he added.

"Don't believe him," cried the old man; "don't look at it! It's a wretched old barrack—not to be compared with this."

"I don't know—I can't judge," said the girl, smiling at Lord Warburton.

In this discussion Ralph Touchett took no interest whatever; he stood with his hands in his pockets, looking greatly as if he should like to renew his conversation with his new-found cousin.

"Are you very fond of dogs?" he enquired by way of beginning. He seemed to recognise that it was an awkward beginning for a clever man.

"Very fond of them indeed."

"You must keep the terrier, you know," he went on, still awkwardly.

"I'll keep him while I'm here, with pleasure."

"That will be for a long time, I hope."

"You're very kind. I hardly know. My aunt must settle that."

"I'll settle it with her—at a quarter to seven." And Ralph looked at his watch again.

"I'm glad to be here at all," said the girl.

"I don't believe you allow things to be settled for you."

"Oh yes; if they're settled as I like them."

"I shall settle this as I like it," said Ralph. It's most unaccountable that we should never have known you."

"I was there—you had only to come and see me."

"There? Where do you mean?"

"In the United States: in New York and Albany and other American places."

"I've been there—all over, but I never saw you. I can't make it out."

Miss Archer just hesitated. "It was because there had been some disagreement between your mother and my father, after my mother's death, which took place when I was a child. In consequence of it we never expected to see you."

"Ah, but I don't embrace all my mother's quarrels—heaven forbid!" the young man cried. "You've lately lost your father?" he went on more gravely.

"Yes; more than a year ago. After that my aunt was very kind to me; she came to see me and proposed that I should come with her to Europe."

"I see," said Ralph. "She has adopted you."

"Adopted me?" The girl stared, and her blush came back to her, together with a momentary look of pain which gave her interlocutor some alarm. He had underestimated the effect of his words. Lord Warburton, who appeared constantly desirous of a nearer view of Miss Archer, strolled toward the two cousins at the moment, and as he did so she rested her wider eyes on him.

"Oh no; she has not adopted me. I'm not a candidate for

adoption." "I beg a thousand pardons," Ralph murmured. "I meant—I meant—"

He hardly knew what he meant. "You meant she has taken me up. Yes; she likes to take people up. She has been very kind to me; but," she added with a certain visible eagerness of desire to be explicit, "I'm very fond of my liberty."

"Are you talking about Mrs. Touchett?" the old man called out from his chair. "Come here, my dear, and tell me about her. I'm always thankful for information."

The girl hesitated again, smiling. "She's really very benevolent," she answered; after which she went over to her uncle, whose mirth was excited by her words.

Lord Warburton was left standing with Ralph Touchett, to whom in a moment he said: "You wished a while ago to see my idea of an interesting woman. There it is!"

Chapter 7

The two amused themselves, time and again, with talking of theattitude of the British public as if the young lady had been in aposition to appeal to it; but in fact the British public remainedfor the present profoundly indifferent to Miss Isabel Archer,whose fortune had dropped her, as her cousin said, into thedullest house in England. Her gouty uncle received very littlecompany, and Mrs. Touchett, not having cultivated relations withher husband's neighbours, was not warranted in expecting visitsfrom them. She had, however, a peculiar taste; she liked toreceive cards. For what is usually called social intercourse shehad very little relish; but nothing pleased her more than to findher hall-table whitened with oblong morsels of symbolicpasteboard. She flattered herself that she was a very just woman,and had mastered the sovereign truth that nothing in this worldis got for nothing. She had played no social part as mistress ofGardencourt, and it was not to be supposed that, in thesurrounding country, a minute account should be kept of hercomings and goings. But it is by no means certain that she didnot feel it to be wrong that so little notice was taken of themand that her failure (really very gratuitous) to make herselfimportant in the neighbourhood had not much to do with theacrimony of her allusions to her husband's adopted country.

Isabel presently found herself in the singular situation of defending the British constitution against her aunt; Mrs. Touchett having formed the habit of sticking pins into this venerable instrument. Isabel always felt an impulse to pull out the pins; not that she imagined they inflicted any damage on thetough old parchment, but because it seemed to her her aunt mightmake better use of her sharpness. She was very critical herself—it was incidental to her age, her sex and her nationality; butshe was very sentimental as well, and there was something in Mrs.Touchett's dryness that set her own moral fountains flowing.

"Now what's your point of view?" she asked of her aunt. "When youcriticise everything here you should have a point of view. Yoursdoesn't seem to be American—you thought everything over there sodisagreeable. When I criticise I have mine; it's thoroughlyAmerican!""My dear young lady," said Mrs. Touchett, "there are as manypoints of view in the world as there are people of sense to takethem. You may say that doesn't make them very numerous! American?Never in the world; that's shockingly narrow. My point of view,thank God, is personal!"

Isabel thought this a better answer than she admitted; it was atolerable description of her own manner of judging, but it wouldnot have sounded well for her to say so. On the lips of a personless advanced in life and less enlightened by experience thanMrs. Touchett such a declaration would savour of immodesty, evenof arrogance. She risked it nevertheless in talking with Ralph,with whom she talked a great deal and with whom her conversationwas of a sort that gave a large licence to extravagance. Hercousin used, as the phrase is, to chaff her; he very soonestablished with her a reputation for treating everything as ajoke, and he was not a man to neglect the privileges such areputation conferred. She accused him of an odious want ofseriousness, of laughing at all things, beginning with himself.Such slender faculty of reverence as he possessed centred whollyupon his father; for the rest, he exercised his wit indifferentlyupon his father's son, this gentleman's weak lungs, his uselesslife, his fantastic mother, his friends (Lord Warburton inespecial), his adopted, and his native country, his charmingnew-found cousin. "I keep a band of music in my ante-room," hesaid once to her. "

It has orders to play without stopping; itrenders me two excellent services. It keeps the sounds of theworld from reaching the private apartments, and it makes theworld think that dancing's going on within." It was dance-musicindeed that you usually heard when you came within ear-shot ofRalph's band; the liveliest waltzes seemed to float upon the air.Isabel often found herself irritated by this perpetual fiddling;she would have liked to pass through the ante-room, as her cousincalled it, and enter the private apartments. It mattered littlethat he had assured her they were a very dismal place; she wouldhave been glad to undertake to sweep them and set them in order.It was but half-hospitality to let her remain outside; to punishhim for which Isabel administered innumerable taps with theferule of her straight young wit.

It must be said that her witwas exercised to a large extent in self-defence, for her cousinamused himself with calling her "Columbia" and accusing her of apatriotism so heated that it scorched. He drew a caricature ofher in which she was represented as a very pretty young womandressed, on the lines of the prevailing fashion, in the folds ofthe national banner. Isabel's chief dread in life at this periodof her development was that she should appear narrow-minded; whatshe feared next afterwards was that she should really be so. Butshe nevertheless made no scruple of abounding in her cousin'ssense and pretending to sigh for the charms of her native land.She would be as American as it pleased him to regard her, and ifhe chose to laugh at her she would give him plenty of occupation.She defended England against his mother, but when Ralph sang itspraises on purpose, as she said, to work her up, she foundherself able to differ from him on a variety of points. In fact,the quality of this small ripe country seemed as sweet to her asthe taste of an October pear; and her satisfaction was at theroot of the good spirits which enabled her to take her cousin'schaff and return it in kind. If her good-humour flagged atmoments it was not because she thought herself ill-used, butbecause she suddenly felt sorry for Ralph. It seemed to her hewas talking as a blind and had little heart in what he said."I don't know what's the matter with you," she observed to himonce; "but I suspect you're a great humbug."

"That's your privilege," Ralph answered, who had not been used to being so crudely addressed.

"I don't know what you care for; I don't think you care for anything. You don't really care for England when you praise it; you don't care for America even when you pretend to abuse it."

"I care for nothing but you, dear cousin," said Ralph.

"If I could believe even that, I should be very glad."

"Ah well, I should hope so!" the young man exclaimed.

Isabel might have believed it and not have been far from the truth. He thought a great deal about her; she was constantly present to his mind. At a time when his thoughts had been a good deal of a burden to him her sudden arrival, which promised nothing and was an open-handed gift of fate, had refreshed and quickened them, given them wings and something to fly for. PoorRalph had been for many weeks steeped in melancholy; his outlook,habitually sombre, lay under the shadow of a deeper cloud. He hadgrown anxious about his father, whose gout, hitherto confined tohis legs, had begun to ascend into regions more vital.

The oldman had been gravely ill in the spring, and the doctors hadwhispered to Ralph that another attack would be less easy to dealwith. Just now he appeared disburdened of pain, but Ralph couldnot rid himself of a suspicion that this was a subterfuge of theenemy, who was waiting to take him off his guard. If themanoeuvre should succeed there would be little hope of any greatresistance. Ralph had always taken for granted that his fatherwould survive him—that his own name would be the first grimlycalled. The father and son had been close companions, and theidea of being left alone with the remnant of a tasteless life onhis hands was not gratifying to the young man, who had always andtacitly counted upon his elder's help in making the best of apoor business. At the prospect of losing his great motive Ralphlost indeed his one inspiration.

If they might die at the sametime it would be all very well; but without the encouragement ofhis father's society he should barely have patience to await hisown turn. He had not the incentive of feeling that he wasindispensable to his mother; it was a rule with his mother tohave no regrets. He bethought himself of course that it had beena small kindness to his father to wish that, of the two, theactive rather than the passive party should know the felt wound;he remembered that the old man had always treated his ownforecast of an early end as a clever fallacy, which he should bedelighted to discredit so far as he might by dying first. But ofthe two triumphs, that of refuting a sophistical son andthat of holding on a while longer to a state of being which, withall abatements, he enjoyed, Ralph deemed it no sin to hope thelatter might be vouchsafed to Mr. Touchett.

These were nice questions, but Isabel's arrival put a stop to hispuzzling over them. It even suggested there might be acompensation for the intolerable ennui of surviving his genialsire. He wondered whether he were harbouring "love" for thisspontaneous young woman from Albany; but he judged that on thewhole he was not. After he had known her for a week he quite madeup his mind to this, and every day he felt a little more sure.Lord Warburton had been right about her; she was a reallyinteresting little figure. Ralph wondered how their neighbour hadfound it out so soon; and then he said it was only another proofof his friend's high abilities, which he had always greatlyadmired. If his cousin were to be nothing more than anentertainment to him, Ralph was conscious she was an entertainmentof a high order. "A character like that," he said to himself—"a real little passionate force to see at play is the finestthing in nature. It's finer than the finest work of art—than aGreek bas-relief, than a great Titian, than a Gothic cathedral.It's very pleasant to be so well treated where one had leastlooked for it. I had never been more blue, more bored, than for aweek before she came; I had never expected less that anythingpleasant would happen. Suddenly I receive a Titian, by the post,to hang on my wall—a Greek bas-relief to stick over mychimney-piece. The key of a beautiful edifice is thrust into myhand, and I'm told to walk in and admire. My poor boy, you'vebeen sadly ungrateful, and now you had better keep very quiet andnever grumble again."

The sentiment of these reflexions was veryjust; but it was not exactly true that Ralph Touchett had had akey put into his hand. His cousin was a very brilliant girl, whowould take, as he said, a good deal of knowing; but she neededthe knowing, and his attitude with regard to her, though it wascontemplative and critical, was not judicial. He surveyed theedifice from the outside and admired it greatly; he looked in atthe windows and received an impression of proportions equallyfair. But he felt that he saw it only by glimpses and that he hadnot yet stood under the roof. The door was fastened, and thoughhe had keys in his pocket he had a conviction that none ofthem would fit. She was intelligent and generous; it was a finefree nature; but what was she going to do with herself? Thisquestion was irregular, for with most women one had no occasionto ask it. Most women did with themselves nothing at all; theywaited, in attitudes more or less gracefully passive, for a manto come that way and furnish them with a destiny. Isabel'soriginality was that she gave one an impression of havingintentions of her own. "Whenever she executes them," said Ralph,"may I be there to see!"

It devolved upon him of course to do the honours of the place.Mr. Touchett was confined to his chair, and his wife's positionwas that of rather a grim visitor; so that in the line of conductthat opened itself to Ralph duty and inclination wereharmoniously mixed. He was not a great walker, but he strolledabout the grounds with his cousin—a pastime for which theweather remained favourable with a persistency not allowed for inIsabel's somewhat lugubrious prevision of the climate; and in thelong afternoons, of which the length was but the measure of hergratified eagerness, they took a boat on the river, the dearlittle river, as Isabel called it, where the opposite shoreseemed still a part of the foreground of the landscape; or droveover the country in a phaeton—a low, capacious, thick-wheeledphaeton formerly much used by Mr. Touchett, but which he had nowceased to enjoy.

Isabel enjoyed it largely and, handling thereins in a manner which approved itself to the groom as"knowing," was never weary of driving her uncle's capital horsesthrough winding lanes and byways full of the rural incidents shehad confidently expected to find; past cottages thatched andtimbered, past ale-houses latticed and sanded, past patches ofancient common and glimpses of empty parks, between hedgerowsmade thick by midsummer. When they reached home they usuallyfound tea had been served on the lawn and that Mrs. Touchett hadnot shrunk from the extremity of handing her husband his cup. Butthe two for the most part sat silent; the old man with his headback and his eyes closed, his wife occupied with her knitting andwearing that appearance of rare profundity with which some ladiesconsider the movement of their needles.

One day, however, a visitor had arrived. The two young persons,after spending an hour on the river, strolled back to the houseand perceived Lord Warburton sitting under the trees and engagedin conversation, of which even at a distance the desultorycharacter was appreciable, with Mrs. Touchett. He had driven overfrom his own place with a portmanteau and had asked, as thefather and son often invited him to do, for a dinner and alodging. Isabel, seeing him for half an hour on the day of herarrival, had discovered in this brief space that she liked him;he had indeed rather sharply registered himself on her fine senseand she had thought of him several times. She had hoped sheshould see him again—hoped too that she should see a few others.Gardencourt was not dull; the place itself was sovereign, heruncle was more and more a sort of golden grandfather, and Ralphwas unlike any cousin she had ever encountered—her idea ofcousins having tended to gloom. Then her impressions were stillso fresh and so quickly renewed that there was as yet hardly ahint of vacancy in the view. But Isabel had need to remindherself that she was interested in human nature and that herforemost hope in coming abroad had been that she should see agreat many people.

When Ralph said to her, as he had done severaltimes, "I wonder you find this endurable; you ought to see someof the neighbours and some of our friends, because we have reallygot a few, though you would never suppose it"—when he offered toinvite what he called a "lot of people" and make her acquaintedwith English society, she encouraged the hospitable impulse andpromised in advance to hurl herself into the fray. Little, however,for the present, had come of his offers, and it may be confidedto the reader that if the young man delayed to carry them out itwas because he found the labour of providing for his companionby no means so severe as to require extraneous help. Isabel hadspoken to him very often about "specimens;" it was a word thatplayed a considerable part in her vocabulary; she had given himto understand that she wished to see English societyillustrated by eminent cases.

"Well now, there's a specimen," he said to her as they walked up from the riverside and he recognised Lord Warburton.

"A specimen of what?" asked the girl.

"A specimen of an English gentleman."

"Do you mean they're all like him?"

"Oh no; they're not all like him."

"He's a favourable specimen then," said Isabel; "because I'm sure he's nice."

"Yes, he's very nice. And he's very fortunate."

The fortunate Lord Warburton exchanged a handshake with our heroine and hoped she was very well. "But I needn't ask that," he said, "since you've been handling the oars."

"I've been rowing a little," Isabel answered; "but how should you know it?"

"Oh, I know he doesn't row; he's too lazy," said his lordship, indicating Ralph Touchett with a laugh.

"He has a good excuse for his laziness," Isabel rejoined, lowering her voice a little.

"Ah, he has a good excuse for everything!" cried Lord Warburton, still with his sonorous mirth.

"My excuse for not rowing is that my cousin rows so

well," said Ralph. "She does everything well. She touches nothing that she doesn't adorn!"

"It makes one want to be touched, Miss Archer," Lord Warburton declared.

"Be touched in the right sense and you'll never look the worse for it," said Isabel, who, if it pleased her to hear it said thather accomplishments were numerous, was happily able to reflectthat such complacency was not the indication of a feeble mind,inasmuch as there were several things in which she excelled. Herdesire to think well of herself had at least the element ofhumility that it always needed to be supported by proof.

Lord Warburton not only spent the night at Gardencourt, but hewas persuaded to remain over the second day; and when the secondday was ended he determined to postpone his departure till themorrow. During this period he addressed many of his remarks toIsabel, who accepted this evidence of his esteem with a very goodgrace. She found herself liking him extremely; the firstimpression he had made on her had had weight, but at the end ofan evening spent in his society she scarce fell short of seeinghim—though quite without luridity—as a hero of romance.

Sheretired to rest with a sense of good fortune, with a quickenedconsciousness of possible felicities. "It's very nice to know twosuch charming people as those," she said, meaning by "those" hercousin and her cousin's friend. It must be added moreover that anincident had occurred which might have seemed to put hergood-humour to the test. Mr. Touchett went to bed at half-pastnine o'clock, but his wife remained in the drawing-room with theother members of the party. She prolonged her vigil for somethingless than an hour, and then, rising, observed to Isabel that itwas time they should bid the gentlemen good-night. Isabel had asyet no desire to go to bed; the occasion wore, to her sense, afestive character, and feasts were not in the habit ofterminating so early. So, without further thought, she replied,very simply—

"Need I go, dear aunt? I'll come up in half an hour."

"It's impossible I should wait for you," Mrs. Touchett

answered. "Ah, you needn't wait! Ralph will light my candle," Isabel gaily engaged.

"I'll light your candle; do let me light your candle, Miss Archer!" Lord Warburton exclaimed. "Only I beg it shall not be before midnight."

Mrs. Touchett fixed her bright little eyes upon him a moment and transferred them coldly to her niece. "You can't stay alone with the gentlemen. You're not—you're not at your blest Albany, my dear."

Isabel rose, blushing. "I wish I were," she said.

"Oh, I say, mother!" Ralph broke out.

"My dear Mrs. Touchett!" Lord Warburton murmured.

"I didn't make your country, my lord," Mrs. Touchett said majestically. "I must take it as I find it."

"Can't I stay with my own cousin?" Isabel enquired.

"I'm not aware that Lord Warburton is your cousin."

"Perhaps I had better go to bed!" the visitor suggested. "That will arrange it."

Mrs. Touchett gave a little look of despair and sat down again.

"Oh, if it's necessary I'll stay up till midnight."

Ralph meanwhile handed Isabel her candlestick. He had been watching her; it had seemed to him her temper was involved—an accident that might be interesting. But if he had expected anything of a flare he was disappointed, for the girl simply laughed a little, nodded good-night and withdrew accompanied by her aunt. For himself he was annoyed at his mother, though he thought she was right. Above-stairs the two ladies separated at Mrs. Touchett's door. Isabel had said nothing on her way up.

"Of course you're vexed at my interfering with you," said Mrs. Touchett.

Isabel considered. "I'm not vexed, but I'm surprised—and a good deal mystified. Wasn't it proper I should remain in the drawing-room?"

"Not in the least. Young girls here—in decent houses—don't sit alone with the gentlemen late at night."

"You were very right to tell me then," said Isabel. "I don't understand it, but I'm very glad to know it.

"I shall always tell you," her aunt answered, "whenever I see you taking what seems to me too much liberty."

"Pray do; but I don't say I shall always think your remonstrance just."

"Very likely not. You're too fond of your own ways."

"Yes, I think I'm very fond of them. But I always want to know the things one shouldn't do."

"So as to do them?" asked her aunt.

"So as to choose," said Isabel.

Chapter 8

As she was devoted to romantic effects Lord Warburton ventured to express a hope that she would come some day and see his house, a very curious old place. He extracted from Mrs. Touchett a promise that she would bring her niece to Lockleigh, and Ralph signified his willingness to attend the ladies if his father should be able to spare him. Lord Warburton assured our heroine that in the mean time his sisters would come and see her. She knew something about his sisters, having sounded him, during the hours they spent together while he was at Gardencourt, on many points connectedwith his family. When Isabel was interested she asked a greatmany questions, and as her companion was a copious talker sheurged him on this occasion by no means in vain. He told her hehad four sisters and two brothers and had lost both his parents.The brothers and sisters were very good people—"not particularlyclever, you know," he said, "but very decent and pleasant;" andhe was so good as to hope Miss Archer might know them well. Oneof the brothers was in the Church, settled in the family living,that of Lockleigh, which was a heavy, sprawling parish, and wasan excellent fellow in spite of his thinking differently fromhimself on every conceivable topic. And then Lord Warburtonmentioned some of the opinions held by his brother, which wereopinions Isabel had often heard expressed and that she supposedto be entertained by a considerable portion of the human family.

Many of them indeed she supposed she had held herself,

till heassured her she was quite mistaken, that it was reallyimpossible, that she had doubtless imagined she entertained them,but that she might depend that, if she thought them over alittle, she would find there was nothing in them. When sheanswered that she had already thought several of the questionsinvolved over very attentively he declared that she was onlyanother example of what he had often been struck with—the factthat, of all the people in the world, the Americans were the mostgrossly superstitious. They were rank Tories and bigots, everyone of them; there were no conservatives like Americanconservatives. Her uncle and her cousin were there to prove it;nothing could be more medieval than many of their views; they hadideas that people in England nowadays were ashamed to confess to;and they had the impudence moreover, said his lordship, laughing,to pretend they knew more about the needs and dangers of thispoor dear stupid old England than he who was born in it and owneda considerable slice of it—the more shame to him!

From all ofwhich Isabel gathered that Lord Warburton was a nobleman of thenewest pattern, a reformer, a radical, a contemner of ancientways. His other brother, who was in the army in India, was ratherwild and pig-headed and had not been of much use as yet but tomake debts for Warburton to pay—one of the most preciousprivileges of an elder brother. "I don't think I shall pay anymore," said her friend; "he lives a monstrous deal better than Ido, enjoys unheard-of luxuries and thinks himself a much finergentleman than I. As I'm a consistent radical I go in only forequality; I don't go in for the superiority of the youngerbrothers." Two of his four sisters, the second and fourth, weremarried, one of them having done very well, as they said, theother only so-so. The husband of the elder, Lord Haycock, was avery good fellow, but unfortunately a horrid Tory; and his wife,like all good English wives, was worse than her husband. Theother had espoused a smallish squire in Norfolk and, thoughmarried but the other day, had already five children.

Thisinformation and much more Lord Warburton imparted to his youngAmerican listener, taking pains to make many things clear and tolay bare to her apprehension the peculiarities of English life.Isabel was often amused at his explicitness and at the smallallowance he seemed to make either for her own experience or forher imagination. "He thinks I'm a barbarian," she said, "and thatI've never seen forks and spoons;" and she used to ask himartless questions for the pleasure of hearing him answerseriously. Then when he had fallen into the trap, "It's a pityyou can't see me in my war-paint and feathers," she remarked; "ifI had known how kind you are to the poor savages I would havebrought over my native costume!" Lord Warburton had travelledthrough the United States and knew much more about them thanIsabel; he was so good as to say that America was the mostcharming country in the world, but his recollections of itappeared to encourage the idea that Americans in England wouldneed to have a great many things explained to them.

"If I hadonly had you to explain things to me in America!" he said. "I wasrather puzzled in your country; in fact I was quite bewildered,and the trouble was that the explanations only puzzled me more.You know I think they often gave me the wrong ones on purpose;they're rather clever about that over there. But when I explainyou can trust me; about what I tell you there's no mistake."There was no mistake at least about his being very intelligentand cultivated and knowing almost everything in the world.Although he gave the most interesting and thrilling glimpsesIsabel felt he never did it to exhibit himself, and though he hadhad rare chances and had tumbled in, as she put it, for highprizes, he was as far as possible from making a merit of it. Hehad enjoyed the best things of life, but they had not spoiled hissense of proportion. His quality was a mixture of the effect ofrich experience—oh, so easily come by!—with a modesty at timesalmost boyish; the sweet and wholesome savour of which—it was asagreeable as something tasted—lost nothing from the addition ofa tone of responsible kindness.

"I like your specimen English gentleman very much," Isabel said to Ralph after Lord Warburton had gone.

"I like him too—I love him well," Ralph returned. "But I

pity him more." Isabel looked at him askance. "Why, that seems to me his only fault—that one can't pity him a little. He appears to have everything, to know everything, to be everything."

"Oh, he's in a bad way!" Ralph insisted.

"I suppose you don't mean in health?"

"No, as to that he's detestably sound. What I mean is that he's a man with a great position who's playing all sorts of tricks with it. He doesn't take himself seriously."

"Does he regard himself as a joke?"

"Much worse; he regards himself as an imposition—as an abuse." "Well, perhaps he is," said Isabel.

"Perhaps he is—though on the whole I don't think so. But in that case what's more pitiable than a sentient, self-conscious abuse planted by other hands, deeply rooted but aching with a sense of its injustice? For me, in his place, I could be as solemn as a statue of Buddha. He occupies a position that appeals to my imagination. Great responsibilities, great opportunities, great consideration, great wealth, great power, a natural share in the public affairs of a great country. But he's all in a muddle about himself, his position, his power, and indeed about everything in the world. He's the victim of a critical age; he has ceased to believe in himself and he doesn't know what to believe in. When I attempt to tell him (because if I were he I know very well what I should believe in) he calls me a pampered bigot. I believe he seriously thinks me an awful Philistine; he says I don't understand my time. I understand it certainly better than he, who can neither abolish himself as a nuisance nor maintain himself as an institution."

"He doesn't look very wretched," Isabel observed.

"Possibly not; though, being a man of a good deal of charming taste, I think he often has uncomfortable hours. But what is it to say of a being of his opportunities that he's not miserable?

Besides, I believe he is."

"I don't," said Isabel.

"Well," her cousin rejoined, "if he isn't he ought to be!"

In the afternoon she spent an hour with her uncle on the

lawn, where the old man sat, as usual, with his shawl over his legs and his large cup of diluted tea in his hands. In the course of conversation he asked her what she thought of their late visitor.

Isabel was prompt. "I think he's charming."

"He's a nice person," said Mr. Touchett, "but I don't recommend you to fall in love with him."

"I shall not do it then; I shall never fall in love but on your recommendation. Moreover," Isabel added, "my cousin gives me rather a sad account of Lord Warburton."

"Oh, indeed? I don't know what there may be to say, but you must remember that Ralph must talk."

"He thinks your friend's too subversive—or not subversive enough! I don't quite understand which," said Isabel.

The old man shook his head slowly, smiled and put down his cup.

"I don't know which either. He goes very far, but it's quite possible he doesn't go far enough. He seems to want to do away with a good many things, but he seems to want to remain himself. I suppose that's natural, but it's rather inconsistent."

"Oh, I hope he'll remain himself," said Isabel. "If he were to be done away with his friends would miss him sadly."

"Well," said the old man, "I guess he'll stay and amuse his friends. I should certainly miss him very much here at Gardencourt. He always amuses me when he comes over, and I think he amuses himself as well. There's a considerable number like him, round in society; they're very fashionable just now. I don't know what they're trying to do—whether they're trying to get up a revolution. I hope at any rate they'll put it off till after I'm gone. You see they want to disestablish everything; but I'm a pretty big landowner here, and I don't want to be disestablished.

I wouldn't have come over if I had thought they were going to behave like that," Mr. Touchett went on with expanding hilarity.

"I came over because I thought England was a safe country. I call it a regular fraud if they are going to introduce any considerable changes; there'll be a large number disappointed in that case."

"Oh, I do hope they'll make a revolution!" Isabel exclaimed. "I should delight in seeing a revolution."

"Let me see," said her uncle, with a humorous intention; "I forget whether you're on the side of the old or on the side of the new. I've heard you take such opposite views."

"I'm on the side of both. I guess I'm a little on the side of everything. In a revolution—after it was well begun—I think I should be a high, proud loyalist. One sympathises more with them, and they've a chance to behave so exquisitely. I mean so picturesquely."

"I don't know that I understand what you mean by behaving picturesquely, but it seems to me that you do that always, my dear."

"Oh, you lovely man, if I could believe that!" the girl interrupted.

"I'm afraid, after all, you won't have the pleasure of going gracefully to the guillotine here just now," Mr. Touchett went on. "If you want to see a big outbreak you must pay us a long visit. You see, when you come to the point it wouldn't suit them to be taken at their word."

"Of whom are you speaking?"

"Well, I mean Lord Warburton and his friends—the radicals of the upper class. Of course I only know the way it strikes me. They talk about the changes, but I don't think they quite realise. You and I, you know, we know what it is to have lived under democratic institutions: I always thought them very comfortable, but I wasused to them from the first. And then I ain't a lord; you're alady, my dear, but I ain't a lord. Now over here I don't think itquite comes home to them. It's a matter of every day and everyhour, and I don't think many of them would find it as pleasant aswhat they've got. Of course if they want to try, it's their ownbusiness; but I expect they won't try very hard." "Don't you think they're sincere?" Isabel asked.

"Well, they want to FEEL earnest," Mr. Touchett allowed; "but it seems as if they took it out in theories mostly. Their radical views are a kind of amusement; they've got to have someamusement, and they might have coarser tastes than that. You seethey're very luxurious, and these progressive ideas are abouttheir biggest luxury. They make them feel moral and yet don'tdamage their position. They think a great deal of their position;don't let one of them ever persuade you he doesn't, for if youwere to proceed on that basis you'd be pulled up very short."Isabel followed her uncle's argument, which he unfolded with hisquaint distinctness, most attentively, and though she wasunacquainted with the British aristocracy she found it in harmonywith her general impressions of human nature. But she felt movedto put in a protest on Lord Warburton's behalf. "I don't believeLord Warburton's a humbug; I don't care what the others are. Ishould like to see Lord Warburton put to the test."

"Heaven deliver me from my friends!" Mr. Touchett answered. "LordWarburton's a very amiable young man—a very fine young man. Hehas a hundred thousand a year. He owns fifty thousand acres ofthe soil of this little island and ever so many other thingsbesides. He has half a dozen houses to live in. He has a seat inParliament as I have one at my own dinner-table. He has eleganttastes—cares for literature, for art, for science, for charmingyoung ladies. The most elegant is his taste for the new views. Itaffords him a great deal of pleasure—more perhaps than anythingelse, except the young ladies. His old house over there—whatdoes he call it, Lockleigh?—is very attractive; but I don'tthink it's as pleasant as this. That doesn't matter, however—hehas so many others. His views don't hurt any one as far as I cansee; they certainly don't hurt himself. And if there were to be arevolution he would come off very easily. They wouldn't touchhim, they'd leave him as he is: he's too much liked.""Ah, he couldn't be a martyr even if he wished!" Isabel sighed."That's a very poor position."

"He'll never be a martyr unless you make him one," said the oldman.Isabel shook her head; there might have been something laughablein the fact that she did it with a touch of melancholy. "I shallnever make any one a martyr.""You'll never be one, I hope.""I hope not. But you don't pity Lord

Warburton then as Ralphdoes?"Her uncle looked at her a while with genial acuteness. "Yes, Ido, after all!"

Chapter 14

Miss Stackpole would have prepared to start immediately; butIsabel, as we have seen, had been notified that Lord Warburtonwould come again to Gardencourt, and she believed it her duty toremain there and see him. For four or five days he had made noresponse to her letter; then he had written, very briefly, to sayhe would come to luncheon two days later. There was something inthese delays and postponements that touched the girl and renewedher sense of his desire to be considerate and patient, not toappear to urge her too grossly; a consideration the more studiedthat she was so sure he "really liked" her. Isabel told her uncleshe had written to him, mentioning also his intention of coming;and the old man, in consequence, left his room earlier than usualand made his appearance at the two o'clock repast. This was by nomeans an act of vigilance on his part, but the fruit of abenevolent belief that his being of the company might help tocover any conjoined straying away in case Isabel should givetheir noble visitor another hearing.

That personage drove overfrom Lockleigh and brought the elder of his sisters with him, ameasure presumably dictated by reflexions of the same order asMr. Touchett's. The two visitors were introduced to MissStackpole, who, at luncheon, occupied a seat adjoining LordWarburton's. Isabel, who was nervous and had no relish for theprospect of again arguing the question he had so prematurelyopened, could not help admiring his good-humoured self-possession,which quite disguised the symptoms of that preoccupation with herpresence it was natural she should suppose him to feel. Heneither looked at her nor spoke to her, and the only sign of hisemotion was that he avoided meeting her eyes. He had plenty oftalk for the others, however, and he appeared to eat his luncheonwith discrimination and appetite. Miss Molyneux, who had asmooth, nun-like forehead and wore a large silver crosssuspended from her neck, was evidently preoccupied with HenriettaStackpole, upon whom her eyes constantly rested in a mannersuggesting a conflict between deep alienation and yearningwonder. Of the two ladies from Lockleigh she was the one Isabelhad liked best; there was such a world of hereditary quiet inher. Isabel was sure moreover that her mild forehead and silvercross referred to some weird Anglican mystery—some delightfulreinstitution perhaps of the quaint office of the canoness.

Shewondered what Miss Molyneux would think of her if she knew MissArcher had refused her brother; and then she felt sure that MissMolyneux would never know—that Lord Warburton never told hersuch things. He was fond of her and kind to her, but on the wholehe told her little. Such, at least, was Isabel's theory; when, attable, she was not occupied in conversation she was usuallyoccupied in forming theories about her neighbours. According toIsabel, if Miss Molyneux should ever learn what had passedbetween Miss Archer and Lord Warburton she would probably beshocked at such a girl's failure to rise; or no, rather (this wasour heroine's last position) she would impute to the youngAmerican but a due consciousness of inequality.Whatever Isabel might have made of her opportunities, at allevents, Henrietta Stackpole was by no means disposed to neglectthose in which she now found herself immersed. "Do you knowyou're the first lord I've ever seen?" she said very promptly toher neighbour. "I suppose you think I'm awfully benighted."

"You've escaped seeing some very ugly men," Lord Warburton answered, looking a trifle absently about the table.

"Are they very ugly? They try to make us believe in America that they're all handsome and magnificent and that they wear wonderful robes and crowns."

"Ah, the robes and crowns are gone out of fashion," said Lord Warburton, "like your tomahawks and revolvers."

"I'm sorry for that; I think an aristocracy ought to be splendid," Henrietta declared. "If it's not that, what is it?"

"Oh, you know, it isn't much, at the best," her neighbour allowed. "Won't you have a potato?"

"I don't care much for these European potatoes. I

shouldn't know you from an ordinary American gentleman."

"Do talk to me as if I were one," said Lord Warburton. "I don't see how you manage to get on without potatoes; you must find so few things to eat over here."

Henrietta was silent a little; there was a chance he was not sincere. "I've had hardly any appetite since I've been here," she went on at last; "so it doesn't much matter. I don't approve of you, you know; I feel as if I ought to tell you that."

"Don't approve of me?"

"Yes; I don't suppose any one ever said such a thing to you before, did they? I don't approve of lords as an institution. I think the world has got beyond them—far beyond."

"Oh, so do I. I don't approve of myself in the least. Sometimes it comes over me—how I should object to myself if I were not myself, don't you know? But that's rather good, by the way—not to be vainglorious."

"Why don't you give it up then?" Miss Stackpole enquired.

"Give up—a—?" asked Lord Warburton, meeting her harsh inflexion with a very mellow one.

"Give up being a lord."

"Oh, I'm so little of one! One would really forget all about it if you wretched Americans were not constantly reminding one. However, I do think of giving it up, the little there is left of it, one of these days."

"I should like to see you do it!" Henrietta exclaimed rather grimly.

"I'll invite you to the ceremony; we'll have a supper and a dance."

"Well," said Miss Stackpole, "I like to see all sides. I don't approve of a privileged class, but I like to hear what they have to say for themselves."

"Mighty little, as you see!"

"I should like to draw you out a little more," Henrietta continued. "But you're always looking away. You're afraid of meeting my eye. I see you want to escape me."

"No, I'm only looking for those despised potatoes."

"Please explain about that young lady—your sister—then.

I don't understand about her. Is she a Lady?" "She's a capital good girl."

"I don't like the way you say that—as if you wanted to change the subject. Is her position inferior to yours?"

"We neither of us have any position to speak of; but she's better off than I, because she has none of the bother."

"Yes, she doesn't look as if she had much bother. I wish I had as little bother as that. You do produce quiet people over here, whatever else you may do."

"Ah, you see one takes life easily, on the whole," said Lord Warburton. "And then you know we're very dull. Ah, we can be dull when we try!" "I should advise you to try something else. I shouldn't know what to talk to your sister about; she looks so different. Is that silver cross a badge?"

"A badge?"

"A sign of rank."

Lord Warburton's glance had wandered a good deal, but at this it met the gaze of his neighbour. "Oh yes," he answered in a moment; "the women go in for those things. The silver cross is worn by the eldest daughters of Viscounts." Which was his harmless revenge for having occasionally had his credulity too easily engaged in America. After luncheon he proposed to Isabel to come into the gallery and look at the pictures; and though she knew he had seen the pictures twenty times she complied without criticising this pretext. Her conscience now was very easy; ever since she sent him her letter she had felt particularly light of spirit. He walked slowly to the end of the gallery, staring at its contents and saying nothing; and then he suddenly broke out:

"I hoped you wouldn't write to me that way."

"It was the only way, Lord Warburton," said the girl. "Do try and believe that."

"If I could believe it of course I should let you alone. But we can't believe by willing it; and I confess I don't understand. I could understand your disliking me; that I could understand well. But that you should admit you do—"

"What have I admitted?" Isabel interrupted, turning slightly pale.

"That you think me a good fellow; isn't that it?" She said nothing, and he went on: "You don't seem to have any reason, and that gives me a sense of injustice."

"I have a reason, Lord Warburton." She said it in a tone that made his heart contract.

"I should like very much to know it."

"I'll tell you some day when there's more to show for it."

"Excuse my saying that in the mean time I must doubt of it."

"You make me very unhappy," said Isabel.

"I'm not sorry for that; it may help you to know how I feel. Will you kindly answer me a question?" Isabel made no audible assent, but he apparently saw in her eyes something that gave him courage to go on. "Do you prefer some one else?"

"That's a question I'd rather not answer."

"Ah, you do then!" her suitor murmured with bitterness.

The bitterness touched her, and she cried out: "You're mistaken! I don't."

He sat down on a bench, unceremoniously, doggedly, like a man in trouble; leaning his elbows on his knees and staring at the floor. "I can't even be glad of that," he said at last, throwing himself back against the wall; "for that would be an excuse."

She raised her eyebrows in surprise. "An excuse? Must I excuse myself?"

He paid, however, no answer to the question. Another idea had come into his head. "Is it my political opinions? Do you think I go too far?"

"I can't object to your political opinions, because I don't understand them."

"You don't care what I think!" he cried, getting up. "It's all the same to you."

Isabel walked to the other side of the gallery and stood there showing him her charming back, her light slim figure, the length of her white neck as she bent her head, and the density of her dark braids. She stopped in front of a small picture as if for the purpose of examining it; and there was something so young and free in her movement that her very pliancy seemed to mock at him. Her eyes, however, saw nothing; they had suddenly been suffused with tears. In a moment he followed her, and by this time she had brushed her tears away; but when she turned round her face was pale and the expression of her eyes strange. "That reason that I wouldn't tell you—I'll tell it you after all. It's that I can't escape my fate."

"Your fate?"

"I should try to escape it if I were to marry you."

"I don't understand. Why should not that be your fate as well as anything else?"

"Because it's not," said Isabel femininely. "I know it's not. It's not my fate to give up—I know it can't be."

Poor Lord Warburton stared, an interrogative point in either eye.

"Do you call marrying me giving up?"

"Not in the usual sense. It's getting—getting—getting a great deal. But it's giving up other chances."

"Other chances for what?"

"I don't mean chances to marry," said Isabel, her colour quickly coming back to her. And then she stopped, looking down with a deep frown, as if it were hopeless to attempt to make her meaning clear.

"I don't think it presumptuous in me to suggest that you'll gain more than you'll lose," her companion observed.

"I can't escape unhappiness," said Isabel. "In marrying you I shall be trying to."

"I don't know whether you'd try to, but you certainly would: that I must in candour admit!" he exclaimed with an anxious laugh.

"I mustn't—I can't!" cried the girl.

"Well, if you're bent on being miserable I don't see why you should make me so. Whatever charms a life of misery may have for you, it has none for me."

"I'm not bent on a life of misery," said Isabel. "I've always been intensely determined to be happy, and I've often believed I should be. I've told people that; you can ask them. But it comes over me every now and then that I can never be happy in any extraordinary way; not by turning away, by separating myself." "By separating yourself from what?"

"From life. From the usual chances and dangers, from what most people know and suffer."

Lord Warburton broke into a smile that almost denoted hope. "Why, my dear Miss Archer," he began to explain with the most considerate eagerness, "I don't offer you any exoneration from life or from any chances or dangers whatever. I wish I could; depend upon it I would! For what do you take me, pray? Heaven help me, I'm not the Emperor of China! All I offer you is the chance of taking the common lot in a comfortable sort of way. The common lot? Why, I'm devoted to the common lot! Strike an alliance with me, and I promise you that you shall have plenty of it. You shall separate from nothing whatever—not even from your friend Miss Stackpole."

"She'd never approve of it," said Isabel, trying to smile and take advantage of this side-issue; despising herself too, not a little,

"Are we speaking of Miss Stackpole?" his lordship asked impatiently. "I never saw a person judge things on such theoretic grounds."

"Now I suppose you're speaking of me," said Isabel with humility; and she turned away again, for she saw Miss Molyneux enter the gallery, accompanied by Henrietta and by Ralph.

Lord Warburton's sister addressed him with a certain timidity and reminded him she ought to return home in time for tea, as she was expecting company to partake of it. He made no answer—apparently not having heard her; he was preoccupied, and with good reason.

Miss Molyneux—as if he had been Royalty—stood like a lady-in-waiting.

"Well, I never, Miss Molyneux!" said Henrietta Stackpole. "If I wanted to go he'd have to go. If I wanted my brother to do a thing he'd have to do it."

"Oh, Warburton does everything one wants," Miss Molyneux answered with a quick, shy laugh. "How very many pictures you have!" she went on, turning to Ralph.

"They look a good many, because they're all put together," said Ralph. "But it's really a bad way."

"Oh, I think it's so nice. I wish we had a gallery at Lockleigh. I'm so very fond of pictures," Miss Molyneux went on, persistently, to Ralph, as if she were afraid Miss Stackpole would address her again. Henrietta appeared at once to fascinate and to frighten her.

"Ah yes, pictures are very convenient," said Ralph, who appeared to know better what style of reflexion was acceptable to her.

"They're so very pleasant when it rains," the young lady continued. "It has rained of late so very often."

"I'm sorry you're going away, Lord Warburton," said Henrietta. "I wanted to get a great deal more out of you."

"I'm not going away," Lord Warburton answered.

"Your sister says you must. In America the gentlemen obey the ladies."

"I'm afraid we have some people to tea," said Miss Molyneux, looking at her brother.

"Very good, my dear. We'll go."

"I hoped you would resist!" Henrietta exclaimed. "I wanted to see what Miss Molyneux would do."

"I never do anything," said this young lady.

"I suppose in your position it's sufficient for you to exist!" Miss Stackpole returned. "I should like very much to see you at home."

"You must come to Lockleigh again," said Miss Molyneux, very sweetly, to Isabel, ignoring this remark of Isabel's friend. Isabel looked into her quiet eyes a moment, and for that moment seemed to see in their grey depths the reflexion of everything she had rejected in rejecting Lord Warburton—the peace, the kindness, the honour, the possessions, a deep security and a great exclusion. She kissed Miss Molyneux and then she said: "I'm afraid I can never come again."

"Never again?"

"I'm afraid I'm going away."

"Oh, I'm so very sorry," said Miss Molyneux. "I think that's so very wrong of you."

Lord Warburton watched this little passage; then he turned away and stared at a picture. Ralph, leaning against the rail before the picture with his hands in his pockets, had for the moment been watching him.

"I should like to see you at home," said Henrietta, whom Lord Warburton found beside him. "I should like an hour's talk with you; there are a great many questions I wish to ask you." "I shall be delighted to see you," the proprietor of Lockleigh answered; "but I'm certain not to be able to answer many of your questions. When will you come?"

"Whenever Miss Archer will take me. We're thinking of going to London, but we'll go and see you first. I'm determined to get some satisfaction out of you."

"If it depends upon Miss Archer I'm afraid you won't get much. She won't come to Lockleigh; she doesn't like the place."

"She told me it was lovely!" said Henrietta.

Lord Warburton hesitated. "She won't come, all the same. You had better come alone," he added.

Henrietta straightened herself, and her large eyes expanded.

"Would you make that remark to an English lady?" she enquired with soft asperity.

Lord Warburton stared. "Yes, if I liked her enough."

"You'd be careful not to like her enough. If Miss Archer won't visit your place again it's because she doesn't want to take me.

I know what she thinks of me, and I suppose you think the same— that I oughtn't to bring in individuals." Lord Warburton was at a loss; he had not been made acquainted with Miss Stackpole's professional character and failed to catch her allusion. "Miss Archer has been warning you!" she therefore went on.

"Warning me?"

"Isn't that why she came off alone with you here—to put you on your guard?"

"Oh dear, no," said Lord Warburton brazenly; "our talk had no such solemn character as that."

"Well, you've been on your guard—intensely. I suppose

it's natural to you; that's just what I wanted to observe. And so, too, Miss Molyneux—she wouldn't commit herself. You have been warned, anyway," Henrietta continued, addressing this young lady; "but for you it wasn't necessary."

"I hope not," said Miss Molyneux vaguely.

"Miss Stackpole takes notes," Ralph soothingly explained. "She's a great satirist; she sees through us all and she works us up."

"Well, I must say I never have had such a collection of bad material!" Henrietta declared, looking from Isabel to Lord Warburton and from this nobleman to his sister and to Ralph. "There's something the matter with you all; you're as dismal as if you had got a bad cable."

"You do see through us, Miss Stackpole," said Ralph in a low tone, giving her a little intelligent nod as he led the party out of the gallery. "There's something the matter with us all." Isabel came behind these two; Miss Molyneux, who decidedly liked her immensely, had taken her arm, to walk beside her over the polished floor. Lord Warburton strolled on the other side with his hands behind him and his eyes lowered. For some moments he said nothing; and then, "Is it true you're going to London?" he asked.

"I believe it has been arranged."

"And when shall you come back?"

"In a few days; but probably for a very short time. I'm going to Paris with my aunt."

"When, then, shall I see you again?"

"Not for a good while," said Isabel. "But some day or other, I hope."

"Do you really hope it?"

"Very much."

He went a few steps in silence; then he stopped and put out his hand. "Good-bye." "Good-bye," said Isabel. Miss Molyneux kissed her again, and she let the two depart. After it, without rejoining Henrietta and Ralph, she retreated to her own room; in which apartment, before dinner, she was found by Mrs. Touchett, who had stopped on her way to the salon. "I may as well tell you," said that lady, "that your uncle has informed me of your relations with Lord Warburton." Isabel considered. "Relations? They're hardly relations. That's the strange part of it: he has seen me but three or four times."

"Why did you tell your uncle rather than me?" Mrs. Touchett dispassionately asked.

Again the girl hesitated. "Because he knows Lord Warburton better."

"Yes, but I know you better."

"I'm not sure of that," said Isabel, smiling.

"Neither am I, after all; especially when you give me that rather conceited look. One would think you were awfully pleased with yourself and had carried off a prize! I suppose that when you refuse an offer like Lord Warburton's it's because you expect to do something better."

"Ah, my uncle didn't say that!" cried Isabel, smiling still.

Chapter 21

Mrs. Touchett, before arriving in Paris, had fixed the day for her departure and by the middle of February had begun to travel southward. She interrupted her journey to pay a visit to her son, who at San Remo, on the Italian shore of the Mediterranean, had been spending a dull, bright winter beneath a slow-moving white umbrella. Isabel went with her aunt as a matter of course, though Mrs. Touchett, with homely, customary logic, had laid before her a pair of alternatives.

"Now, of course, you're completely your own mistress and are as free as the bird on the bough. I don't mean you were not so before, but you're at present on a different footing—property erects a kind of barrier. You can do a great many things if you're rich which would be severely criticised if you were poor.

You can go and come, you can travel alone, you can have your own establishment: I mean of course if you'll take a companion—some decayed gentlewoman, with a darned cashmere and dyed hair, whopaints on velvet. You don't think you'd like that? Of course youcan do as you please; I only want you to understand how muchyou're at liberty.

You might take Miss Stackpole as your dame decompagnie; she'd keep people off very well. I think, however, thatit's a great deal better you should remain with me, in spite ofthere being no obligation. It's better for several reasons, quiteapart from your liking it. I shouldn't think you'd like it, but Irecommend you to make the sacrifice. Of course whatever noveltythere may have been at first in my society has quite passed away,and you see me as I am—a dull, obstinate, narrow-minded old woman." "I don't think you're at all dull," Isabel had replied to this.

"But you do think I'm obstinate and narrow-minded? I told you so!"said Mrs. Touchett with much elation at being justified.Isabel remained for the present with her aunt, because, in spiteof eccentric impulses, she had a great regard for what was usuallydeemed decent, and a young gentlewoman without visible relationshad always struck her as a flower without foliage. It was truethat Mrs. Touchett's conversation had never again appeared sobrilliant as that first afternoon in Albany, when she sat in herdamp waterproof and sketched the opportunities that Europe wouldoffer to a young person of taste. This, however, was in a greatmeasure the girl's own fault; she had got a glimpse of her aunt'sexperience, and her imagination constantly anticipated thejudgements and emotions of a woman who had very little of the samefaculty.

Apart from this, Mrs. Touchett had a great merit; she wasas honest as a pair of compasses. There was a comfort in herstiffness and firmness; you knew exactly where to find her andwere never liable to chance encounters and concussions. On her ownground she was perfectly present, but was never over-inquisitive asregards the territory of her neighbour. Isabel came at last tohave a kind of undemonstrable pity for her; there seemedsomething so dreary in the condition of a person whose naturehad, as it were, so little surface—offered so limited a face tothe accretions of human contact. Nothing tender, nothingsympathetic, had ever had a chance to fasten upon it—nowind-sown blossom, no familiar softening moss. Her offered, herpassive extent, in other words, was about that of a knife-edge.Isabel had reason to believe none the less that as she advanced inlife she made more of those concessions to the sense of somethingobscurely distinct from convenience—more of them than sheindependently exacted. She was learning to sacrifice consistencyto considerations of that inferior order for which the excuse mustbe found in the particular case. It was not to the credit of herabsolute rectitude that she should have gone the longest way roundto Florence in order to spend a few weeks with her invalid son;since in former years it had been one of her most definiteconvictions that when Ralph wished to see her he was at liberty toremember that Palazzo Crescentini contained a large apartmentknown as the quarter of the signorino.

"I want to ask you something," Isabel said to this young man theday after her arrival at San Remo—"something I've thought morethan once of asking you by letter, but that I've hesitated on thewhole to write about. Face to face, nevertheless, my questionseems easy enough. Did you know your father intended to leave meso much money?"

Ralph stretched his legs a little further than usual and gazed alittle more fixedly at the Mediterranean."What does it matter, my dear Isabel, whether I knew? My fatherwas very obstinate."

"So," said the girl, "you did know."

"Yes; he told me. We even talked it over a little." "What did hedo it for?" asked Isabel abruptly. "Why, as a kind of compliment."

"A compliment on what?"

"On your so beautifully existing."

"He liked me too much," she presently declared.

"That's a way we all have."

"If I believed that I should be very unhappy. Fortunately I don'tbelieve it. I want to be treated with justice; I want nothing butthat."

"Very good. But you must remember that justice to a lovely being is after all a florid sort of sentiment."

"I'm not a lovely being. How can you say that, at the very moment when I'm asking such odious questions? I must seem to you delicate!"

"You seem to me troubled," said Ralph.

"I am troubled."

"About what?"

For a moment she answered nothing; then she broke out: "Do you think it good for me suddenly to be made so rich? Henrietta doesn't."

"Oh, hang Henrietta!" said Ralph coarsely, "If you ask me I'm delighted at it."

"Is that why your father did it—for your amusement?"

"I differ with Miss Stackpole," Ralph went on more gravely. "I think it very good for you to have means."

Isabel looked at him with serious eyes. "I wonder whether you know what's good for me—or whether you care."

"If I know depend upon it I care. Shall I tell you what it is? Not to torment yourself."

"Not to torment you, I suppose you mean."

"You can't do that; I'm proof. Take things more easily. Don't askyourself so much whether this or that is good for you. Don'tquestion your conscience so much—it will get out of tune like astrummed piano. Keep it for great occasions. Don't try so muchto form your character—it's like trying to pull open a tight,tender young rose. Live as you like best, and your character willtake care of itself. Most things are good for you; the exceptionsare very rare, and a comfortable income's not one of them." Ralphpaused, smiling; Isabel had listened quickly. "You've too much powerof thought—above all too much conscience," Ralph added. "It's outof all reason, the number of things you think wrong. Put backyour watch. Diet your fever. Spread your wings; rise above theground. It's never wrong to do that."

She had listened eagerly, as I say; and it was her nature tounderstand quickly. "I wonder if you appreciate what you say. Ifyou do, you take a great responsibility.""You frighten me a little, but I think I'm right," said Ralph,persisting in cheer."All the same what you say is very true," Isabel pursued. "Youcould say nothing more true. I'm absorbed in myself—I look at lifetoo much as a doctor's prescription. Why indeed should weperpetually be thinking whether things are good for us, as if wewere patients lying in a hospital? Why should I be so afraid ofnot doing right? As if it mattered to the world whether I doright or wrong!""You're a capital person to advise," said Ralph; "you take thewind out of my sails!"

She looked at him as if she had not heard him—though she wasfollowing out the train of reflexion which he himself had kindled."I try to care more about the world than about myself—but Ialways come back to myself. It's because I'm afraid." She stopped;her voice had trembled a little. "Yes, I'm afraid; I can't tellyou. A large fortune means freedom, and I'm afraid of that. It'ssuch a fine thing, and one should make such a good use of it. Ifone shouldn't one would be ashamed. And one must keep thinking;it's a constant effort. I'm not sure it's not a greater happinessto be powerless."

"For weak people I've no doubt it's a greater happiness. For weakpeople the effort not to be contemptible must be great.""And how do you know I'm not weak?" Isabel asked."Ah," Ralph answered with a flush that the girl noticed, "if youare I'm awfully sold!"The charm of the Mediterranean coast only deepened for our heroineon acquaintance, for it was the threshold of Italy, the gate ofadmirations. Italy, as yet imperfectly seen and felt, stretchedbefore her as a land of promise, a land in which a love of thebeautiful might be comforted by endless knowledge. Whenever shestrolled upon the shore with her cousin—and she was the companionof his daily walk—she looked across the sea, with longing eyes,to where she knew that Genoa lay.

She was glad to pause, however,on the edge of this larger adventure; there was such a thrill evenin the preliminary hovering. It affected her moreover as a peacefulinterlude, as a hush of the drum and fife in a career which shehad little warrant as yet for regarding as agitated, but whichnevertheless she was constantly picturing to herself by the lightof her hopes, her fears, her fancies, her ambitions, herpredilections, and which reflected these subjective accidents in amanner sufficiently dramatic. Madame Merle had predicted to Mrs.Touchett that after their young friend had put her hand into herpocket half a dozen times she would be reconciled to the idea thatit had been filled by a munificent uncle; and the event justified,as it had so often justified before, that lady's perspicacity.Ralph Touchett had praised his cousin for being morallyinflammable, that is for being quick to take a hint that was meantas good advice.

His advice had perhaps helped the matter; she hadat any rate before leaving San Remo grown used to feeling rich. Theconsciousness in question found a proper place in rather a denselittle group of ideas that she had about herself, and often itwas by no means the least agreeable. It took perpetually forgranted a thousand good intentions. She lost herself in a mazeof visions; the fine things to be done by a rich, independent,generous girl who took a large human view of occasions andobligations were sublime in the mass. Her fortune therefore becameto her mind a part of her better self; it gave her importance, gaveher even, to her own imagination, a certain ideal beauty. What itdid for her in the imagination of others is another affair, andon this point we must also touch in time. The visions I have justspoken of were mixed with other debates. Isabel liked better tothink of the future than of the past; but at times, as shelistened to the murmur of the Mediterranean waves, her glancetook a backward flight.

It rested upon two figures which, inspite of increasing distance, were still sufficiently salient;they were recognisable without difficulty as those of CasparGoodwood and Lord Warburton. It was strange how quickly theseimages of energy had fallen into the background of our younglady's life. It was in her disposition at all times to lose faithin the reality of absent things; she could summon back her faith,in case of need, with an effort, but the effort was often painfuleven when the reality had been pleasant. The past was apt to lookdead and its revival rather to show the livid light of ajudgement-day. The girl moreover was not prone to take forgranted that she herself lived in the mind of others—she had notthe fatuity to believe she left indelible traces. She was capableof being wounded by the discovery that she had been forgotten;but of all liberties the one she herself found sweetest was theliberty to forget. She had not given her last shilling,sentimentally speaking, either to Caspar Goodwood or to LordWarburton, and yet couldn't but feel them appreciably in debt toher. She had of course reminded herself that she was to hear fromMr. Goodwood again; but this was not to be for another yearand a half, and in that time a great many things might happen.She had indeed failed to say to herself that her American suitormight find some other girl more comfortable to woo; because,though it was certain many other girls would prove so, she hadnot the smallest belief that this merit would attract him. Butshe reflected that she herself might know the humiliation ofchange, might really, for that matter, come to the end of thethings that were not Caspar (even though there appeared so manyof them), and find rest in those very elements of his presencewhich struck her now as impediments to the finer respiration. Itwas conceivable that these impediments should some day prove asort of blessing in disguise—a clear and quiet harbour enclosedby a brave granite breakwater. But that day could only come inits order, and she couldn't wait for it with folded hands.

ThatLord Warburton should continue to cherish her image seemed to hermore than a noble humility or an enlightened pride ought to wishto reckon with. She had so definitely undertaken to preserve norecord of what had passed between them that a correspondingeffort on his own part would be eminently just. This was not, asit may seem, merely a theory tinged with sarcasm. Isabel candidlybelieved that his lordship would, in the usual phrase, get overhis disappointment. He had been deeply affected—this shebelieved, and she was still capable of deriving pleasure from thebelief; but it was absurd that a man both so intelligent and sohonourably dealt with should cultivate a scar out of proportionto any wound. Englishmen liked moreover to be comfortable, saidIsabel, and there could be little comfort for Lord Warburton, inthe long run, in brooding over a self-sufficient American girlwho had been but a casual acquaintance. She flattered herselfthat, should she hear from one day to another that he had marriedsome young woman of his own country who had done more to deservehim, she should receive the news without a pang even of surprise.It would have proved that he believed she was firm—which waswhat she wished to seem to him. That alone was grateful to herpride.

Chapter 22

On one of the first days of May, some six months after old Mr.Touchett's death, a small group that might have been described bya painter as composing well was gathered in one of the many roomsof an ancient villa crowning an olive-muffled hill outside of theRoman gate of Florence. The villa was a long, ratherblank-looking structure, with the far-projecting roof whichTuscany loves and which, on the hills that encircle Florence,when considered from a distance, makes so harmonious a rectanglewith the straight, dark, definite cypresses that usually rise ingroups of three or four beside it. The house had a front upon alittle grassy, empty, rural piazza which occupied a part of thehill-top; and this front, pierced with a few windows in irregularrelations and furnished with a stone bench lengthily adjusted tothe base of the structure and useful as a lounging-place to oneor two persons wearing more or less of that air of undervaluedmerit which in Italy, for some reason or other, always gracefullyinvests any one who confidently assumes a perfectly passiveattitude—this antique, solid, weather-worn, yet imposing fronthad a somewhat incommunicative character.

It was the mask, notthe face of the house. It had heavy lids, but no eyes; the housein reality looked another way—looked off behind, into splendidopenness and the range of the afternoon light. In that quarterthe villa overhung the slope of its hill and the long valley ofthe Arno, hazy with Italian colour. It had a narrow garden, inthe manner of a terrace, productive chiefly of tangles of wildroses and other old stone benches, mossy and sun-warmed. Theparapet of the terrace was just the height to lean upon, andbeneath it the ground declined into the vagueness of olive-cropsand vineyards. It is not, however, with the outside of the placethat we are concerned; on this bright morning of ripened springits tenants had reason to prefer the shady side of the wall. Thewindows of the ground-floor, as you saw them from the piazza,were, in their noble proportions, extremely architectural; buttheir function seemed less to offer communication with the worldthan to defy the world to look in.

They were massivelycross-barred, and placed at such a height that curiosity, even ontiptoe, expired before it reached them. In an apartment lightedby a row of three of these jealous apertures—one of the severaldistinct apartments into which the villa was divided and whichwere mainly occupied by foreigners of random race long residentin Florence—a gentleman was seated in company with a young girland two good sisters from a religious house. The room was,however, less sombre than our indications may have represented,for it had a wide, high door, which now stood open into thetangled garden behind; and the tall iron lattices admitted onoccasion more than enough of the Italian sunshine.

It wasmoreover a seat of ease, indeed of luxury, telling ofarrangements subtly studied and refinements frankly proclaimed,and containing a variety of those faded hangings of damask andtapestry, those chests and cabinets of carved and time-polishedoak, those angular specimens of pictorial art in frames aspedantically primitive, those perverse-looking relics of medievalbrass and pottery, of which Italy has long been the not quiteexhausted storehouse. These things kept terms with articles ofmodern furniture in which large allowance had been made for alounging generation; it was to be noticed that all the chairswere deep and well padded and that much space was occupied by awriting-table of which the ingenious perfection bore the stamp ofLondon and the nineteenth century.

There were books in profusionand magazines and newspapers, and a few small, odd, elaboratepictures, chiefly in water-colour. One of these productions stoodon a drawing-room easel before which, at the moment we begin tobe concerned with her, the young girl I have mentioned had placedherself. She was looking at the picture in silence.

Silence—absolute silence—had not fallen upon her companions;but their talk had an appearance of embarrassed continuity. Thetwo good sisters had not settled themselves in their respectivechairs; their attitude expressed a final reserve and their facesshowed the glaze of prudence. They were plain, ample,mild-featured women, with a kind of business-like modesty towhich the impersonal aspect of their stiffened linen and of theserge that draped them as if nailed on frames gave an advantage.One of them, a person of a certain age, in spectacles, with afresh complexion and a full cheek, had a more discriminatingmanner than her colleague, as well as the responsibility of theirerrand, which apparently related to the young girl. This objectof interest wore her hat—an ornament of extreme simplicity andnot at variance with her plain muslin gown, too short for heryears, though it must already have been "let out." The gentlemanwho might have been supposed to be entertaining the two nuns wasperhaps conscious of the difficulties of his function, it beingin its way as arduous to converse with the very meek as with thevery mighty.

At the same time he was clearly much occupied withtheir quiet charge, and while she turned her back to him his eyesrested gravely on her slim, small figure. He was a man of forty,with a high but well-shaped head, on which the hair, still dense,but prematurely grizzled, had been cropped close. He had a fine,narrow, extremely modelled and composed face, of which the onlyfault was just this effect of its running a trifle too much topoints; an appearance to which the shape of the beard contributednot a little. This beard, cut in the manner of the portraits ofthe sixteenth century and surmounted by a fair moustache, ofwhich the ends had a romantic upward flourish, gave its wearer aforeign, traditionary look and suggested that he was a gentlemanwho studied style.

His conscious, curious eyes, however, eyes atonce vague and penetrating, intelligent and hard, expressive ofthe observer as well as of the dreamer, would have assured youthat he studied it only within well-chosen limits, and that in sofar as he sought it he found it. You would have been much at aloss to determine his original clime and country; he had none ofthe superficial signs that usually render the answer to thisquestion an insipidly easy one. If he had English blood in hisveins it had probably received some French or Italian commixture;but he suggested, fine gold coin as he was, no stamp nor emblemof the common mintage that provides for general circulation; hewas the elegant complicated medal struck off for a specialoccasion. He had a light, lean, rather languid-looking figure,and was apparently neither tall nor short. He was dressed as aman dresses who takes little other trouble about it than to haveno vulgar things.

"Well, my dear, what do you think of it?" he asked of the younggirl. He used the Italian tongue, and used it with perfect ease;but this would not have convinced you he was Italian.The child turned her head earnestly to one side and the other."It's very pretty, papa. Did you make it yourself?""Certainly I made it. Don't you think I'm clever?""Yes, papa, very clever; I also have learned to make pictures."And she turned round and showed a small, fair face painted with afixed and intensely sweet smile."You should have brought me a specimen of your powers.""I've brought a great many; they're in my trunk.""She draws very—very carefully," the elder of the nuns remarked,speaking in French.

"I'm glad to hear it. Is it you who have instructed her?"

"Happily no," said the good sister, blushing a little. "Ce n'est pas ma partie. I teach nothing; I leave that to those who are wiser. We've an excellent drawing-master, Mr.—Mr.—what is his name?" she asked of her companion.

Her companion looked about at the carpet. "It's a German name," she said in Italian, as if it needed to be translated.

"Yes," the other went on, "he's a German, and we've had him many years."

The young girl, who was not heeding the conversation, had wandered away to the open door of the large room and stood looking into the garden. "And you, my sister, are French," said the gentleman.

"Yes, sir," the visitor gently replied. "I speak to the pupils in my own tongue. I know no other. But we have sisters of other countries—English, German, Irish. They all speak their proper language."

The gentleman gave a smile. "Has my daughter been under the care of one of the Irish ladies?" And then, as he saw that his visitors suspected a joke, though failing to understand it, "You're very complete," he instantly added.

"Oh, yes, we're complete. We've everything, and everything's of the best."

"We have gymnastics," the Italian sister ventured to remark. "But not dangerous."

"I hope not. Is that YOUR branch?" A question which provoked much candid hilarity on the part of the two ladies; on the subsidence of which their entertainer, glancing at his daughter, remarked that she had grown.

"Yes, but I think she has finished. She'll remain—not big," said the French sister.

"I'm not sorry. I prefer women like books—very good and not too long. But I know," the gentleman said, "no particular reason why my child should be short."

The nun gave a temperate shrug, as if to intimate that such things might be beyond our knowledge. "She's in very good health; that's the best thing."

"Yes, she looks sound." And the young girl's father watched her a moment. "What do you see in the garden?" he asked in French.

"I see many flowers," she replied in a sweet, small voice and with an accent as good as his own.

"Yes, but not many good ones. However, such as they are, go out and gather some for ces dames."

The child turned to him with her smile heightened by pleasure. "May I, truly?"

"Ah, when I tell you," said her father.

The girl glanced at the elder of the nuns. "May I, truly, ma mere?"

"Obey monsieur your father, my child," said the sister, blushing again.

The child, satisfied with this authorisation, descended from the threshold and was presently lost to sight. "You don't spoil them," said her father gaily.

"For everything they must ask leave. That's our system. Leave is freely granted, but they must ask it."

"Oh, I don't quarrel with your system; I've no doubt it's

excellent. I sent you my daughter to see what you'd make of her. I had faith."

"One must have faith," the sister blandly rejoined, gazing through her spectacles.

"Well, has my faith been rewarded What have you made of her?"

The sister dropped her eyes a moment. "A good Christian, monsieur."

Her host dropped his eyes as well; but it was probable that the movement had in each case a different spring. "Yes, and what else?"

He watched the lady from the convent, probably thinking she would say that a good Christian was everything; but for all her simplicity she was not so crude as that. "A charming young lady —a real little woman—a daughter in whom you will have nothing but contentment."

"She seems to me very gentille," said the father. "She's really pretty."

"She's perfect. She has no faults."

"She never had any as a child, and I'm glad you have given her none."

"We love her too much," said the spectacled sister with dignity.

"And as for faults, how can we give what we have not? Le couvent n'est pas comme le monde, monsieur. She's our daughter, as you may say. We've had her since she was so small."

"Of all those we shall lose this year she's the one we shall miss most," the younger woman murmured deferentially.

"Ah, yes, we shall talk long of her," said the other. "We shall hold her up to the new ones." And at this the good sister appeared to find her spectacles dim; while her companion, after fumbling a moment, presently drew forth a pocket-handkerchief of durable texture. "It's not certain you'll lose her; nothing's settled yet," their host rejoined quickly; not as if to anticipate their tears, but in the tone of a man saying what was most agreeable to himself.

"We should be very happy to believe that. Fifteen is very

young to leave us." "Oh," exclaimed the gentleman with more vivacity than he had yet used, "it is not I who wish to take her away. I wish you could keep her always!"

"Ah, monsieur," said the elder sister, smiling and getting up, "good as she is, she's made for the world. Le monde y gagnera."

"If all the good people were hidden away in convents how would the world get on?" her companion softly enquired, rising also.

This was a question of a wider bearing than the good woman apparently supposed; and the lady in spectacles took a harmonising view by saying comfortably: "Fortunately there are good people everywhere."

"If you're going there will be two less here," her host remarked gallantly.

For this extravagant sally his simple visitors had no answer, and they simply looked at each other in decent deprecation; but their confusion was speedily covered by the return of the young girl with two large bunches of roses—one of them all white, the other red.

"I give you your choice, mamman Catherine," said the child. "It's only the colour that's different, mamman Justine; there are just as many roses in one bunch as in the other."

The two sisters turned to each other, smiling and hesitating, with "Which will you take?" and "No, it's for you to choose."

"I'll take the red, thank you," said Catherine in the spectacles. "I'm so red myself. They'll comfort us on our way back to Rome."

"Ah, they won't last," cried the young girl. I wish I could give you something that would last!"

"You've given us a good memory of yourself, my daughter. That will last!" "I wish nuns could wear pretty things. I would give you my blue beads," the child went on.

"And do you go back to Rome to-night?" her father enquired.

"Yes, we take the train again. We've so much to do labas." "Are you not tired?"

"We are never tired."

"Ah, my sister, sometimes," murmured the junior votaress.

"Not to-day, at any rate. We have rested too well here. Que Dieu vows garde, ma fine."

Their host, while they exchanged kisses with his daughter, went forward to open the door through which they were to pass; but as he did so he gave a slight exclamation, and stood looking beyond.

The door opened into a vaulted ante-chamber, as high as a chapel and paved with red tiles; and into this antechamber a lady had just been admitted by a servant, a lad in shabby livery, who was now ushering her toward the apartment in which our friends were grouped. The gentleman at the door, after dropping hisc exclamation, remained silent; in silence too the lady advanced.

He gave her no further audible greeting and offered her no hand, but stood aside to let her pass into the saloon. At the threshold she hesitated. "Is there any one?" she asked.

"Some one you may see."

She went in and found herself confronted with the two nuns and their pupil, who was coming forward, between them, with a hand in the arm of each. At the sight of the new visitor they all paused, and the lady, who had also stopped, stood looking at them. The young girl gave a little soft cry: "Ah, Madame Merle!"

The visitor had been slightly startled, but her manner the next instant was none the less gracious. "Yes, it's Madame Merle, come to welcome you home." And she held out two hands to the girl, who immediately came up to her, presenting her forehead to be kissed. Madame Merle saluted this portion of her charming little person and then stood smiling at the two nuns. They acknowledged her smile with a decent obeisance, but permitted themselves no direct scrutiny of this imposing, brilliant woman, who seemed to bring in with her something of the radiance of the outer world.

"These ladies have brought my daughter home, and now they return to the convent," the gentleman explained.

"Ah, you go back to Rome? I've lately come from there. It's very lovely now," said Madame Merle.

The good sisters, standing with their hands folded into their sleeves, accepted this statement uncritically; and the master of the house asked his new visitor how long it was since she had left Rome. "She came to see me at the convent," said the young girl before the lady addressed had time to reply.

"I've been more than once, Pansy," Madame Merle declared. "Am I not your great friend in Rome?"

"I remember the last time best," said Pansy, "because you told me I should come away."

"Did you tell her that?" the child's father asked.

"I hardly remember. I told her what I thought would please her. I've been in Florence a week. I hoped you would come to see me."

"I should have done so if I had known you were there. One doesn't know such things by inspiration—though I suppose one ought. You had better sit down."

These two speeches were made in a particular tone of voice—a tone half-lowered and carefully quiet, but as from habit rather than from any definite need. Madame Merle looked about her, choosing her seat. "You're going to the door with these women? Let me of course not interrupt the ceremony. Je vous salue, mesdames," she added, in French, to the nuns, as if to dismiss them.

"This lady's a great friend of ours; you will have seen her at the convent," said their entertainer. "We've much faith in her judgement, and she'll help me to decide whether my daughter shall return to you at the end of the holidays."

"I hope you'll decide in our favour, madame," the sister in spectacles ventured to remark.

"That's Mr. Osmond's pleasantry; I decide nothing," said Madame Merle, but also as in pleasantry. "I believe you've a very good school, but Miss Osmond's friends must remember that she's very naturally meant for the world."

"That's what I've told monsieur," sister Catherine answered. "It's precisely to fit her for the world," she murmured, glancing at Pansy, who stood, at a little distance, attentive to Madame Merle's elegant apparel. "Do you hear that, Pansy? You're very naturally meant for the world," said Pansy's father.

The child fixed him an instant with her pure young eyes. "Am I not meant for you, papa?" Papa gave a quick, light laugh. "That doesn't prevent it! I'm of the world, Pansy."

"Kindly permit us to retire," said sister Catherine. "Be good and wise and happy in any case, my daughter."

"I shall certainly come back and see you," Pansy returned, recommencing her embraces, which were presently interrupted by Madame Merle.

"Stay with me, dear child," she said, "while your father takes the good ladies to the door."

Pansy stared, disappointed, yet not protesting. She was evidently impregnated with the idea of submission, which was due to any one who took the tone of authority; and she was a passive spectator of the operation of her fate. "May I not see mamman Catherine get into the carriage?" she nevertheless asked very gently.

"It would please me better if you'd remain with me," said Madame Merle, while Mr. Osmond and his companions, who had bowed low again to the other visitor, passed into the antechamber.

"Oh yes, I'll stay," Pansy answered; and she stood near Madame Merle, surrendering her little hand, which this lady took. She stared out of the window; her eyes had filled with tears.

"I'm glad they've taught you to obey," said Madame Merle. "That's what good little girls should do."

"Oh yes, I obey very well," cried Pansy with soft eagerness, almost with boastfulness, as if she had been speaking of her piano-playing. And then she gave a faint, just audible sigh. Madame Merle, holding her hand, drew it across her own fine palm and looked at it. The gaze was critical, but it found nothing to deprecate; the child's small hand was delicate and fair. "I hope they always see that you wear gloves," she said in a moment.

"Little girls usually dislike them."

"I used to dislike them, but I like them now," the child made answer.

"Very good, I'll make you a present of a dozen."

"I thank you very much. What colours will they be?" Pansy demanded with interest.

Madame Merle meditated. "Useful colours."

"But very pretty?"

"Are you very fond of pretty things?"

"Yes; but—but not too fond," said Pansy with a trace of asceticism.

"Well, they won't be too pretty," Madame Merle returned with a laugh. She took the child's other hand and drew her nearer; after which, looking at her a moment, "Shall you miss mother Catherine?" she went on.

"Yes—when I think of her."

"Try then not to think of her. Perhaps some day," added Madame Merle, "you'll have another mother."

"I don't think that's necessary," Pansy said, repeating her little soft conciliatory sigh. "I had more than thirty mothers at the convent."

Her father's step sounded again in the antechamber, and Madame Merle got up, releasing the child. Mr. Osmond came in and closed the door; then, without looking at Madame Merle, he pushed one or two chairs back into their places. His visitor waited a moment for him to speak, watching him as he moved about. Then at last she said: "I hoped you'd have come to Rome. I thought it possible you'd have wished yourself to fetch Pansy away."

"That was a natural supposition; but I'm afraid it's not the first time I've acted in defiance of your calculations."

"Yes," said Madame Merle, "I think you very perverse."

Mr. Osmond busied himself for a moment in the room—there was plenty of space in it to move about—in the fashion of a manmechanically seeking pretexts for not giving an attention whichmay be embarrassing. Presently, however, he had exhausted hispretexts; there was nothing left for him—unless he took up abook—but to stand with his hands behind him looking at Pansy."Why didn't you come and see the last of mamman Catherine?" heasked of her abruptly in French. Pansy hesitated a moment, glancing at Madame Merle. "I asked her to stay with me," said this lady, who had seated herself again in another place.

"Ah, that was better," Osmond conceded. With which he dropped into a chair and sat looking at Madame Merle; bent forward a little, his elbows on the edge of the arms and his hands interlocked.

"She's going to give me some gloves," said Pansy.

"You needn't tell that to every one, my dear," Madame Merle observed.

"You're very kind to her," said Osmond. "She's supposed to have everything she needs."

"I should think she had had enough of the nuns."

"If we're going to discuss that matter she had better go out of the room."

"Let her stay," said Madame Merle. "We'll talk of something else."

"If you like I won't listen," Pansy suggested with an appearance of candour which imposed conviction.

"You may listen, charming child, because you won't understand," her father replied. The child sat down, deferentially, near the open door, within sight of the garden, into which she directed her innocent, wistful eyes; and Mr. Osmond went on irrelevantly, addressing himself to his other companion. "You're looking particularly well."

"I think I always look the same," said Madame Merle.

"You always ARE the same. You don't vary. You're a wonderful woman." "Yes, I think I am."

"You sometimes change your mind, however. You told me on your return from England that you wouldn't leave Rome again for the present."

"I'm pleased that you remember so well what I say. That was my intention. But I've come to Florence to meet some friends who have lately arrived and as to whose movements I was at that time uncertain."

"That reason's characteristic. You're always doing something for your friends."

Madame Merle smiled straight at her host. "It's less characteristic than your comment upon it which is perfectly insincere. I don't, however, make a crime of that," she added, "because if you don't believe what you say there's no reason why you should. I don't ruin myself for my friends; I don't deserve your praise. I care greatly for myself."

"Exactly; but yourself includes so many other selves—so much of every one else and of everything. I never knew a person whose life touched so many other lives."

"What do you call one's life?" asked Madame Merle. "One's appearance, one's movements, one's engagements, one's society?"

"I call YOUR life your ambitions," said Osmond.

Madame Merle looked a moment at Pansy. "I wonder if she understands that," she murmured.

"You see she can't stay with us!" And Pansy's father gave rather a joyless smile. "Go into the garden, mignonne, and pluck a flower or two for Madame Merle," he went on in French.

"That's just what I wanted to do," Pansy exclaimed, rising with promptness and noiselessly departing. Her father followed her to the open door, stood a moment watching her, and then came back, but remained standing, or rather strolling to and fro, as if to cultivate a sense of freedom which in another attitude might be wanting.

"My ambitions are principally for you," said Madame Merle, looking up at him with a certain courage.

"That comes back to what I say. I'm part of your life—I and a thousand others. You're not selfish—I can't admit that. If you were selfish, what should I be? What epithet would properly describe me?"

"You're indolent. For me that's your worst fault."

"I'm afraid it's really my best."

"You don't care," said Madame Merle gravely.

"No; I don't think I care much. What sort of a fault do you call that? My indolence, at any rate, was one of the reasons I didn't go to Rome. But it was only one of them."

"It's not of importance—to me at least—that you didn't

go; though I should have been glad to see you. I'm glad you're not in Rome now—which you might be, would probably be, if you had gone there a month ago. There's something I should like you to do at present in Florence."

"Please remember my indolence," said Osmond.

"I do remember it; but I beg you to forget it. In that way you'll have both the virtue and the reward. This is not a great labour, and it may prove a real interest. How long is it since you made a new acquaintance?"

"I don't think I've made any since I made yours."

"It's time then you should make another. There's a friend of mine I want you to know."

Mr. Osmond, in his walk, had gone back to the open door again and was looking at his daughter as she moved about in the intense sunshine. "What good will it do me?" he asked with a sort of genial crudity.

Madame Merle waited. "It will amuse you." There was nothing crude in this rejoinder; it had been thoroughly well considered.

"If you say that, you know, I believe it," said Osmond, coming toward her. "There are some points in which my confidence in you is complete. I'm perfectly aware, for instance, that you know good society from bad."

"Society is all bad."

"Pardon me. That isn't—the knowledge I impute to you—a common sort of wisdom. You've gained it in the right way—experimentally; you've compared an immense number of more or less impossible people with each other."

"Well, I invite you to profit by my knowledge."

"To profit? Are you very sure that I shall?"

"It's what I hope. It will depend on yourself. If I could only induce you to make an effort!"

"Ah, there you are! I knew something tiresome was coming. What in the world—that's likely to turn up here—is worth an effort?"

Madame Merle flushed as with a wounded intention. "Don't be foolish, Osmond. No one knows better than you what IS worth an effort. Haven't I seen you in old days?"

"I recognise some things. But they're none of them probable in this poor life."

"It's the effort that makes them probable," said Madame Merle.

"There's something in that. Who then is your friend?"

"The person I came to Florence to see. She's a niece of Mrs. Touchett, whom you'll not have forgotten."

"A niece? The word niece suggests youth and ignorance. I see what you're coming to."

"Yes, she's young—twenty-three years old. She's a great friend of mine. I met her for the first time in England, several months ago, and we struck up a grand alliance. I like her immensely, and I do what I don't do every day—I admire her. You'll do the same."

"Not if I can help it."

"Precisely. But you won't be able to help it."

"Is she beautiful, clever, rich, splendid, universally intelligent and unprecedentedly virtuous? It's only on those conditions that I care to make her acquaintance. You know I asked you some time ago never to speak to me of a creature who shouldn't correspond to that description. I know plenty of dingy people; I don't want to know any more."

"Miss Archer isn't dingy; she's as bright as the morning. She corresponds to your description; it's for that I wish you to know her. She fills all your requirements."

"More or less, of course."

"No; quite literally. She's beautiful, accomplished, generous and, for an American, well-born. She's also very clever and very amiable, and she has a handsome fortune."

Mr. Osmond listened to this in silence, appearing to turn it over in his mind with his eyes on his informant. "What do you want to do with her?" he asked at last.

"What you see. Put her in your way."

"Isn't she meant for something better than that?"

"I don't pretend to know what people are meant for," said Madame Merle. "I only know what I can do with them."

"I'm sorry for Miss Archer!" Osmond declared.

Madame Merle got up. "If that's a beginning of interest

in her I take note of it." The two stood there face to face; she settled her mantilla,

looking down at it as she did so. "You're looking very well," Osmond repeated still less relevantly than before. "You have some idea. You're never so well as when you've got an idea; they're always becoming to you."

In the manner and tone of these two persons, on first meeting atany juncture, and especially when they met in the presence ofothers, was something indirect and circumspect, as if they hadapproached each other obliquely and addressed each other byimplication. The effect of each appeared to be to intensify to anappreciable degree the self-consciousness of the other. MadameMerle of course carried off any embarrassment better than herfriend; but even Madame Merle had not on this occasion the formshe would have liked to have—the perfect self-possession shewould have wished to wear for her host.

The point to be made is,however, that at a certain moment the element between them,whatever it was, always levelled itself and left them more closelyface to face than either ever was with any one else. This was whathad happened now. They stood there knowing each other well andeach on the whole willing to accept the satisfaction of knowing asa compensation for the inconvenience—whatever it might be—ofbeing known. "I wish very much you were not so heartless," MadameMerle quietly said. "It has always been against you, and it willbe against you now."

"I'm not so heartless as you think. Every now and then somethingtouches me—as for instance your saying just now that yourambitions are for me. I don't understand it; I don't see how orwhy they should be. But it touches me, all the same."

"You'll probably understand it even less as time goes on. There are some things you'll never understand. There's no particular need you should." "You, after all, are the most remarkable of women," said Osmond. "You have more in you than almost any one. I don't see why you think Mrs. Touchett's niece should matter very much to me, when— when—" But he paused a moment.

"When I myself have mattered so little?"

"That of course is not what I meant to say. When I've known and appreciated such a woman as you."

"Isabel Archer's better than I," said Madame Merle. Her companion gave a laugh. "How little you must think of her to say that!"

"Do you suppose I'm capable of jealousy? Please answer me that." "With regard to me? No; on the whole I don't."

"Come and see me then, two days hence. I'm staying at Mrs. Touchett's—Palazzo Crescentini—and the girl will be there."

"Why didn't you ask me that at first simply, without speaking of the girl?" said Osmond. "You could have had her there at any rate."

Madame Merle looked at him in the manner of a woman whom no question he could ever put would find unprepared. "Do you wish to know why? Because I've spoken of you to her." Osmond frowned and turned away. "I'd rather not know that." Then in a moment he pointed out the easel supporting the little water-colour drawing. "Have you seen what's there—my last?"

Madame Merle drew near and considered. "Is it the Venetian Alps—one of your last year's sketches?"

"Yes—but how you guess everything!"

She looked a moment longer, then turned away. "You know I don't care for your drawings."

"I know it, yet I'm always surprised at it. They're really so much better than most people's."

"That may very well be. But as the only thing you do—well, it's so little. I should have liked you to do so many other things: those were my ambitions."

"Yes; you've told me many times—things that were impossible."

"Things that were impossible," said Madame Merle. And then in quite a different tone: "In itself your little picture's very good." She looked about the room—at the old cabinets, pictures, tapestries, surfaces of faded silk. "Your rooms at least are perfect. I'm struck with that afresh whenever I come back; I know none better anywhere. You understand this sort of thing as nobody anywhere does. You've such adorable taste."

"I'm sick of my adorable taste," said Gilbert Osmond.

"You must nevertheless let Miss Archer come and see it. I've told her about it."

"I don't object to showing my things—when people are not idiots."

"You do it delightfully. As cicerone of your museum you appear to particular advantage."

Mr. Osmond, in return for this compliment, simply looked at once colder and more attentive. "Did you say she was rich?"

"She has seventy thousand pounds."

"En ecus bien comptes?"

"There's no doubt whatever about her fortune. I've seen it, as I may say."

"Satisfactory woman!—I mean you. And if I go to see her shall I see the mother?"

"The mother? She has none—nor father either."

"The aunt then—whom did you say?—Mrs. Touchett. I can easily keep her out of the way."

"I don't object to her," said Osmond; "I rather like Mrs. Touchett. She has a sort of old-fashioned character that's passing away—a vivid identity. But that long jackanapes the son—is he about the place?"

"He's there, but he won't trouble you."

"He's a good deal of a donkey."

"I think you're mistaken. He's a very clever man. But he's not fond of being about when I'm there, because he doesn't like me."

"What could he be more asinine than that? Did you say she has looks?" Osmond went on.

"Yes; but I won't say it again, lest you should be disappointed in them. Come and make a beginning; that's all I ask of you." "A beginning of what?"

Madame Merle was silent a little. "I want you of course to marry her."

"The beginning of the end? Well, I'll see for myself. Have you told her that?"

"For what do you take me? She's not so coarse a piece of

machinery—nor am I." "Really," said Osmond after some meditation, "I don't understand your ambitions."

"I think you'll understand this one after you've seen Miss Archer. Suspend your judgement." Madame Merle, as she spoke, had drawn near the open door of the garden, where she stood a moment looking out. "Pansy has really grown pretty," she presently added.

"So it seemed to me."

"But she has had enough of the convent."

"I don't know," said Osmond. "I like what they've made of her. It's very charming."

"That's not the convent. It's the child's nature."

"It's the combination, I think. She's as pure as a pearl."

"Why doesn't she come back with my flowers then?" Madame Merle asked. "She's not in a hurry."

"We'll go and get them."

"She doesn't like me," the visitor murmured as she raised her parasol and they passed into the garden.

Chapter 23

Madame Merle, who had come to Florence on Mrs. Touchett's arrival at the invitation of this lady—Mrs. Touchett offering her for a month the hospitality

Chapter 27

I may not attempt to report in its fulness our young woman'sresponse to the deep appeal of Rome, to analyse her feelings asshe trod the pavement of the Forum or to number her pulsations asshe crossed the threshold of Saint Peter's. It is enough to saythat her impression was such as might have been expected of aperson of her freshness and her eagerness. She had always beenfond of history, and here was history in the stones of the streetand the atoms of the sunshine. She had an imagination thatkindled at the mention of great deeds, and wherever she turnedsome great deed had been acted. These things strongly moved her,but moved her all inwardly. It seemed to her companions that shetalked less than usual, and Ralph Touchett, when he appeared tobe looking listlessly and awkwardly over her head, was reallydropping on her an intensity of observation. By her own measureshe was very happy; she would even have been willing to takethese hours for the happiest she was ever to know.

The sense ofthe terrible human past was heavy to her, but that of somethingaltogether contemporary would suddenly give it wings that itcould wave in the blue. Her consciousness was so mixed that shescarcely knew where the different parts of it would lead her, andshe went about in a repressed ecstasy of contemplation, seeingoften in the things she looked at a great deal more than wasthere, and yet not seeing many of the items enumerated in herMurray. Rome, as Ralph said, confessed to the psychologicalmoment. The herd of reechoing tourists had departed and most ofthe solemn places had relapsed into solemnity. The sky was ablaze of blue, and the plash of the fountains in their mossyniches had lost its chill and doubled its music. On the cornersof the warm, bright streets one stumbled on bundles of flowers.Our friends had gone one afternoon—it was the third of theirstay—to look at the latest excavations in the Forum, theselabours having been for some time previous largely extended.

Theyhad descended from the modern street to the level of the SacredWay, along which they wandered with a reverence of step which wasnot the same on the part of each. Henrietta Stackpole was struckwith the fact that ancient Rome had been paved a good deal likeNew York, and even found an analogy between the deep chariot-rutstraceable in the antique street and the overjangled iron grooveswhich express the intensity of American life. The sun had begunto sink, the air was a golden haze, and the long shadows ofbroken column and vague pedestal leaned across the field of ruin.Henrietta wandered away with Mr. Bantling, whom it was apparently-delightful to her to hear speak of Julius Caesar as a "cheeky oldboy," and Ralph addressed such elucidations as he was prepared tooffer to the attentive ear of our heroine. One of the humblearcheologists who hover about the place had put himself at thedisposal of the two, and repeated his lesson with a fluency whichthe decline of the season had done nothing to impair. A processof digging was on view in a remote corner of the Forum, and hepresently remarked that if it should please the signori to goand watch it a little they might see something of interest. Theproposal commended itself more to Ralph than to Isabel, weary with much wandering; so that she admonished her companion tosatisfy his curiosity while she patiently awaited his return. Thehour and the place were much to her taste—she should enjoy beingbriefly alone. Ralph accordingly went off with the cicerone whileIsabel sat down on a prostrate column near the foundations of theCapitol. She wanted a short solitude, but she was not long toenjoy it. Keen as was her interest in the rugged relics of theRoman past that lay scattered about her and in which thecorrosion of centuries had still left so much of individual life,her thoughts, after resting a while on these things, had wandered,by a concatenation of stages it might require some subtlety totrace, to regions and objects charged with a more active appeal.From the Roman past to Isabel Archer's future was a long stride,but her imagination had taken it in a single flight and now hoveredin slow circles over the nearer and richer field.

She was soabsorbed in her thoughts, as she bent her eyes upon a row ofcracked but not dislocated slabs covering the ground at her feet,that she had not heard the sound of approaching footsteps before ashadow was thrown across the line of her vision. She looked up andsaw a gentleman—a gentleman who was not Ralph come back to saythat the excavations were a bore. This personage was startled asshe was startled; he stood there baring his head to her perceptiblypale surprise.

"Lord Warburton!" Isabel exclaimed as she rose.

"I had no idea it was you. I turned that corner and came upon you."

She looked about her to explain. "I'm alone, but my companions have just left me. My cousin's gone to look at the work over there."

"Ah yes; I see." And Lord Warburton's eyes wandered vaguely in the direction she had indicated. He stood firmly before her now; he had recovered his balance and seemed to wish to show it, though very kindly. "Don't let me disturb you," he went on, looking at her dejected pillar. "I'm afraid you're tired."

"Yes, I'm rather tired." She hesitated a moment, but sat down again. "Don't let me interrupt you," she added.

"Oh dear, I'm quite alone, I've nothing on earth to do. I had no idea you were in Rome. I've just come from the East. I'm only passing through."

"You've been making a long journey," said Isabel, who had learned from Ralph that Lord Warburton was absent from England.

"Yes, I came abroad for six months—soon after I saw you last. I've been in Turkey and Asia Minor; I came the other day from Athens." He managed not to be awkward, but he wasn't easy, and after a longer look at the girl he came down to nature. "Do you wish me to leave you, or will you let me stay a little?" She took it all humanely. "I don't wish you to leave me, Lord Warburton; I'm very glad to see you." "Thank you for saying that. May I sit down?"

The fluted shaft on which she had taken her seat would have afforded a resting-place to several persons, and there was plenty of room even for a highly-developed Englishman. This fine specimen of that great class seated himself near our young lady, and in the course of five minutes he had asked her several questions, taken rather at random and to which, as he put some of them twice over, he apparently somewhat missed catching the answer; had given her too some information about himself which was not wasted upon her calmer feminine sense.

He repeated more than once that he had not expected to meet her, and it was evident that the encounter touched him in a way that would have made preparation advisable. He began abruptly to pass from the impunity of things to their solemnity, and from their being delightful to their being impossible. He was splendidly sunburnt; even his multitudinous beard had been burnished by the fire of Asia.

He was dressed in the loose-fitting, heterogeneous garments in which the English traveller in foreign lands is wont to consult his comfort and affirm his nationality; and with hispleasant steady eyes, his bronzed complexion, fresh beneath itsseasoning, his manly figure, his minimising manner and hisgeneral air of being a gentleman and an explorer, he was such arepresentative of the British race as need not in any clime havebeen disavowed by those who have a kindness for it. Isabel notedthese things and was glad she had always liked him. He had kept,evidently in spite of shocks, every one of his merits—propertiesthese partaking of the essence of great decent houses, as onemight put it; resembling their innermost fixtures and ornaments,not subject to vulgar shifting and removable only by some wholebreak-up.

They talked of the matters naturally in order; heruncle's death, Ralph's state of health, the way she had passedher winter, her visit to Rome, her return to Florence, her plansfor the summer, the hotel she was staying at; and then of LordWarburton's own adventures, movements, intentions, impressionsand present domicile. At last there was a silence, and it said somuch more than either had said that it scarce needed his finalwords. "I've written to you several times."

"Written to me? I've never had your letters."

"I never sent them. I burned them up."

"Ah," laughed Isabel, "it was better that you should do thatthan I!""I thought you wouldn't care for them," he went on with asimplicity that touched her. "It seemed to me that after all Ihad no right to trouble you with letters.""I should have been very glad to have news of you. You know how Ihoped that—that—" But she stopped; there would be such aflatness in the utterance of her thought."I know what you're going to say. You hoped we should alwaysremain good friends." This formula, as Lord Warburton uttered it,was certainly flat enough; but then he was interested in makingit appear so.She found herself reduced simply to "Please don't talk of allthat"; a speech which hardly struck her as improvement on theother."It's a small consolation to allow me!" her companion exclaimedwith force."I can't pretend to console you," said the girl, who, all stillas she sat there, threw herself back with a sort of inwardtriumph on the answer that had satisfied him so little six monthsbefore.

He was pleasant, he was powerful, he was gallant; therewas no better man than he. But her answer remained."It's very well you don't try to console me; it wouldn't be inyour power," she heard him say through the medium of her strangeelation."I hoped we should meet again, because I had no fear you wouldattempt to make me feel I had wronged you. But when you do that—the pain's greater than the pleasure." And she got up with asmall conscious majesty, looking for her companions."I don't want to make you feel that; of course I can't say that.I only just want you to know one or two things—in fairness tomyself, as it were. I won't return to the subject again. I feltvery strongly what I expressed to you last year; I couldn't thinkof anything else. I tried to forget—energetically,systematically.

I tried to take an interest in somebody else. Itell you this because I want you to know I did my duty. I didn'tsucceed. It was for the same purpose I went abroad—as far awayas possible. They say travelling distracts the mind, but itdidn't distract mine. I've thought of you perpetually, ever sinceI last saw you. I'm exactly the same. I love you just as much,and everything I said to you then is just as true. This instantat which I speak to you shows me again exactly how, to my greatmisfortune, you just insuperably charm me. There—I can't sayless. I don't mean, however, to insist; it's only for a moment. Imay add that when I came upon you a few minutes since, withoutthe smallest idea of seeing you, I was, upon my honour, in thevery act of wishing I knew where you were." He had recovered hisself-control, and while he spoke it became complete. He mighthave been addressing a small committee—making all quietly andclearly a statement of importance; aided by an occasional look ata paper of notes concealed in his hat, which he had not again puton. And the committee, assuredly, would have felt the pointproved. "I've often thought of you, Lord Warburton," Isabel answered. "You may be sure I shall always do that." And she added in a tone of which she tried to keep up the kindness and keep down themeaning: "There's no harm in that on either side."They walked along together, and she was prompt to ask about hissisters and request him to let them know she had done so. He madefor the moment no further reference to their great question, butdipped again into shallower and safer waters. But he wished toknow when she was to leave Rome, and on her mentioning the limitof her stay declared he was glad it was still so distant."Why do you say that if you yourself are only passing through?"she enquired with some anxiety.

"Ah, when I said I was passing through I didn't mean that onewould treat Rome as if it were Clapham Junction. To pass throughRome is to stop a week or two.""Say frankly that you mean to stay as long as I do!"His flushed smile, for a little, seemed to sound her. "You won'tlike that. You're afraid you'll see too much of me.""It doesn't matter what I like. I certainly can't expect you toleave this delightful place on my account. But I confess I'mafraid of you."

"Afraid I'll begin again? I promise to be very careful."They had gradually stopped and they stood a moment face to face."Poor Lord Warburton!" she said with a compassion intended to begood for both of them."Poor Lord Warburton indeed! But I'll be careful.""You may be unhappy, but you shall not make ME so. That I can'tallow.""If I believed I could make you unhappy I think I should try it."At this she walked in advance and he also proceeded. "I'll neversay a word to displease you.""Very good. If you do, our friendship's at an end.""Perhaps some day—after a while—you'll give me leave.""Give you leave to make me unhappy?"He hesitated. "To tell you again—" But he checked himself. "I'llkeep it down. I'll keep it down always."Ralph Touchett had been joined in his visit to the excavation byMiss Stackpole and her attendant, and these three now emergedfrom among the mounds of earth and stone collected round theaperture and came into sight of Isabel and her companion. PoorRalph hailed his friend with joy qualified by wonder, andHenrietta exclaimed in a high voice "Gracious, there's thatlord!" Ralph and his English neighbour greeted with the austeritywith which, after long separations, English neighbours greet, andMiss Stackpole rested her large intellectual gaze upon thesunburnt traveller. But she soon established her relation to thecrisis. "I don't suppose you remember me, sir." "Indeed I do remember you," said Lord Warburton. "I asked you tocome and see me, and you never came.""I don't go everywhere I'm asked," Miss Stackpole answeredcoldly. "Ah well, I won't ask you again," laughed the master ofLockleigh."If you do I'll go; so be sure!"Lord Warburton, for all his hilarity, seemed sure enough. Mr.Bantling had stood by without claiming a recognition, but he nowtook occasion to nod to his lordship, who answered him with afriendly "Oh, you here, Bantling?" and a hand-shake."Well," said Henrietta, "I didn't know you knew him!""I guess you don't know every one I know," Mr. Bantling rejoinedfacetiously.

"I thought that when an Englishman knew a lord he always toldyou.""Ah, I'm afraid Bantling was ashamed of me," Lord Warburtonlaughed again. Isabel took pleasure in that note; she gave asmall sigh of relief as they kept their course homeward.The next day was Sunday; she spent her morning over two longletters—one to her sister Lily, the other to Madame Merle; butin neither of these epistles did she mention the fact that arejected suitor had threatened her with another appeal. Of aSunday afternoon all good Romans (and the best Romans are oftenthe northern barbarians) follow the custom of going to vespers at Saint Peter's; and it had been agreed among our friends that theywould drive together to the great church. After lunch, an hourbefore the carriage came, Lord Warburton presented himself at theHotel de Paris and paid a visit to the two ladies, Ralph Touchettand Mr. Bantling having gone out together. The visitor seemed tohave wished to give Isabel a proof of his intention to keep thepromise made her the evening before; he was both discreet andfrank—not even dumbly importunate or remotely intense. He thusleft her to judge what a mere good friend he could be. He talkedabout his travels, about Persia, about Turkey, and when MissStackpole asked him whether it would "pay" for her to visit thosecountries assured her they offered a great field to femaleenterprise. Isabel did him justice, but she wondered what hispurpose was and what he expected to gain even by proving thesuperior strain of his sincerity. If he expected to melt her byshowing what a good fellow he was, he might spare himself thetrouble. She knew the superior strain of everything about him,and nothing he could now do was required to light the view.Moreover his being in Rome at all affected her as a complicationof the wrong sort—she liked so complications of the right.Nevertheless, when, on bringing his call to a close, he said hetoo should be at Saint Peter's and should look out for her andher friends, she was obliged to reply that he must follow hisconvenience.

In the church, as she strolled over its tesselated acres, hewas the first person she encountered. She had not been one of thesuperior tourists who are "disappointed" in Saint Peter's andfind it smaller than its fame; the first time she passed beneaththe huge leathern curtain that strains and bangs at the entrance,the first time she found herself beneath the far-arching dome andsaw the light drizzle down through the air thickened with incenseand with the reflections of marble and gilt, of mosaic andbronze, her conception of greatness rose and dizzily rose. Afterthis it never lacked space to soar. She gazed and wondered like achild or a peasant, she paid her silent tribute to the seatedsublime.

Lord Warburton walked beside her and talked of SaintSophia of Constantinople; she feared for instance that he wouldend by calling attention to his exemplary conduct. The servicehad not yet begun, but at Saint Peter's there is much to observe,and as there is something almost profane in the vastness of theplace, which seems meant as much for physical as for spiritualexercise, the different figures and groups, the mingledworshippers and spectators, may follow their various intentionswithout conflict or scandal. In that splendid immensityindividual indiscretion carries but a short distance. Isabel andher companions, however, were guilty of none; for thoughHenrietta was obliged in candour to declare that Michael Angelo'sdome suffered by comparison with that of the Capitol atWashington, she addressed her protest chiefly to Mr. Bantling'sear and reserved it in its more accentuated form for the columnsof the Interviewer. Isabel made the circuit of the church withhis lordship, and as they drew near the choir on the left of theentrance the voices of the Pope's singers were borne to them overthe heads of the large number of persons clustered outside thedoors.

They paused a while on the skirts of this crowd, composedin equal measure of Roman cockneys and inquisitive strangers, andwhile they stood there the sacred concert went forward. Ralph,with Henrietta and Mr. Bantling, was apparently within, whereIsabel, looking beyond the dense group in front of her, saw theafternoon light, silvered by clouds of incense that seemed tomingle with the splendid chant, slope through the embossedrecesses of high windows. After a while the singing stopped andthen Lord Warburton seemed disposed to move off with her. Isabelcould only accompany him; whereupon she found herself confrontedwith Gilbert Osmond, who appeared to have been standing at ashort distance behind her. He now approached with all the forms—he appeared to have multiplied them on this occasion to suitthe place.

"So you decided to come?" she said as she put out her hand.

"Yes, I came last night and called this afternoon at your hotel. They told me you had come here, and I looked about for you."

"The others are inside," she decided to say.

"I didn't come for the others," he promptly returned.

She looked away; Lord Warburton was watching them; perhaps he had heard this. Suddenly she remembered it to be just what he had said to her the morning he came to Gardencourt to ask her tomarry him. Mr. Osmond's words had brought the colour to hercheek, and this reminiscence had not the effect of dispelling it.She repaired any betrayal by mentioning to each companion thename of the other, and fortunately at this moment Mr. Bantlingemerged from the choir, cleaving the crowd with British valourand followed by Miss Stackpole and Ralph Touchett. I sayfortunately, but this is perhaps a superficial view of thematter; since on perceiving the gentleman from Florence RalphTouchett appeared to take the case as not committing him to joy.

He didn't hang back, however, from civility, and presentlyobserved to Isabel, with due benevolence, that she would soonhave all her friends about her. Miss Stackpole had met Mr. Osmondin Florence, but she had already found occasion to say to Isabelthat she liked him no better than her other admirers—than Mr.Touchett and Lord Warburton, and even than little Mr. Rosier inParis. "I don't know what it's in you," she had been pleased toremark, "but for a nice girl you do attract the most unnaturalpeople. Mr. Goodwood's the only one I've any respect for, andhe's just the one you don't appreciate.""What's your opinion of Saint Peter's?" Mr. Osmond was meanwhileenquiring of our young lady."It's very large and very bright," she contented herself withreplying.

"It's too large; it makes one feel like an atom."

"Isn't that the right way to feel in the greatest of human temples?" she asked with rather a liking for her phrase.

"I suppose it's the right way to feel everywhere, when one IS nobody. But I like it in a church as little as anywhere else."

"You ought indeed to be a Pope!" Isabel exclaimed, remembering something he had referred to in Florence.

"Ah, I should have enjoyed that!" said Gilbert Osmond.

Lord Warburton meanwhile had joined Ralph Touchett, and the two strolled away together. "Who's the fellow speaking to Miss

Archer?" his lordship demanded.

"His name's Gilbert Osmond—he lives in Florence," Ralph said.

"What is he besides?"

"Nothing at all. Oh yes, he's an American; but one forgets that—

he's so little of one."

"Has he known Miss Archer long?"

"Three or four weeks."

"Does she like him?"

"She's trying to find out."

"And will she?"

"Find out—?" Ralph asked.

"Will she like him?"

"Do you mean will she accept him?"

"Yes," said Lord Warburton after an instant; "I suppose that's what I horribly mean."

"Perhaps not if one does nothing to prevent it," Ralph replied.

His lordship stared a moment, but apprehended. "Then we must be perfectly quiet?"

"As quiet as the grave. And only on the chance!" Ralph added.

"The chance she may?"

"The chance she may not?"

Lord Warburton took this at first in silence, but he spoke again.

"Is he awfully clever?"

"Awfully," said Ralph.

His companion thought. "And what else?"

"What more do you want?" Ralph groaned.

"Do you mean what more does SHE?"

Ralph took him by the arm to turn him: they had to rejoin the others. "She wants nothing that WE can give her."

"Ah well, if she won't have You—!" said his lordship handsomely as they went.

Chapter 13

Study Questions and Answers

Q. Discuss the Importance of Chapter Six in The Turn of the Screw

Or

Q. Write a short summary of Chapter Six

Chapter Six is an important section of The Turn of the Screw, as it involves many of the themes of the story, as well as reflecting its general narrative structure. James' novel is phenomenally complex; it has an incredible ambiguity to it, which allows for some very outlandish and far-fetched ideas to be formulated. A 'theme' can almost be drawn from almost every other sentence, if one so desires. It is deciding which issues have a little more to them than there may seem at first and which are what they appear, nothing more, which is difficult. As with many books of its ilk, over-analysing is a serious essay writing hazard.

To take things one aspect at a time, and to begin with the narrative structure. Whilst not exactly a key issue' of the story, the narrative structure can often inŸuence how those issues are revealed and detailed to readers, so still holds some relevance to the essay title. Chapter Six' overall structure is very similar to that of the story as a whole. It begins quietly, after the climax at the end of the previous chapter (as with the main part of The Turn of the Screw after the prologue, which creates a great deal of anticipation) and begins to increase in tension slowly throughout, with a slight lull in the middle, where the narrative becomes very reŸective and introspective, with the Governess writing her thoughts seemingly as they enter her head, creating a somewhat rambling, dense prose.

Finally, when readers are least expecting it, the plot suddenly leaps into view once again, creating an exciting žnale "Then I again shifted my eyes-I faced what I had to face. which leaves many plot threads open to interpretation as with the žnal words of the žnal chapter, "Œand his little heart, dispossessed, had stopped-Chapter Six is something of a microcosm of the rest of the story, at least in terms of the narrative structure.

More important, however, is how the key issues of the story are represented in this chapter. These issues come in two distinct categories. The žrst involve the various themes of the story, involving the characters, the plot and reality itself. The second type consists of the various techniques James uses in the Governess' language to depict her character and set the tone for the book.

Taking the latter žrst; the Governess' language is very distinctive. It is very verbose and detailed, examining events and people very closely, using as many words as possible to describe even the simplest of things. For example, towards the end of Chapter Six she is trying to think of rational alternatives for the presence of Miss Jessel on the opposite side of the lake. When she fails, she writes "Nothing was more natural than that these things should be the other things they absolutely were not. This style of writing is extremely difficult to understand in places, making the book heavy reading in places, and creating a somewhat monotonous and depressing atmosphere at times. This may be due to James' own writing style, or a deliberate attempt to dežne the Governess' own writing traits; it is difficult to tell. Either way, it creates a very dark feel for the story.

As for the themes, there are probably almost an inžnite number of interpretations that could be theorised from the text. Readers have to determine how much they are willing to accept. There are some themes which are not explored in this particular chapter; nevertheless, there are still a surprising number of them squeezed into a mere seven pages.

One recurring theme is evident in the conversation between Mrs. Grose and the Governess. The two characters have a tendency to complete each other's sentences, to speak almost as if they are of one mind. Two incidences here are particularly noticeable:

It does strike me that my pupils have never mentioned -!'

She looked at me hard as I musingly pulled up. His having been here and the time they were with him?'

And:

I continued to think. It is rather odd.'

That he has never spoken of him?'

This leads into another, incredibly important theme of the book. That of appearance and reality. On the surface, The Turn of the Screw appears to be a disturbing and unusual ghost story. However, several other theories have been discussed over the years, all of which question the Governess' sanity to some extent-some suggest she is writing the entire story in a mental home; others think that Douglas is in fact an adult Miles (which requires a new interpretation of the ending, of course). As can be seen, these theories can become wilder and more exotic until the speculation goes too far. The theme of the Governess and Mrs. Grose talking as one is part of the theory that suggests that Mrs Grose is, in fact, a žgment of the Governess' warped and disturbed imagination. Or, if one was to follow the mental home idea, Mrs Grose could be a nurse who is counselling the Governess, hence her continued support and understanding, even when the narrator becomes increasingly deluded and disturbed.

It is a mineželd of misinformation and over-active imaginations, a mineželd in which mines are being planted as each page goes by, due to the ambiguity of the writing. One of the best examples of this ambiguity happens to be in Chapter Six, when Mrs Grose is talking about Quint's relationship with Miles: Quint was much too free.'

This gave me, straight from my vision of his face-such a face!-a sudden sickness of disgust. Too free with my boy?'

Too free with every one!'

This could clearly be interpreted any number of ways. It could mean that Quint was too friendly with the child, given their respective social positions, or that he was too generous towards Miles. There is also a more sinister point of view; that

Quint was abusing the boy. This theory possibly stems from James' alleged paedophilia, but some of the language elsewhere in the text is decidedly suspicious (using words such as intercourse', for example, to describe a normal conversation). This disturbing idea is supported by the Freudian images in the text.

Again, this depends upon the readers own disposition towards Freudian ideas. However, supporters of the philosophy have an immense amount of material to work with in The Turn of the Screw. In the žnal chapter there are several decidedly ambiguous references during the Governess' conversation with Miles that could be interpreted in a sexual way ("I let the impulse Ÿame up to convert the climax of his dismay into the very proof of his liberation.. Earlier in the text, Quint is seen standing atop a tower-an image which Freudians insist is representative or male sexual organs, a theme supposedly continued in Chapter Six, when Miss Jessel is seen across a lake, representing the female side of the issue. Personally, I do not put much weight in this very deep Freudian insight'-it seems, to me, that this is reading too much into the text.

Chapter Six also shows the Governess making unfounded assumptions about events. From seeing Quint twice, both times when she was alone, she suddenly leaps to the conclusion that he is searching for Miles. These frequent assumptions, made throughout the story, lend weight to the theory that she is insane, and that the ghosts are merely hallucinations on her part, or artefacts of a deranged imagination.

Finally, Chapter Six represents in places what this novel is at the core-a Gothic story. This is most evident when Miss Jessel appears across the lake. This is a particularly Gothic image, made all the more vivid in the following chapter, when she is described as "a žgure of quite as unmistakable horror and evil: a woman in black, pale and dreadful.• In retrospect, this makes the end of Chapter Six seem even more Gothic.

Chapter Six reŸects many of the key issues of the story, more so than most chapters. However, The Turn of the Screw is a very intense book, and every sentence seems to have hints of some deeper, darker deliberation on the part of James' writing. It is not unusual in this story to have a single chapter that contains a great deal of important information and relevance to the rest of the book-Chapter Six does tend to explore more issues in such a short space than other sections of the story, however.

Q. Write a Brief Essay on "Enter ethics, whose specialty is articulating the relation between freedom and necessity, desire and the law."

"Enter ethics, whose specialty is articulating the relation between freedom and necessity, desire and the law."

In this paper, I want to use a definition of ethics taken from one of the leading writers on the subject of literature and ethics as a springboard for a reading of The Portrait of a Lady. Yet, though I find Harpham's definition useful, I do not wholly share his view that the relation between his keyterms is best articulated by noting that "the stark ought of ethics the law to a creature who is presumed to be free to follow it or not. If human beings were not free, there would be no need for urging, but if they were not in fact bound by the law, there would be nothing to urge".

I want to complicate this picture by bringing in another pair of terms—metaphor and metonymy—that have the added virtue of belonging to the field of rhetoric and are thus arguably more properly literary than Harpham's keywords. My intention is not to align either of these figures with one of the poles in Harpham's definition. Rather, I aim to show how paying due attention to the complex operation of these tropes in The Portrait of a Lady enables us to see that freedom and necessity, desire and the law, are not the neatly opposed poles that they might appear to be. The most intensely charged ethical moments in this novel occur when the fraught interpenetration of these realms is at its most pronounced.

Since the time when Roman Jakobson offered powerful evidence for the deep structural distinction between metaphor and metonymy, most students of rhetoric have agreed that these two tropes together form a basic skeleton, to which all other figures may be related. When one takes this perspective, then one is of course using metaphor and metonymy as what Hans Kellner calls " 'inflatable tropes' that can be understood as 'figures of words,' 'figures of thought,' 'figures of comprehension,' and 'figures of discourse,' " referring respectively to the paradigmatic and the syntagmatic. For Jakobson, too, metaphor and metonymy are shorthand terms for what he calls the "two different semantic lines" along which a stretch of discourse may develop: "one topic," he writes, "may lead to another either through their similarity [belonging to the same paradigm] or their contiguity [belonging to the same syntagm]".

"Similarity" is the key feature of metaphor, yet this statement needs to be importantly modified. In the classic textbook example of metaphor, "he was a lion in the fight," it is clear that the subject of the sentence displayed a similarity to a lion, yet it is equally clear that this subject was not, in actual fact, a lion. Metaphor, David Lodge comments, "creates a relationship of similarity between dissimilars". Metaphor, to quote another rhetorical definition, "creates the relation between its objects," a relationship that consists in the essential quality that the objects are thought to share, no matter how unrelated they are in actual fact. Metonymy for its part deals in items that are intimately linked to one another in real, syntagmatic contexts, without anyone claiming that they share a paradigmatic quality—not even temporarily, not even for the duration of the figure of speech.

When you say "The White House has decided," the White House is a metonymy for the American President, not because that mansion would somehow enjoy the same power as this political leader, but because the White House happens to be the executive residence of the President of the United States. The link between that building and political power is "habitually and conventionally known and accepted. ... We must already know that the [two things] are related, if the metonymy is to be ... understood"

Delightfully unconventional creature that she is, the heroine of The Portrait of a Lady is of course drawn more to strikingly metaphorical ways of thinking about her own character than to socially sanctioned metonymical ones. In a famous passage early in the novel, the narrator thus recounts of Isabel Archer that "Her nature had, in her conceit, a certain garden-like quality, a suggestion of perfume and murmuring boughs, of shady bowers and lengthening vistas, which made her feel that introspection was, after all, an exercise in the open air". There is, for Isabel, a likeness between her nature and richly appointed gardens that is hardly merely conventional; rather: it is the essential quality of her own self as opposed to other people's that can thus be captured. "But she was often reminded that there were other gardens in the world than those of her remarkable soul, and that there were moreover a great many places which were not gardens at all—only dusky pestiferous tracts, planted thick with ugliness and misery".

Isabel's attitude is contrasted to that of Madame Merle, for whom context is of central importance. The point in one of their early conversations when, as the narrator informs us, Madame Merle becomes "very metaphysical" is worth quoting at some length:

When you've lived as long as I you'll see that every human being has his shell and that you must take the shell into account. By the shell I mean the whole envelope of circumstances. There's no such thing as an isolated man or woman; we're each of us made up of some cluster of appurtenances. What shall we call our 'self'? Where does it begin? where does it end? It overflows into everything that belongs to us—and then it flows back again. I know a large part of myself is in the clothes I choose to wear. I've a great respect for things! One's self—for other people—is one's expression of one's self; and one's house, one's furniture, one's garments, the books one reads, the company one keeps—these things are all expressive.

In this little speech, Madame Merle not merely points to the crucial role played by a person's context—one's "shell," "circumstances," "appurtenances"—; she goes quite a bit further in identifying such an "envelope," such a "cluster," as "expressive" of "one's self." The self for one thing cannot be restricted to some essential core that belongs solely to "an isolated man or woman"; rather, it "overflows" into the syntagmatic realm that envelops it. For another, the self is determined just as much by this context ("and then it flows back again"; "we're made up of some cluster of appurten ances"). As a whole, the speech gives voice to the metonymical idea that the context of a thing or person may stand in for the latter. For Isabel, the things that Madame Merle rhapsodizes are more handicaps than assets.

"Nothing that belongs to me is any measure of me; everything's on the contrary a limit, a barrier, and a perfectly arbitrary one". Far from being able to act as representative of the essential self, one's context is a social imposition that stands in the way of true self-realization. This is one of the reasons, perhaps the key one, why Isabel Archer is unwilling to marry a suitor for her hand that would have struck many of her contemporaries as too good a catch to be true. "Lord Warburton loomed up before her, largely and brightly, as a collection of attributes and powers which were not to be measured by simple rule .... What she felt was that a territorial, a political, a social magnate had conceived the design of drawing her into the system in which he rather invidiously lived and moved". To marry Lord Warburton would be to embrace all the extensions and limitations that, to reactivate Madame Merle's phrase, a large "cluster of appurtenances" brings with it. "She couldn't marry Lord Warburton; the idea failed to support any enlightened prejudice in favour of the free exploration of life that she had hitherto entertained or was now capable of entertaining".

Isabel is eager for the freedom to discover not just life in general, but her own life in particular: "you could have made her colour, any day in the year, by calling her a rank egoist. She was always planning out her development, desiring her perfection, observing her progress". The "introspection" that she regularly indulges in is motivated by a desire to know what she is really like—how she may be paradigmatically understood. Her imagination is oriented towards the discovery of her true nature, and examines the latter by means of the metaphorical avenue that was illustrated earlier by the extended garden simile. Isabel Archer is bent on testing the limits of her world and is therefore grateful to her aunt for taking her from the provincial American town in which only books can feed her imagination to the European theater that provides a more appropriate stage for someone who wishes to develop her essential nature, perfect it, witness its progress. The portrait of a lady of the novel's title may thus be thought of to some extent as reflecting Isabel Archer's tendency to idealize her own person.

Even more than his aunt, Ralph Touchett enters into the spirit of Isabel's enterprise. Plagued by the weakness of his lungs, he cannot himself live up to the ambitions that he might have cherished. His desire to "put a little wind in sails," to enable her "to meet the requirements of imagination," can be seen as an attempt to live vicariously through the young woman. When Ralph completes the statement I have just quoted by observing that "Isabel has a great deal of imagination," his father's retort, "So have you, my son," makes explicit the paradigmatic link that exists between Isabel's character and Ralph's own. Pushing the point, we could say that Ralph treats Isabel metaphorically, in this sense that he recognizes a fundamental similarity between their natures, and wishes to see her act out the Ralph, as it were, that he cannot be due to the limitations that his health has placed on him.

He wishes to see Isabel behave as the enterprising explorer that he believes himself essentially to be; he wishes to see her flourish freely in the active worlds that have been closed to him by his handicap.

Yet is such a metaphorical account of Ralph's relation to Isabel the only one possible? Could we not say with equal justification that the life Isabel leads as a rich woman is actually metonymically indebted to Ralph? After all, it is really, unbeknownst to her, Ralph's fortune that has transformed Isabel's identity from a young lady with a great deal of imagination into one who commands the wherewithal to enact her imaginings. Regarded from Ralph's perspective, his secret endowment of Isabel with half his fortune turns his cousin into a syntagmatic extension of his own self. Here is someone who will for the rest of her life be indelibly linked to him no matter what she does—no matter how different she may in the end prove to be from himself—merely by virtue of the fact that he has split "the whole envelope of his circumstances" (to quote another of Madame Merle's phrases) neatly into two financially equal halves and ensured that she possess one.

The rhetorical complexity that marks Ralph's philosophy and conduct is quite absent from Isabel's course of action for most of the book. If her early exchanges with Madame Merle give voice to her preference for the metaphorical, Isabel's conscious decision to marry Osmond is entirely based on this predilection too. Defending her choice to a sceptical Ralph, Isabel singles out the fact that Osmond is "so independent, so individual". When Ralph points to Osmond's lack of importance in the world, Isabel counters by saying that she is "far more struck with what he has and what he represents than with what he may lack".

It is clear that "what represents" is not to be taken metonymically, as it was in the case of a Warburton, but metaphorically, like Isabel's view of herself. Indeed, the portrait that this lady paints of herself is matched by the idealized portrait she creates of this "gentleman" who she believes "knows everything, ... understands everything, ... has the kindest, gentlest, highest spirit". Osmond to Isabel embodies the supreme realization of the very values that she had detected in her own beautiful nature. They thus belong to the same paradigm, and it is this fact that makes him stand out favourably in comparison with Lord Warburton, who can best be defined by his syntagmatic accoutrements.

Isabel's ethical life at this stage centers on a rearticulation of the concept of freedom, which now manifests itself in her strongheaded determination to marry a man who stands firm in his pursuit of non-material values, in his "wilful renunciation" of the "grubbing and grabbing" that goes on in the world. Osmond, to Isabel, is a highly moral creature—"a very honest man"). The fortune she has inherited affords Isabel the opportunity to use her freedom to moral effect, by marrying a man whose material success has been negligible.

There is an ironical contrast, of course, between the emphasis Isabel is constantly placing on her freedom, as well as the fondness she shows for a metaphorical understanding of the nature of the self, and the reality that she is the object of all sorts of manipulations that prove that her position in the world is heavily determined by metonymical processes. There is first of all Ralph's role in making her rich; and Ralph's ensuring that Isabel should not know about his agency by metonymically substituting his father's "will" for what was in fact his own. Then there is Madame Merle's scheming so as to "put" Isabel in Osmond's "way" and her arranging their first meeting so that it takes place at Osmond's house, since she knows that "As cicerone of your museum you appear to particular advantage". Serena Merle never wavers in her faith in the power of the metonymical—her belief that persons' surroundings may perfectly stand in for them and show them in a much better light than anything they do or say.

Finally, there is the curious role played by Osmond's daughter Pansy in ensuring that Isabel accept Osmond, a role that I have discussed in greater detail elsewhere. Let me here just mention my conclusion that a wavering Isabel is brought round when she pays a visit, on her own, to Pansy Osmond, at Osmond's request, during which she is immensely struck by the very aspect that Pansy presents to the observer—"how prettily she had been directed and fashioned; and yet how simple, how natural, how innocent she had been kept!".

It is as though Osmond, sensing that he is not making much headway in his direct wooing of Isabel, decides to withdraw into the background himself (where he remains for something like ten months, while Isabel and Serena Merle tour the East), but not without first having ensured that he would in the meantime be indirectly represented to Isabel's memory by the young girl that he has taken such pains to shape into a pleasing little thing—simple, natural, innocent. Osmond has cunningly put into practice Madame Merle's insight that context may act more powerfully for a person than anything they themselves might undertake. Pansy, as a metonymical substitute for her father, has actually won Isabel for him.

How can the framework I have been sketching help us make sense of the concluding scenes of The Portrait of a Lady? One fundamental point is that Isabel has come to recognize that the choices she believed she had made freely, independently, in this manner confirming her own paradigmatic essence, were in fact orchestrated by those around her. She has been caught in a web that was spun not just by the "evil"-intentioned Serena Merle and Gilbert Osmond but also, unintentionally, by the more happily inspired Ralph Touchett. The latter fact in particular makes it clear that life in society involves one in all sorts of contiguities, no matter how much one may be inclined to introspection and the cultivation of metaphors of the free and independent self.

When Caspar Goodwood offers Isabel a chance to escape from what she has meanwhile come to regard as the misery of her marriage, his words are seductive indeed. They appeal forcefully to that side of Isabel that would still be swayed by the romance of freedom: "We can do absolutely as we please; to whom under the sun do we owe anything?.... The world's all before us—and the world's very big". Goodwood's understanding of the independent self is very much like Isabel's in the earlier parts of the novel: "It would be an insult to you to assume that you care for the look of the thing, for what people will say, for the bottomless idiocy of the world. We've nothing to do with all that; we're quite out of it; we look at things as they are". A firmer rejection of Madame Merle's strong emphasis on "the company one keeps" as an expression of the self is hard to imagine.

It is not just Goodwood's words that are seductive; so is his manner. Especially in the version James revised for the New York Edition, the final scene of the novel is as erotically charged as one is likely to find anywhere in Jamesn). The imagery is of "float in fathomless waters," and undergoing "a rushing torrent." Even before Goodwood acts, Isabel is thinking that "she had never been loved before. She had believed it, but this was different; this was the hot wind of the desert, at the approach of which the others dropped dead, like mere sweet airs of the garden". Isabel believes that "to let him take her in his arms would be the next best thing to dying," a belief that is "a kind of rapture, in which she felt herself sink and sink." These descriptions indicate a vividly aroused desire, to be sure, and when Isabel finally "felt his arms about her and his lips on her own lips," the sensation is not an unpleasant one that she tries to get rid of immediately. Rather, "His kiss was like white lightning, a flash that spread, and spread again, and stayed." What is more, the narrator notes that "while she took "—note the active involvement that the verb "to take" implies—"it was extraordinarily as if ... she felt each thing in his hard manhood that had least pleased her, each aggressive fact of his face, his figure, his presence, justified of its intense identity and made one with this act of possession." What is so extraordinary is that what Isabel had disliked from a distance, now becomes "justified" in the close proximity of the kiss, in her submission to "this act of possession" that is so much in line with the "intense identity" of these traits of Goodwood's "hard manhood."

But the upshot of this emotional experience is not, as one might have thought, that Isabel accepts the sensuous side of her character, acknowledging that, for the sake of desire, she has to allow herself to be thus possessed by a man. In fact, the reverse may be said to happen. The imagery of the scene is sensuous, yet it also clearly brings out the bound and unfree condition that giving in to such sensuality involves, a condition that is like being drowned, exposed to lightning and submitted to possession. There is, in other words, a sharp contrast between Goodwood's talk of freedom and independence and the force with which he imposes his sexual power on Isabel, appealing directly to what she has called early in the book "the deepest thing" within her soul: the "belief that if a certain light should dawn she could give herself completely". It is such a complete surrender of the self that Caspar Goodwood is really demanding of Isabel, and on which depends the sexual fulfilment that he holds out.

It is worth recalling here Harpham's description of ethics as an articulation of "the relation between freedom and necessity, desire and the law." What is so crucial about the long scene with Goodwood, it seems to me, is that it helps Isabel to realize that the opposition between "freedom and necessity, desire and the law" can be a fatuous one. Implying as it does that freedom and desire belong together, just as do necessity and the law, Harpham's formulation cannot do justice to the final scene of The Portrait of a Lady, and the ethical decision in which it culminates: Isabel's choice of the "very straight path" that leads back to Rome. As we have just seen, Goodwood's "act of possession" makes it clear that desire can be the opposite of freedom. Sexual fulfilment may depend on a complete relinquishing of a person's freedom and independence. The choice that Isabel faces at the end of the story is between a bound condition that masks itself in metaphors of freedom while exacting a surrender of the essential self and a bound condition that is situated at the more superficial level of "the observance of a magnificent form" that Osmond expects of her.

Osmond's "wish to preserve appearances," we could say, amounts to a metonymical bondage only: it requires Isabel to live by Madame Merle's rule that "One's self—for other people—is one's expression of one's self; ... one's house, one's furniture, one's garments, ..., the company one keeps" It does not draw on her fund of "passion," guarded "within herself, deep down," hoarded "like a large sum stored in a bank—which there was a terror in having to begin to spend". Paradoxically, there is likely to be more freedom for Isabel at Palazzo Roccanera—Osmond's "house of darkness" —than in the "very big" world Goodwood proposes to explore with her, causing her to respond "as if he were pressing something that hurt her," and sealing their putative compact with a kiss that is "like white lightning".

We should not be misled by James's imagery of light and dark here. The white lightning that Goodwood produces may be erotically pleasurable. "But when darkness returned she was free" Adrian Poole cogently argues that the privileged term in The Portrait of a Lady is "dusk," rather than light. It would seem that the overabundance of white light that Goodwood produces (recall also that "if a certain light should dawn she could give herself completely"—a prospect that Isabel has consistently dreaded) needs to be first offset by complete darkness before a measure of freedom can be recovered. The location that then allows the heroine to come to a final decision about the direction of her life is the highly liminal one of the Gardencourt doorsill. She is attracted to the house on her flight from Caspar by the "lights in the windows," yet is never shown to enter its brightness, instead pausing with "her hand on the latch," in the dusk of that threshold. It is here that Isabel sees "a very straight path."

Thus, desire and freedom are surprisingly at odds in the denouement of James's novel. But so, it could be argued, are necessity and the law, to turn to the two remaining terms from Harpham's schema. If Isabel, in the early parts of the novel, tries to base her decisions on moral principles (which Harpham would dub "laws") that Ralph thinks of disparagingly as "fine theor" with little relation to reality, joined in this sentiment by Isabel herself in the fireside chapter, this tendency is much reduced by the end. Though Harpham is not talking about James in his observations on the ethics of literature, his other keyterm, necessity, may be usefully invoked not as the near-synonym of "law" that he intends it to be, but as a shorthand phrase for another type of ethical imperative, that I have elsewhere summarized as "the ethics of metonymy."

Reaching the insight that a bound condition is unavoidable in social life, Isabel Archer is well on her way towards embracing an ethical attitude that will become much more pronounced in later Jamesian works, such as The Ambassadors and The Wings of the Dove. This attitude places less emphasis on abstract laws and general principles—on the need to find a "good ... formula" to account for one's actions, as Isabel puts it to herself in chapter 55 —and more on the need to react to the demands of a situation in which one finds oneself. These two alternatives may be termed metaphorical and metonymical in character respectively, the basic modus operandi of metaphor as a figure of thought applying to the former in that a paradigmatic connection is perceived between discrete ethical decisions that share their rootedness in a certain law or principle; that of metonymy to the latter because a syntagmatic connection is seen to exist between a moral agent and the situation that calls for an ethical decision. Like the rhetorical figures of metaphor and metonymy, neither of these ethical alternatives should be thought of as superior to the other; rather, they are complementary.

If I here tend to privilege the metonymical it is because it has received scanter attention than the metaphorical, even though its relevance to many of the ethical problems posed in modern literature is high. In the closing scenes of The Portrait of a Lady, Isabel Archer's recognition of the decisive role played by metonymy in her life also results in her tentative embrace of an ethics of metonymy. When she arrives in London, en route for Gardencourt to be with the dying Ralph, Isabel already indicates to Henrietta Stackpole her intention to return to Rome, explaining that this is the promise she made to Pansy Osmond. When Henrietta questions the rationale for this undertaking, Isabel agrees:

"I'm not sure I myself see now," Isabel replied. "But I did then."

"If you've forgotten your reason perhaps you won't return."

Isabel waited a moment. "Perhaps I shall find another."

"You'll certainly never find a good one."

"In default of a better my having promised will do," Isabel suggested.

The fact that Isabel is "not sure ... now" but was "then" can be explained in respect of the type of ethical attitude that I have briefly sketched: an ethics in which the demands of a particular situation at a particular time prompt one to take up a responsibility that one cannot easily explain with reference to any clear law; rather, one undertakes to fulfil the obligation simply because one is there. Isabel has "forgotten reason" because there never was "a good one"—there never was a readily identifiable ground on which to commit herself to the daughter of her tyrannical husband and his deceptive one-time lover. The Isabel who strongly disagreed with Madame Merle over the nature of the self—insisting on its supreme sovereignty over against her friend's assertion that we are intimately tied up with what happens to be our context—that Isabel seems to have changed considerably when she is prepared to return to a husband (who she knows will make her "a scene of the rest of my life]) for no other reason than that she made a promise not to abandon this man's daughter.

It is also this altered Isabel who ultimately proves resistant to Goodwood's siren song of absolute freedom. In fact, as we saw, it may well be in the dissonant clash between the metaphors of the sovereign self that he spouts and the imprisonment of a sexual bondage that he really exacts that Isabel finds that "better" reason for returning to her husband that she is looking for upon her arrival in England hus Isabel's adoption of the "very straight path" back to the Osmonds must be regarded as a high-level ethical negotiation of the relation between freedom and necessity, desire and the law.

Recognizing that her earlier pursuit of lofty principles could not protect her from the mundane manipulations of down-to-earth reality, and that the hot breath of desire extinguishes any measure of freedom, Isabel willingly submits to the necessity that the situation in which she finds herself presents. The "abrupt and unsatisfactory" ending that many readers have noted reflects the tentative nature of the ethical resolution that James here develops. It will only be in later works that he arrives at a more fully elaborated ethics of metonymy that can stand the test of further plotting.

Q. Reading James is something of an evasion of the real work of the world. Discuss

Henry James studies today are as vibrant as they have ever been. Yet, no matter how great the fascination with the Jamesian text, a large number of readers cannot get rid of a sense of shame at their enjoyment of it. They feel that reading James is something of an evasion of the real work of the world. If earlier generations located that guilty feeling within the ivory tower that James's formal experimentation offered them, a technically more blase generation has associated its unease more often with the politically ambiguous, or plainly incorrect, stance the Master adopts. This is particularly true with regard to The American Scene, at present one of the hottest texts in James studies. Noting 'the commonplace racial slurs punctuating' that text, Bryan Washington, for instance, has a hard time resisting the book's 'liberal, eminently civilized voice, sometimes sustained for pages at a time, becomes so seductive, so powerful, that we forget about the racial slurs, the cultural stereotypes...'. Washington regrets that the primary subject of his book, James Baldwin, succumbed to the seduction and appeared to undertake an 'iterative valorization' of Henry James throughout his work. 'If such writing [as The American Scene's] is representative, symptomatic of James's nativism and of his elitism, then why did Baldwin, by contrast a progressive, bother to read him at all?' Implicitly admitting an inability to come up with a satisfactory reply, Washington writes: 'There can be only speculation here, but... Baldwin almost certainly gave James the benefit of the doubt'.

A similar sense of embarrassment troubles Kenneth Warren in the course of his engagement with James in Black and White Strangers. While resenting what he feels is undue pressure on the African-American critic to remain dedicated to 'a criticism and politics centered upon... black difference', Warren does feel a need to confess that, at a 'mundane level, the time spent reading James... is admittedly time away from the black-authored texts that have been neglected'.

'If we are not to overvalue James's exquisitely ambiguous critiques of capitalism and racism [in The American Scene]', Warren has more recently wondered, 'how should we value him? Why, indeed, should we value him at all?' Sounding as apologetic about his enthusiasm for James as Washington is with regard to Baldwin's discipleship, Warren goes on to offer his personal reasons for 'Still Reading Henry James' (as the title of his piece puts it). They are proffered in a strikingly diffident manner that I want to highlight by eliding, for now, the actual arguments (they appear in the attached footnote): 'Here, all I can do is to say that what makes James of continual interest to me is that... And while answering this question is not the most pressing political issue of our time... And for those of us sometimes embarrassed by the fact that James has managed to stick around... nothing more should be required than...'. This diffidence is in sharp contrast to the terms Warren uses in discussing W.E.B. Du Bois, who enacts the political drama of the intellect wrestling with the temptation to instrumentalize itself for the legitimation of the prevailing order. He performs for us the difficulty of thinking differently... e are warned to be aware of how similar our own intellectual techniques may be to those we contest, but we are also able to find some self-justification in our predicament. Our sense of the difficulty of our enterprise also makes it clear why the hard intellectual work we do is 'necessary'.

If with regard to James, 'all can do is to say ', Du Bois with greater virility 'enacts the political drama of... wrestling'. Instead of merely chattering about it, Du Bois 'performs... the difficulty'. Whereas a Jamesian question 'is not the most pressing issue', we do 'contest' manfully when we are under the wings of Du Bois. If James can make 'us' feel 'embarrassed' we are fortunate to find some moral 'self-justification' thanks to Du Bois. In short, with Du Bois we feel reassured that our 'intellectual work' as literary critics is 'hard', as a man's job should be, rather than 'exquisitely ambiguous'.

The terms I have italicized show that there is a distinctly gendered side to the unease some critics register over James. A closer look at The Henry James Review's 'Race Forum' suggests that the key 'political' objection voiced against The American Scene, and Jamesian realism in general, is actually that it is insufficiently masculine, and therefore immoral. Like the seductive snares of a wanton woman, the purple patches of James's irresponsible prose are in need of correction by the critics (if they are not to be guiltily enjoyed by the same). When contributors to the 'Race Forum' seek to redeem James from the charge of 'political incorrectness consequent on failures of racial sympathy', they tend to replicate the gendered and moral assumptions of his censors, attempting to demonstrate that the Jamesian aesthetic responsibly performs serious cultural work worthy of comparison with real, hard politics.

Consider Ross Posnock's 'Henry James and the Limits of Historicism'. Posnock reminds us that for Kenneth Warren The

American Scene's 'handling of the race problem falls dreadfully short of the clear denunciations of lynching and mob violence that prevailing conditions called for'. As Posnock comments:

However one assesses the fairness of this judgment, it does carry force — its stark, obdurate literalism becomes the ceiling against which shatter all analogical arguments for James's openness as a cultural critic (including those found in my own work on James). One can revel in and demonstrate in ever-ingenious ways the subtleties of James's serpentine negotiation with otherness. But Warren's judgment will remain unmoved and unmovable.

The privileged terms in Posnock's gloss perform a yoking of masculinity and morality: a moral 'judgment' regarding James's silence in the face of racist violence need not be considered in the light of 'fairness' but of 'force'. That is to say, the critical assessment of James's silence on violence itself becomes a form of violence: it 'shatter' 'arguments', it opposes to any attempt at 'negotiation with otherness' the 'unmoved and unmovable' violence of 'stark, obdurate' power. It is striking how easily these complimentary phrases could be associated with the very attitude that marked the lynchers and mobsters which The American Scene should have denounced. Refusing any 'negotiation with otherness', 'unmoved' by the suffering of black people, white autocratic men closed their ears to any liberal 'arguments for... openness' and were proud to 'remain... unmovable', applying the 'stark, obdurate literalism' of the lynching pole. In a feminist vein, one could even find the 'literalis... ceiling' reminiscent of the glass 'ceiling' — 'unmoved and unmovable' — that places a patriarchal 'reality check' on the upward mobility of women.

The passage seems to serve mainly as an act of white male contrition. The bracketed aside suggests that the critic feels uncomfortable about having joined the women in 'revel in... subtleties', 'overestimat the range of James's empathic powers', while all along that work was so '"disappointing"' to black people. Yet, the essay's final paragraph does attempt to undertake a redemption of James from those intractable charges by appealing to such qualities as might stand the test of implacable scrutiny, such Jamesian strategies as even 'Du Bois might have admired and valued'.{14} The American Scene, Posnock argues, 'does possess an "alternate trajectory"... commit to immersion, hazard, contingency, and... this trajectory displays political power and even courage though not precisely of the sort Warren asks for embracing what Du Bois called "a certain tingling challenge of risk"... Henry James... enact a pragmatism that turns aesthetics from contemplation to action that cuts against the grain of capitalist efficiency and utility'. Posnock's James is in the thick of the struggle, 'committ', 'immers', exposed to 'hazard', needing 'courage' in the face of a rousing 'challenge of risk', manfully 'cut against the grain', heroically turning mere aesthetics to 'action'. This James may truly assume an honourable place in the fight for 'political power'.

Even when critics are secure in their admiration of James's work and do not feel called upon to defend his political correctness they still tend to discuss The American Scene in terms of a rhetorical logic in which political progress is only to be expected from taking an active stand in a battle over power. For Sara Blair, of 'particular concern... is James's pursuit of two entangled aims: to contest the nation-building power of emergent mass visual culture, and to create a space of cultural agency...'. The author of The American Scene is fired by a 'contestatory and deeply social intention', demonstrates his 'performative embattlement', has a 'contestatory interest in the framing of racial and national fate'. y the end of the book, Blair claims, James has achieved a 'posture intensifies his contest for the power of producing America's cultural design' and 'positions himself so as to contest' other designing moves (271; emphasis added). The word 'contest' and all its derivations are chanted as a kind of mantra throughout the piece, sometimes twice in the same line), and if James did not exactly take a firm stand on the question of Jim Crow racism, at least he 'position himself' in a properly radical fashion at a more general level. While the emphasis here is less on the hardness that needs to be mustered to succeed on the cultural battlefield, for this critic too politics is clearly the privileged term over aesthetics, as when Blair tries to defend 'James's notoriously aestheticized cultural politics'. Responding in the same issue of The Henry James Review to Posnock's challenge that her 'analogical arguments for James's openness' 'shatter' against the reality of his failure to condemn Southern lynchings, Blair admits that '... James indubitably preserves the "literary", the high cultural, as a space of social performance at the cost of more radical attacks on the politics of hierarchy, of race supremacy, of margin and center themselves'. The italicized phrase again underlines the preferability of 'radical attack' as a means of working social change. The literary can only play second fiddle to the political on Blair's account, which turns out to be not so different from Posnock's once one attends to the way both try to invest the aesthetic with combative rhetorical force.

But what if we could regard the Jamesian literary not as a means of performing at the cost of more radical attacks on a certain politics but as a more profitable way of theorizing and practising the political? As one political scientist, Bonnie Honig, has recently argued, 'the test of democratic theory and politics is not so much their ability to resolve the most polarized issues but rather their ability to relax the propensity to polarization...'. Honig's book sets out to 'explore the sites, instruments and goals of... a stealth politics..., noting how certain sites and forms of political action may work to reinscribe citizenship as a political practice rather than as a status'. As such, she differentiates her project from that of multiculturalists who 'see politics as a way to secure the necessary material and juridical conditions to protect existing identities.... They seek to establish equal respect for existing groups, to give overdue recognition to previously neglected minorities...'. The James critics reviewed above tend to locate their project within the context of an openly contestatory fight over status. A better James to their mind would have written about black people as full-fledged subjects possessing the same level of consciousness as his usual heroes and heroines. (This is Warren's main point.) And, of course, a better James would have taken a radical stand, aligning himself outspokenly with

Southern blacks' rights to protection and equal respect. His failure to join liberals of the time (such as his brother William) in denouncing lynchings becomes for these critics a failure to pass what Honig calls the 'litmus tests that sort out who is with "us" and who is against'. What some political theorists are attempting to 'delineate and model' instead, according to Honig, is 'the proper democratic labours of translation and negotiation in order to prevent the development of polarization and litmus-testing'.

There is a striking parallel here with the recent work in moral philosophy of people like Annette Baier and Carol Gilligan. Baier's Moral Prejudices has focused on the contemporary (and the specifically feminist) potential of Hume's philosophy, pointing out that, 'here, on the more contractarian model [of philosophers like Kant and, more recently, Rawls], morality regulates and arbitrates where interests are opposed, on a Humean view, as on Gilligan's [woman interviewees], morality's main task is to rearrange situations so that interests are no longer so opposed', in Honig's words, to relax the propensity to polarization There is, in Baier's work, a clear feminist undertone that such a concept of morality is more readily associated with the traditionally feminine qualities of caring, nurturing, responsiveness, rather than the traditionally masculine ones of lex dura, violence and mutual distrust (necessitating the resort to 'contracts').

It Should be clear that such a gentle philosophy does not imply a Buddhist withdrawal from social interaction into isolated contemplation. To the contrary, Baier emphasizes that her view of morality implies 'both an individual and a social task'. Whereas an appeal to the individual's discrete 'reason' is central to the contractarian tradition, the qualities privileged in Baier's account exist in a social field: 'What matters most, for judging moral wisdom, are corrected sentiments, imagination, and cooperative genius'. In an essay dealing with terrorism, entitled 'Violent Demonstrations', Baier warns against state violence in response to terrorist acts. Rather, emphasizing the importance of language to human transactions, Baier suggests that we look harder for 'the right tactful incantations for the ceremony of graduation into legitimacy [demanded by terrorists]. History surely can give us useful suggestions for tried and true face-saving diplomatic phrases'. Can we tackle 'violence',

Baier wonders, by answering it with 'more verbal violence, and more moralizing or meta-moralizing [i.e. by moral philosophers like herself]'. But since this is such uncharted territory 'we all, like the terrorist, tend sometimes to fall back on homeopathic cures, and so on mere violence as a response to violence'. Are not those who would insist on measuring the Jamesian text by the standard of a 'stark, obdurate literalism' engaging in an act of verbal violence of the type that these philosophical considerations warn against? Calling on James to make a more 'violent demonstration' of his political correctness, they may miss the whole point of his 'tactful incantations', of his expertise at employing such 'face-saving diplomatic phrases' as are so badly needed in the reality of negotiation within democratic societies.

Q. Do you feel that The Portrait is without a Subject?

Or

Q. Discuss the issue of self and nature in the novel.

I was the world in which I walked, and what I saw
Or heard or felt came not but from myself;
And there I found myself more truly and more strange.
(Wallace Stevens, "Tea at the Palaz of Hoon")

To say that Immanuel Kant has ruled Western philosophy for over two hundred years could arguably be a gross understatement. His contribution to historical philosophy, for example, can be traced from "What Is Enlightenment," where he believes that nothing is required for enlightenment but freedom, to "Idea for Universal History with a Cosmopolitan Intent," where he states that the development of humankind's capacities is brought about by antagonism. Kant's writings both dictate and transcend the moral, aesthetic, and rational epistemological systems that govern much of Western philosophy. However, for the sake of being critically succinct, my essay will concern itself with Kant's ideas on the subjectivity of aesthetics as applied to Henry James' masterpiece, The Portrait of a Lady. The primary critical supposition that I will attempt to prove is that James followed a particularly neo-Kantian formulation of aesthetics — sometimes subtle, sometimes conspicuous — that both affirms and modifies the German philosopher's notions in the Critique of Judgment. Using Critique of Judgment as a point of departure, I will attempt to define Kant's subjectivity of aesthetics as well as identify its distinguishable characteristics. Then, my essay will examine this Kantian framework, along with Paul Ricoeur's notions of subject-object relations, as they apply to Jamesian aesthetics in "The Art of Fiction" and The Portrait of a Lady.

Perhaps the first thing needed for such an analysis is to seek a clear definition of the subjectivity of aesthetics that is found within Kant's theoretical matrix in Critique of Judgment. Critique of Judgment is essentially Kant's attempt to categorize aesthetics into a verifiable form, an approximation of the form of beauty with a degree of breadth, scope, and complexity that had not been attempted successfully by any philosopher until this point. To begin discussing Kant's formulations in Critique of Judgment, perhaps we should start with his emphasis on subjective judgment versus objective judgment, building our understanding of the specific definitions and characteristics of his aesthetic schematics as the essay progresses.

A subjective judgment, to Kant, is a non-empirical assertion that takes away the emphasis on the objective representation of an aesthetic object, amplifying the resultant "feeling in the subject as it is affected by the representation". This assertion places the human, discerning subject as a progenitor in the aesthetic process: instead of meaning being placed outside of the receptive subject, Kant is arguing that the receptive subject, via feeling, is active in the process of aesthetic judgment. A judgment becomes specifically "aesthetical" to Kant when, instead of affirming the logical and the rational as standards of judgment, representations are specifically "referred in a judgment to the subject".

Central to Kant's subjectivity of aesthetics, and which

also negates any external prerequisite of judgment, is his critique of a pre-formative conceptual basis of representation. In Critique of Judgment, he makes constant reference to the delimiting basis of conceptual thought. As mentioned previously, concept is connected with objective purposiveness – both of which are forms of critique that rely on an external basis of aesthetic judgment. Rather than invoke a cognitive faculty in subject-object relations, Kant argues that we must purify our aesthetic by disassociating ourselves from such a faculty. A non-conceptual approach to aesthetics allows for the overall "effect" of the aesthetic representation to offer itself to the human faculties.

Basically, the a priori concept, like objective purposiveness, reduces the authenticity of the aesthetic experience. Again, the human subject plays a significant role in this non-conceptual approach. That is, by allowing the superimposition of the effect to shape our aesthetic experience, we, after the fact, contribute by giving what Kant calls understanding and imagination (the "lively play of both mental powers") to a certain representation. The paradox of such an assertion is that by allotting aesthetic experience to the subjective mind as a medium for conceptualization, we somehow commune with what Kant calls the universal. This is how Kant makes an ingenious contradiction about the subjectivity of aesthetics as it relates to conceptualization. That is, by denying conceptualization until encountering the object, we circumvent the fallacy of a priori reasoning; in the process, subjective volition is correlated with what he terms "the conditions of universality". Succinctly, concept should come via inductive reasoning rather than deductive reasoning.

With this aconceptual basis of reasoning comes a unique dictum of Kant's subjectivity of aesthetics. That is, Kant seeks a verifiable form, what he often calls "the unity of relations," that can be projected onto nature itself. Borrowing an idea from Critique of Pure Reason, Kant constantly seeks a substantive form within the cosmos, a method of categorizing the sundry manifestations of nature. In Critique of Judgment, Kant mentions form as being an imperative part of the subjectivity of aesthetics from its correlation to beauty. Beauty, to Kant, is "attributed to the object on account of its form," sensory perception reminds us that we find "every form of the objects of sense...," and ornamental representations are so "only by their form". Perhaps we can best understand Kant's emphasis on form by looking closely at his discussion of color in the section entitled 'Elucidation by Means of Examples' in Critique of Judgment. Kant states that the mind has a two-fold method of perceiving colors: by perception of the sensory effect of colors as well as the reflection of "the regular play of impressions."

This passage suggests that the mind, in its reflective state, perceives colors and thus all visual phenomena with an implicit tendency to find a formal cohesion in the objects being viewed. The "unity of a manifold of sensations" that Kant speaks of here is the mind perceiving singularity where there is multiplicity; that is, Kant examines formal design within the microcosm of color to represent nature as a whole. This relates to two postulations that we have already established about the subjectivity of aesthetics in Critique of Judgment: the idea of the purification of the aesthetic experience and the resultant abstraction that acts as the mind's conduit for its participation in the process. Abstraction here seems to imply a higher essence of understanding, that which gives form to previously amorphous conceptual thought.

Kant says in this passage that for the judgment to be pure in its aesthetic assimilation, we must block out foreign sensations and instead extract its formal unity from the process. He is asserting that form affords a pure aesthetic experience, one that gives tangible definition to previously abstract qualities in nature. The unity of nature seems to be implicit within the cosmos; it is through the mind's tendency to seek singularity that such a teleological projection can occur, however.

Before delving into the discussion of Kant's subjectivity of aesthetics as it relates to James in "The Art of Fiction" and The Portrait of a Lady, I will attempt a condensed overview of Kantian aesthetics. First, one of Kant's major contributions to aesthetic theory is that he moves the locus of emphasis away from objective determination and instead focuses upon the capability of the judging subject. The human mind now plays a vital part in any aesthetic experience. That is, while the object under scrutiny maintains a relative autonomy from the receptive subject in terms of concept, purpose, and beauty, the mind now seeks "essential and universal purposes" in its quest for an ideal of beauty. Coupled with this movement towards extrapolating the universal from an object's representation is an implied Kantian dictum. That is, Kant advocates shifting the interest of the aesthetic object from the reader's subjectivity and her response to art toward concern with the internalism of the work itself. Kant's subjectivity of aesthetics both affirms subjective participation in the aesthetic process while also arguing for the independent self-subsistence of the object in question. My essay will re-address many of these often seemingly contradictory points of Kant's argument as they apply to James' own aesthetic treatment in The Portrait of a Lady and "The Art of Fiction."

Henry James' 1884 publication of "The Art of Fiction" affirms many salient characteristics of Kant's subjectivity of aesthetics. "The Art of Fiction" establishes the Jamesian ethos of aesthetics. James' doctrine of organicism, for example, might best be understood in the context of the aesthetics of subjectivity. From the aforementioned "Elucidation" section of Critique of Judgment, we can assert that the human subject contributes to the aesthetic process by its "reflection the regular play of impressions". By giving semblance to disparate impressions, the subject's ability to "delineate," that is, perceive form within multiplicity, becomes "the essential thing". This formal unity, however, is an attribute of cognitive judgment: the aesthetic "reflection" of judgment is essentially an act of recognition, an act which is subsequent to and a result of the preceding cognitive judgment. Accordingly, in "The Art of Fiction," James attempts to convey an aesthetic with the ability to capture formal unity in the context of the novel; that is, James seeks a Kantian unity in his essay by such statements as "a novel is a living thing, all one and continuous, like any other organism". James' aesthetic seeks form within the individual parts of a novel's form, "the living thing"; he sees description, dialogue, and incident as complementary active forces within the novel's composition. The formal unity that James seeks within the specific framework of the novel must have a specific means for creating such a design.

In "The Art of Fiction," James states that the "needle and thread of the novel," what he concomitantly calls "the idea and the form," are the "story and the novel". While Kant idealistically projects a formal unity upon nature via perception, James imputes the same design of singularity upon the successful novel's creation. By finding that in each of the parts there is something of each of the other parts, James is proposing that the seemingly disparate elements of the novel, the ones that critics often focus on, are actually representative of the organic holism of the text.

The simultaneity of the visual apparatus is key to Jamesian aesthetics. That is, James suggests several implicit dictums of Kant's subjectivity of aesthetics by both viewing the text as an organic whole and by seeking a rendition of life without rearrangement. James critiques the pre-arranged novelistic devices of modern writers, what he calls in conspicuously Kantian terms, the "factitious artificial form". The novelist, to James, must give us the unadulterated portrait of life without the shackles of personal preference; she must not let her particular vision of life distort what is actually portrayed in the literary artifact. Selection, James says, should come after the fact, when the novel has already tried to capture "the strange irregular rhythm of life". If the novel's selection of material is like a visual apparatus of life, James is arguing that the textual representation should be all-inclusive, a form without a pre-conceptual basis of selection.

Besides this attribute, James makes some other statements in "The Art of Fiction" that are reformulated Kantian ideas. In Critique of Judgment, Kant maintains that part of the aesthetic experience must entail a contribution on the part of the subject who is interpreting the representation. That is, Kant states that we connect to the higher purposiveness of aesthetic reflection by a certain degree of abstraction, marked by understanding and imagination. Thus, the mind becomes a variable in the aesthetic equation, offering something that manifests a higher level of aesthetic integration. James also believes that there is a necessary representation between the aesthetic object, in this case a novel, and the mind that creates it. For example, James states that "the deepest quality of a work of art will always be the quality of the mind of the producer".

This can best be understood in Kantian terms; that is, a work of art — the aesthetic representation — is marked by a symbiotic relationship between the object and the producer. The usual distinctions between subject and object, in James and in Kant, are supplanted by this symbiosis, one that connects the object viewed with a higher moral purpose in both writers' view of the subject. The novelist, to James, cannot have a superficial mind devoid of the moral qualities "of the substance of beauty and truth". Kant also seeks a higher moral purposiveness within the integration of subject and object. The specific moral qualities that Kant mentions are those of "goodness of heart, purity, strength, and peace". These traits of higher moral purposiveness are symbolic of the union between object and subject; the latter invokes a superior degree of imaginative connection between the aesthetic representation and one's mind.

Aesthetic representation, within the Kantian universe as well as the Jamesian, also relies on the internal purposiveness of the object in question. As mentioned, internal purposiveness implies a standard of judgment that is not dependent upon any external standard of judgment. In one instance, James criticizes the use of dogmatism concerning subject matter. The dogma, or concept before experiential knowledge, would undermine the aesthetic experience. The most explicit example of how James incorporates an ethos of internal purposiveness, however, comes during his discussion of the execution of the novelist. James states that execution, within the context of criticism, is "the only point of a novel that is open to contention". Later in the essay, he writes that "questions of art are questions (in the widest sense) of execution; questions of morality are quite another affair". In his critique of Besant, James is arguing that one must be careful not to apply a moral purpose to an examination of the literary artifact; he critiques such an approach as one based in "vagueness" and clearly attempts to separate morality and execution into two separate camps, one worthy of critical application, the other, "quite another affair." What James is trying to articulate is that we must grant the writer his donnee, or subject matter, leaving only the carrying out of the aesthetic process open to criticism. In this sense, the novel has its own means to an end, that is, a purposiveness that must be independent from any pre-conceptualized standard of judgment. The artistic failure that James speaks of is a confirmation of the Kantian shift of aesthetics, paradoxically affirming the reader's subjectivity and, at the same time, emphasizing the internal mechanics of the work itself.

Hence, "The Art of Fiction" can be interpreted as the Jamesian manifesto of aesthetic principles, many of which, such as the internal purposiveness of the aesthetic object, are reminiscent of Kant's theories in Critique of Judgment. As my essay has established the similarity between Kant's subjectivity of aesthetics and James' aesthetic manifesto, "The Art of Fiction," what remains to be done is a critical exegesis of how such a theoretical framework can be applied to the novel The Portrait of a Lady. In particular, in what ways does James adhere to such a Kantian approach to aesthetic principles, and how does he modify Kant's definitions? To begin with, the question might be raised concerning how this novel emulates Kant's subjective experience of aesthetics.

Could anyone disaffirm the notion that The Portrait of a Lady involves the reader in a more complex, systematically interwoven textual experience than perhaps any other novel? With an emphasis more on the representation of the mind rather than the body, The Portrait of a Lady indeed follows such a subjective paradigm. Experientially speaking, the novel is as rich a representation of aesthetic subjectivity as one encounters in literature. That is, James' novel invokes the collaborative process of experience, from which we shape meaning after assimilating a textual representation, over the usual method of viewer involvement, the use of action by the author. How does The Portrait of a Lady move forward in any sort of semblance of plot? The answer is characterization. This authorial device corresponds with the novel as being propelled less by a medium of arbitrary plot formulation — such as we see painfully exhibited in other Realist novels such as Howells' The Rise of Silas Lapham — and more towards an immersion into the psychological dimension of James' unique vision.

As one critic states of this dimension of the novel, "the willful neglect of a purely subjective experience could only make for a failure of representation". What James does not neglect, however, is the psychological realism of the novel, what I would define as the subjective involvement that the novel evokes, both affirming the author's unique vision of the world and rendering the reader completely immersed in the psychosomatic dimension of the work. Despite the subjective suggestiveness of the novel, there exists a distinct conflict between James' appropriation of Kantian aesthetics — particularly the novel's emphasis on an aesthetic object's internal purposiveness and interest, manifested in the character of Isabel Archer — and how the aesthetic object's relative independence is compromised by forces around her.

James' particular vision of the world, epitomized in The Portrait of a Lady, is unquestionably marked by a characteristic that Kantian aesthetics attempts to subvert: the quest for possession. In the schematics of Kantian aesthetics, the subject, while at times an integral part of the aesthetic process, comes to enlightenment when he accepts that the object under scrutiny has an independent form of existence with a separate and autonomous purpose. The love plot of The Portrait of a Lady, outside of Ralph Touchett, is marked by men who strive for possession — of an independent object — as a means of sustaining their own subjective visions. This is certainly the case with men who desire to possess the independent aesthetic "object" in the novel, Isabel Archer. The three men who overtly attempt to win Isabel's hand in marriage, Caspar Goodwood, Lord Warburton, and Gilbert Osmond, each represent a different degree of the possessive nature of men in the novel. Gilbert Osmond, however, seeks to convert Isabel into his collection of "pictures... medallions and tapestries". As Gilbert is showing his vast array of priceless antiques and other sundry "romantic objects," he is really showing Isabel what she herself may become in time. As one critic states, "He is a collector of things, and she offers herself up to him as a fine finished object". Unfortunately for Isabel, no one can enter Gilbert's subjective aesthetic without losing that element of autonomy, what Kant terms "self-subsistence," that characterizes an independent object.

Gilbert's awareness of the independent self-subsistence of Isabel essentially only confirms his own subjective vision; he wishes instead to only acknowledge her as his object. Gilbert cryptically foreshadows this when he tells Isabel "A woman's natural mission is to be where she's most appreciated". Certainly, Gilbert's definition of appreciation is the fruition of his subjective vision of the world, one where Isabel is objectified to the point where almost any independent awareness of self, purposiveness, and autonomy is dissolved completely. Later in the novel, James posits a psychological picture of this disintegration via the visual technique of chiaroscuro: "Then the shadows had begun to gather; it was as if Osmond deliberately, almost malignantly, had put the lights out, one by one". The lights in this passage can be interpreted as Isabel's affirmation of herself as an independent object that are, of course, slowly being extinguished; the shadows that have begun to gather are the encroachment of Gilbert's subjective vision.

This brings us to perhaps the most subtle but provocative use of Kant's subjectivity of aesthetics in The Portrait of a Lady. That is, we can read the various shifts in direction within the novel as representative of the conflict of telos that characterizes the novel. As stated, Kant wants to impute a telos or design onto the natural realm, one that would communicate the sundry categories and concepts that implicitly govern the universe. Telos also, by definition, refers to an inherent design in nature that suggests a movement towards a locus of finality.

In The Portrait of a Lady, the novel is characterized by a conflict of telos; that is, each male character attempts to project a design or form onto the lives of other characters. Whether Isabel, the recipient of this artificial design, is aware of the forces at work around her is debatable.

However, some conspicuous examples in the text exemplify how much telos, in this sense being culturally constructed as opposed to naturally, works to control the lives of the characters involved in the textual milieu. For example, Isabel's rejection of Caspar, a man who "showed his appetites and designs too simply and artlessly," is representative of the emphasis on teleological projection in the text. Caspar's fault is that he lacks the artifice to hide his desire for implementing design over Isabel's life. Isabel's trip to Europe can be interpreted as an attempt by the quintessential 'American' woman to follow the telos or design of the Old World, that is, a culture that is firmly entrenched in a historical reality with a beginning and end.

The concept of history to the American woman is one that is incomplete and undeveloped in comparison with the decadence of Europe; in the novel, for example, Isabel, in a moment of prescience concerning her upcoming trip to Europe, does confirm to Mrs. Touchett that she "likes places in which things have happened" — that is, the historical reality embodied by the teleologically-grounded chronology of Europe. The opposite of such a firmly-entrenched design is the American telos represented by Caspar. Isabel's rejection of him is as much one that is averse to his salient desire to impose his design upon her as it is a rejection of the embryonic stage of telos that the American historical reality embodies, one in which identity via a past is limited by the country's shortened sense of a culturally-constructed self.

If the novel is propelled by a sense of teleological conflict, one that affirms the Kantian notion of conceptual and categorical determination, then obviously Gilbert attempts to impose his particular design upon the life of his wife. Isabel does not discern the design inherent in Gilbert's plan to marry her; he is not as obvious in his intentions of imputing telos onto Isabel's life as a character like Caspar. Gilbert knows the subtlety of implementing his particular telos onto Isabel, like he has done with Pansy, intellectually, emotionally, and physically; he works his malignant plan with precision. The contrast between Isabel's two visions of Gilbert, one before the marital consummation and the other after, proves Isabel's naivete in understanding Gilbert's design.

"She had a more wondrous vision of him, fed through charmed senses and oh such a stirred fancy! — she had not read him right.". While it certainly does not help matters that Isabel still is aligned with an overtly quixotic vision of life until her marriage, it is obvious by this statement that her previous a priori conception of Gilbert cannot ascertain the scope of his delimiting design. The voice of Isabel at this moment in the novel has gained the insight of awareness but at the cost of the fulfillment of her own teleological progression. James says, "She remembered perfectly the first sign he had given of it [Gilbert's hatred towards and deception of his wife]- it had been like the bell that was to ring up the curtain upon the real drama of their life". With this statement, Isabel is perceived as finally grasping the realization that her independent telos has been subsumed under the design of another, Gilbert.

While Isabel may be subsumed under the culturally-constructed telos of Gilbert, she might also be aware of the contractual obligations of her marriage, one where her independent subsistence within the misogynistic relationship with her husband is indeed a conscious choice on her part. To invoke a twentieth-century theorist in this regard, Paul Ricoeur, one might argue that Isabel has objectified herself in the marriage contract on some level, however, that is inevitably purposeful. Ricoeur's larger project in his Freedom and Nature: The Voluntary and the Involuntary is to outline a philosophy of the will, positing that the self is simultaneously both an autonomous object and a subject with a vested interest. As Ricoeur writes about subject-object relations, "the you is the other myself". In regards to The Portrait of a Lady, the subject, Isabel, is only slightly aware of the overpowering design of her winning suitor, Gilbert — but she enters into the marriage contract freely. In chapter fifty-one, for example, Gilbert reminds Isabel of her own agency in the act of marrying him. He says to his wife, "You are nearer to me than any human creature, and I'm nearer to you. It may be a disagreeable proximity; it's one, at any rate, of our own deliberate making". From a Ricoeurian vantage, Isabel has entered into the marriage contract as means of "projecting" herself; though Ricoeur is positing the act of self-commitment as a diachronic project taken on the part of the subject, he still creates a theoretical model for the "disagreeable proximity" that exists between Isabel and Gilbert in James' novel.

Isabel, despite being the victim of Gilbert's constrictive teleological design-the same telos that Kant attempts to impute upon nature in his Critique of Judgment-still, if we affirm Ricoeur's argument, maintains a degree of agency in the process. According to Ricoeur, the self "throws itself ahead of itself in posing itself as the object". That is, in any binding commitment, the self circumvents temporality, becomes complicit in the very act of willing itself, and, in a way, becomes part of the eventual outcome of its willing. Gilbert's perception, however malignant when coupled with an actualized design, is one where he reminds Isabel of how she was the causal agent in instigating their shared marriage; that is, her search for an erudite, decorous European suitor has fashioned her into a contract of her own making, a "project" that is the self objectified, to invoke Ricoeur.

Gilbert's standard of judgment, in Kantian terms, lacks any type of value towards Isabel that acknowledges an intrinsic self-worth, that is, one that exists outside of the domain of extrinsic value systems. Gilbert's world, on the other hand, is essentially the superficial world of sensory perception. While an idealist, Gilbert never truly transcends the visceral level. As one critic, Tony Tanner, states about Gilbert, "to care so totally and uncritically for forms, taste, convention is to be absolutely enslaved to mere appearances, never questioning essences or the intrinsic worth of things". Tanner's critique of Gilbert is justified, as Isabel herself realizes that he is of the "artistic, the plastic view". Gilbert's "plastic" view lacks the insight to judge an object as being a free beauty, what Kant defines in the Critique of Judgment to be any object which is not determined in respect to any purpose by concepts. Gilbert only views sensory data as a means to an end, the affirmation of the external standard of judgment that Kant believes reduces the appreciation of an aesthetic object. Tanner further critiques Gilbert's aesthetic by stating his intentions with Isabel "to turn her into a reflector of himself, utterly devoid of any spontaneous life of her own". For all his aspirations of grandiose idealism, for all his self-professed "accumulation of beauty and knowledge," Gilbert does not venture beyond the superficial level of the world of appearances. To do so would imply a realization that Isabel exists with her own degree of internal purposiveness and a standard of judgment that exceeds his own subjective vision.

As we have touched upon James' own subjective vision as it is embodied in the novel The Portrait of a Lady, we could now apply this aesthetic to the novel as it relates to experiential knowledge. As stated before, experience in the novel is imbued with a tremendous amount of psychological involvement on the part of the reader. At times, this is the only connection that we can maintain with the novel because James purposely makes consciousness a shared simulacrum between the characters. States of consciousness in the novel do not flow like disjointed voices in the textual progression as in most novels. Instead, the characters' consciousness, which is what we as readers experience in the novel's ebb and flow, is transformed into a singular aesthetic unity. For example, the whole of chapter forty-two in the novel is such an ebb and flow of consciousness between the mind of Isabel ("she saw," "she had resisted," etc.) and Gilbert ("he had thought," "he had discovered," etc.). Consciousness, as a shared medium between two seemingly antithetical minds, becomes a singular experience in James' aesthetic schematics.

Hence, the paradox of James' aesthetic vision is that while at the same time he is seeking a proper representation of his own subjective angle in The Portrait of a Lady he is also detaching himself, his own Kantian purpose, if you will, from the entire creative process. That is, while The Portrait of a Lady enacts the Jamesian dictum that a novel should be a "personal, direct impression of life," he must also take a laissez-faire approach to his position within the aesthetic process ("The Art of Fiction," 170). This Jamesian characteristic has been observed by the critic John Paterson, who states that James believes "the novelist had to be less the priest or philosopher than the detached and disinterested observer of things".

In The Portrait of a Lady, James' narration is irretrievably detached from the novel's aesthetic conceptualization; the novel, like life itself, had to have an existence, a subjective vision, outside of James' own personality. For example, the novel is not marked by aesthetic dogmatism, whether implicit or explicit. James is distanced from the narrative progression of the text even in those moments where we as readers are most involved. For example, in chapter forty-six, when Isabel is interrogated concerning her last relations with Lord Warburton, Gilbert's desired suitor for Pansy, James writes, "It came over her, after he had said this, that she had once thought him beautiful". In this brief moment, an excerpt of a mere two-sentence paragraph in the novel, James is both efficient in his language and distanced from his subjective judgment concerning the fallen nature of Isabel's relationship with Gilbert. Isabel is only described as once perceiving Gilbert as "beautiful" in a previous state; in this subtle intonation, James, a detached observer of events, merely suggests the unhappy state of Isabel's marriage.

The contours of James' vision are the only vestige of authorial intrusion, and he clearly states in his personal journal that, in The Portrait of a Lady, the "whole... is never told." James, at moments such as this one from chapter forty-six, instead of eliciting the reader's sympathy via a didactic, self-affirming diatribe concerning Isabel's plight, is notably absent from the narrative process. In Kantian terms, James is at once affirming his subjective vision in the novel while also separating his personality from the finished aesthetic product.

The final element of Kant's Critique of Judgment that I

wish to discuss in relation to The Portrait of a Lady concerns the struggle between the moral/aesthetic universe and the world of means. Specifically, the tension that is inherent in The Portrait of a Lady is one marked by various characters' oscillations between these two polarized worlds. These dichotomized ideals can best be understood in terms of a definition that Tanner suggests: "[The moral world] is the world of ends in which everything and everyone has an intrinsic worth and they are all respected for what they are". The moral world, which Kant equates with the higher purposiveness of reason in Critique of Judgment, affirms a pure judgment of taste.

That is, the object in question is representative of a worth that is measured by fulfilling a purpose that corresponds with its own self-subsisting fruition — devoid of conformity to some external standard of judgment. The other world reduces the elevated state of the moral to marketable means; in essence, the individual is commodified to a state of objectification. Tanner describes this lower world as one where "people see other people only as things or instruments, and they work to appropriate them as suits their own ambition". These two levels are the realms between which Isabel must maintain some semblance of existence. She attempts to retain a higher moral level throughout the novel ("her aspirations, her theories") while coming to the stark realization that she has been reduced to the world of means (she becomes accustomed, for example, to the idea of "assisting her husband to be pleased"). It is when Isabel is forced into the lower realm of means — where she is explicitly commodified — that she no longer has access to the aesthetic virtues she aspires to earlier in the novel. Isabel, in Kantian aesthetics, no longer expresses the moral ideal.

In retrospect, the parallel worlds of the aesthetic/moral and the one of means are indicative of the self-contradictions that mark both Kant's subjectivity of aesthetics and James as an inheritor of that tradition. For example, the ontological shift that we see in Critique of Judgment does not actually move the emphasis of aesthetics completely into the subjective persona. This is because the subjective self must realize that while the individual is a pivotal part of the aesthetic process, there exists an autonomy of the aesthetic object, one which measures its intrinsic worth as an end in itself. Also paradoxical about Kant's aesthetic theory is the idea that at the unifying moment of connecting with a self-subsistent object, the subjective mind is able to achieve a higher level of moral purposiveness. The distinction between objective and subjective dualism, as a result, tends to be lessened.

James adheres to antithetical notions of aesthetics in his respective work, as well. For example, while affirming his own subjective vision of aesthetics in his novel The Portrait of a Lady, James is remarkably detached, narratively speaking, from the process as a whole. He also builds tension via paradox in the novel by locating Isabel's idealism within a higher moral framework, while in actuality she is oppressed by the reality of her commodification by Gilbert. This polarity of moral worlds is a not so much a concern for Ricoeur's philosophy of the will; instead of setting up oppositions between many of his premises, Ricoeur seeks a refracted Kantian idea: the unity that Kant sought in the nature is now found in subject-object relations. Ricoeur writes in Freedom and Nature that "there are no two selves, one projecting and one in the project; I affirm myself as the subject precisely in the object of my willing". The "project" of Isabel's marriage, which does include another "subject," Gilbert, is one where she is not disparate from her will; the "object" of her relationship, that is, the resultant marriage with Gilbert, is not a disinterested project.

Review of Acting Beautifully: Henry James and the Ethical Aesthetic

It is reasonable to generalize Henry James scholarship over the past fifty years, at least, as having taken place on two fields: the ethical (which James referred to as "morality") and the aesthetic. As a result, James tends to be read and taught primarily as either an ethical writer concerned with representing human situations or an aesthetic writer concerned with language as art. This is odd since James himself never claimed one field against the other for himself, but, occupying its border territory, crossed regularly between the aesthetic and the ethical. The question of the relation and interplay of ethics to aesthetics was important in James's critical essays throughout his career and thus illustrates the centrality of the ethical aesthetic in his conception of fiction, at least. Representative is this passage on Flaubert and Madame Bovary from an early essay, "The Minor French Novelists," which he wrote while he lived in Paris in the mid-1870s:

> Practically M. Flaubert is a potent moralist; whether, when he wrote his book, he was so theoretically is a matter best known to himself. Every out-and-out realist who provokes curious meditation may claim that he is a moralist, for that, after all, is the most that the moralists can do for us. They sow the seeds of virtue; they can hardly pretend to raise the crop. Excellence in this matter consists in the tale and the moral hanging well together, and this they are certainly more likely to do when there has been a definite intention—that intention of which artists who cultivate "art for art" are usually so extremely mistrustful; exhibiting thereby, surely, a most injurious disbelief in the illimitable alchemy of art. (p. 225 in "The Minor French Novelists." The Galaxy 212 [February 1876]: 219-34)

Acting Beautifully not only works to explain what James names in the passage above as the "alchemy" of Jamesian poetics, at least as far as the ethical aesthetic is concerned (which takes one quite far indeed); in addition, Acting Beautifully itself stages the relation of the aesthetic to the ethical through the discussion of key "events" in The Portrait of a Lady, The Wings of the Dove, and "The Altar of the Dead." Writes Jöttkandt, "Each of the three acts I outline has this one thing in common: they separately represent a singular expression of fidelity to the impossibility encountered in the realm of experience that fundamentally transforms not only the characters' own subjective constitutions but also that of the world in which they live. In every case, we will see how the James heroine explicitly calls on the aesthetic order to perform her act". Reading Jöttkandt's book is a powerful and even moving event in itself because it works in the same ethical-aesthetic borderland as the fiction it discusses. Several concepts from Lacan and elsewhere, including "the Real," "passage à l'acte, desire and drive, and an understanding of ethics as it is detailed in Lacan's seminar on Ethics enable Jöttkandt to map and work in that ethical-aesthetic borderland. For "what James contributes to the psychoanalytic discussion is to confirm the inseparability of aesthetics from Lacanian ethics". In this way, Jöttkandt can show via James the way "ethics intersects, cuts across the registers of the Symbolic and the Real".

Although each chapter attends to a different text and a different central problem, each develops points made earlier. Such a strategy produces a book that works cumulatively, adding to a reader's understanding of the ethical aesthetic chapter by chapter, page by page, sentence by sentence. The argument of the book is so coherent—though dense at points—that it reads as if it were a shorter essay. There are no apparent loose ends, no sprawling digressions. The argument itself is always clearly presented to offer a new way of thinking about James's fiction, at least: "As I have shown, aesthetic experience is nothing but an encounter with the limit of the Symbolic realm, the tuchè, an encounter with the Real which, as such, imposes an ethical demand on us. The ethics of our response lies in our infinitely creative, singular ways of maintaining fidelity to this impossibility at the heart of experience".

The chapter on Isabel Archer, freedom, and The Portrait of a Lady introduces the aesthetic nature of the psychoanalytic narrative of ethical subjectivity, which is foundational to Acting Beautifully: "Through a transposition of the psychoanalytic terminology into the philosophical dialectic of freedom and determination, James's novel helps us to see what is really at stake in the psychoanalytic narrative of ethical subjectivity, namely, the radical philosophical, ethical, and political potential of transcendental freedom. But, significantly, what James additionally draws attention to in the psychoanalytic narrative is the peculiarly aesthetic nature of the psychoanalytical ethical act".

The ethical act under consideration in The Portrait of a

Lady is one of the most vexing in the novel: Isabel's decision to return to Osmond. Jöttkandt establishes the terms of her investigation of the act this way: "it is only by understanding her choice as intentionally empty—that is, made deliberately without reference to empirical considerations—that we can begin to approach the specifically ethical dimension of her act". Such a strategy is typical of the way Jöttkandt finds a way to the borderland between ethics and aesthetics—the third way of understanding James that includes both in the ethical aesthetic. For Isabel, as Jöttkandt reads her, the problem is one of the consequences for choosing because "choice is the means by which Isabel believes she actualizes her freedom".

So then why does she choose Osmond? Because for Isabel Osmond "personifies the act of choice". To Isabel his life is based in defining and knowing and choosing. And for Isabel, to remain free is to live a life in which she can continually choose. In addition, following Acting Beautifully's concentration on third ways, Osmond represents to Isabel a third way of male relationship: he combines the "demands of the sensuous impulse" of Goodwood and also Warburton's "claustrophobic constraints of preexisting social and moral systems". He is a "fantasy of aesthetic reconciliation". Yet the novel also offers itself as a Bildungsroman. Here too, in the terms of the nineteenth-century Bildungsroman, the ethical and the aesthetic are fundamental—even if they become in this novel fundamental to James's satire of the form's narrative logic. Crucial to both that satire and to the logic of the chapter overall is Jöttkandt's explanation of Isabel's decision to act "out of duty toward the moral law itself, which for Kant is the only way through which our transcendental freedom can be realized". Such an act of duty, especially as it is carried out with knowledge of the choice that wasn't present to Isabel the first time she chose Osmond, a feature of "reflective judgment", in turn, enacts the idea of the ethical community.

The second chapter, on Milly Theale and The Wings of the Dove, argues that "the earlier questions of freedom and determination become transposed into the linguistic and representational concerns that haunt the psychoanalytic discourse of hysteria. I suggest that by understanding Milly's illness as an hysterical episode, we are better placed to comprehend what I see as the specifically ethical dimension of her final, aesthetic death in Venice". "Both thematically and formally, The Wings of the Dove poses itself the question: What is the ethical response to the unrepresentable?".

This question is significant because "psychoanalysis poses itself the same question in treating the traumatic neuroses, namely, the relationship of language to the unspeakable trauma or, as Freud later revised his theory, the unspeakable desire that resulted in the hysteria or obsessive compulsion". This, in turn, becomes important as Jöttkandt investigates the possibility of Milly's illness being psychological—hysteria—rather than physiological. Seeing Milly's problem as hysteria foregrounds "the question of the limits of representation and its accompanying dilemma—the ethical approach to the unspeakable—since hysteria is itself a reaction to a certain deadlock or failure of representation". For Milly, "hysteria itself constitutes an ethical stance with regard to the unrepresentable, with important implications for the way we understand Milly's final act and, ultimately, the ethical dimensions of this novel. I suggest that beauty is nothing less than the paradigmatic case of hysteria—hysteria's Ur-narrative—enabling us to appreciate how a primordial aesthetic experience lies at the heart of the psychoanalytic 'ethics of desire'".

Jöttkandt locates third terms that are crucial in Wings as in the other James texts she discusses. In Wings, that third term constitutes a discursive space that enables ethical-aesthetic meaning: "If until now the action has been dominated by oppositional pairs engaged in what might be considered a Hegelian life-or-death power struggle, the addition of this third discursive space has the ability to change these relations". Desire enables the location of that third space and enables one to "begin to understand the ethical dimension of The Wings of the Dove".

Jöttkandt ventures at least two especially risky and rewarding insights in this chapter. The first has to do with what

Milly sees when she looks at the Bronzino: not herself, but an allegorical relation to herself in which tears reveal her realization "of the absolute senselessness of comparing time with the end of time.

Milly's discovery that the meaning of life is death turns all temporal hierarchies into bitter irony, since everyone, no matter how long they live, will eventually die". The consequences that issue from Milly's reading of herself through the portrait are central to the chapter's investigation of how desire, naming, and "'the conspiracy of silence'" work for Milly to ward off death. The second insight, as important to the success of the chapter and the book as the first, has to do with Jöttkandt's Freudian and Lacanian reading of the novel's Christian tropes, which, of course, changes fundamentally the meaning of Christianity in the novel and provides a way to explain Milly's sacrifice not as "the final collapse of a disappointed woman; by sacrificing herself, Milly acts in accordance with her desire. By willing death, in this way, Milly in effect dies in order to 'keep dreaming,' to maintain the fantasy that has sustained her as a desiring subject, and which, in preserving an area of indeterminacy, prevents her from becoming wholly trapped by language".

One of the most sensitively rendered sections of the book has to do with Kate Croy. Here's an excerpt from that section:

Like Milly's, Kate's desire is bound up with the word, or name, that bars access, we might as well now say, to jouissance. Her desire, like Milly's, is therefore also hysterical insofar as hysterical desire involves a defense against—and, as I suggested above, the defense of—the gap that prevents the totality from becoming whole. Although most critics see her as cruelly and coldly calculating when she instructs Densher to pretend to love Milly, if we take literally what the novel tells us, there is no guarantee that Milly will die. In fact, unless Kate has better knowledge about Milly's condition even than Sir Luke Strett, by putting Densher into Milly's way, surely she is creating the only conditions under which, as far as she knows, Milly's life will be saved.

In Kate, herself a kind of third-term or borderland

character, duty and desire are not opposed. For in making a choice for duty—her family, she also makes a choice for desire—for that which was also her mother's desire: "Kate's desire is precisely for the thing that will give body to her mother's desire, the name that substitutes for it in the symbolic order. Kate's duty is thus identical to her desire: to rescue the name that substitutes for, and that fills, the gap in the field of representation. Kate's desire is, therefore, like Milly's, a hysterical desire". However, Kate's ethical orientation, characterized by intensity of her pursuit of the object of her desire—in pursuit of her "name" she "gives it up" by submitting her reputation to Densher's sexual blackmail—is that of the drive. Milly's is of desire.

Jöttkandt's final chapter investigates "The Altar of the Dead" to show how "deconstruction itself epitomizes an aesthetic discourse. at least as represented by De Man and his followers". That discourse "represents a structure of deferral very like what I identified as Milly's hysterical/aesthetic solution. Such an identification then makes it possible to diagnose the deconstructive project as a hysterical discourse, designed to maintain a certain sustaining distance from what Lacan calls the Real—the unrepresentable excessive horror/ enjoyment that underpins the symbolic order but for which deconstruction inevitably, for very specific structural reasons that I outline, must fail to possess a concept". The question "Why should the question of the rites/rights of the dead carry such import to the extent that, at least since Hegel's Antigone, they have come to epitomize for us what is essential to ethics?" organizes the chapter.

The discussion of "The Altar of the Dead" depends in large part on understanding Stransom's altar as a representational system both simple (based on a one-to-one correspondence of signifier and signified) and also infinitely variable. "What is at stake in all of this is quite simply the question of a limit, of the exception that creates the rule. The limit is what makes it possible for us to transcend our merely phenomenal state, and enter, with Isabel Archer, a realm of transcendental freedom, to escape, with Milly Theale, the birdcage of language that otherwise threatens to fully entrap us. The limit is nothing less than the condition of possibility of reason itself, enabling us to be freely acting, conscious beings". The candles on Stransom's altar function for him as a simple "'counting machine'", a metaphor for those whom he wishes to remember—one candle per person. On the other hand, the altar arrangement functions for the woman visitor as if it were a metonym—all the candles are for Hague. The importance of this difference is how the woman's reading "disrupts" Stransom's "fallacy of believing we can derive a vertical relation among contiguous elements in a binary system". The altar, then, functions as zeugma, "both the rhetorical reading strategy of deconstruction, and the name of the irreducible 'event' that occurs when deconstructive or 'metonymical' readings and 'metaphorical' readings occur side by side". What is significant in terms of what I have been calling the "borderland" argument that Jöttkandt develops throughout is that

the 'happening' of James's story takes place not at the level of the Symbolic but at the intersection of the Symbolic and the Real. is James who shows us another way of conceptualizing the 'event' of the tale, such that, instead of condemning us to the endless, senseless repetition of language conceived as a strictly mechanical system of tropes, a different possibility is opened up, enabling us to conceptualize how such a system may after all transcend its limits, but without 'forgetting' the hard-won knowledge produced by deconstruction and reverting back to some externally imposed, mystified 'transcendental signfied'.

And the way such a system, one that would open that "different possibility," could operate depends on theorizing language and action in terms of concepts borrowed from set theory, Kant, and Lacan, which in this portion of Acting Beautifully comprise the new terms, the borderland territory itself, where so much of this book lives and by which it is consistently distinguished. The result of this way of thinking about language and ethics and James's altar, in short, is that regardless of the limits of language, the woman's resistance [to Stransom] embodies the ethical demand that insists on the removal of even that last limit [that ethics can be reduced to laws]; her resistance conveys the way ethics must always escape our attempts to pin it down, to consolidate it, such that, as we know from Kant, we will never cognize the totality of the meaning of our actions, that is, whether or not our act has been ethical. Nevertheless, as Isabel discovered, we must act anyway, we must make choices but, as James expresses so beautifully with this story, true fidelity means maintaining a resistance against ever thinking we can reach the 'ethical' as such, i.e., as a limit that must be defended at all costs. Something, James seems to be saying, always escapes our infinitude—namely, precisely our finitude. It is our finitude that demands we take every moment, every singular situation on a one-by-one basis for action.

Jöttkandt opens her book by telling us that it is and is not about James: "It occurs to me that my title might seem a little misleading once one realizes that my subject implicitly deals at least as much with Lacan as it does with James". In the final part of the book, with the extrapolation of "some of the practical implications exemplified by James's heroine in "The Altar of the Dead", she begins to finish that plan, which does more than explicate or theorize James. Jöttkandt shows some consequences of her reading of James, which is especially significant in terms of Badiou's own rethinking of ethics, his own border territory, "'the rights of the Immortal, affirmed in their own right, or the rights of the Infinite, exercised over the contingency of suffering and death'".

Like the reading she carries out of "The Altar of the Dead," Jöttkandt's understanding of Badiou's ethics, like psychoanalysis, offers a way to find "truth" in the "event." Thus an important marker of the territory Acting Beautifully finds, makes, and maps: "Deconstruction is nothing other than the act of remaining faithful to the 'event' of psychoanalysis. It is a strict 'fidelity,' that is, an act of love toward psychoanalysis, as Derrida himself has suggested. Badiou tells us if we absolutize a truth we slip into evil. Deconstruction shows us how we can remain faithful to an event inasmuch as it escapes us, inasmuch as its 'truth' always remains in excess of the system that has created it. This, too, I think is the significance of the woman's return to the altar ". Sigi Jöttkandt's decision to close Acting Beautifully with a powerful reminder of James's own ethical and personal engagement during World War I and the last years of his life both ends the book fittingly and also reminds us of the ethical-aesthetic importance of James's work not only in his fiction, but in his day-to-day life, his letters and his non-fiction.

The closing, attending so carefully, tenderly, and accessibly to the way "ethics intersects the registers of the Symbolic and the Real", raises the question of whether there has been a reader of James as sensitive and as intellectually engaged with both the nuances of James's aesthetic and the significance of his ethics as Jöttkandt.

Q. Discuss the female potential in The Potrait of a Lady.

The late 1960s and 70s witnessed an extraordinary flowering of James adaptations, especially on BBC television. The Portrait of a Lady was swiftly followed by What Maisie Knew; The Spoils of Poynton appeared in 1970 with The Golden Bowl premiering two years later. Later on in the decade The Ambassadors and The Wings of the Dove were produced. British critics enthusiastically welcomed some of these adaptations: Francis Hope congratulated the BBC for The Portrait of a Lady, which he believed was an example of public service broadcasting at its best. Julian Critchley in the London Times considered What Maisie Knew "great fun", even if James himself might have considered it a serious work.

This article will consider two of these adaptations—The Portrait of a Lady and The Golden Bowl—in detail, focusing in particular on the way in which they conceive their female characters. Before that, however, I will situate the adaptations in context by looking at how classic serials were produced in the 60s and 70s. Both The Portrait of a Lady and The Golden Bowl were adapted by Jack Pulman and directed by James Cellan Jones; following their British premieres, they were broadcast on PBS in the United States in the Masterpiece Theatre series which began in 1971. They were produced by the BBC Serials Department, which at the time provided 140 hours per annum of television, with a staff of six directors and eight producers. Each year the department head proposed a package of programs for broadcast in regular slots—the classic serial on BBC2 every Saturday (with a repeat on Thursday), or the Sunday tea-time classic serial on BBC1. By the late 60s the serial had established through weekly scheduling in seasonal blocks enough regularity to build an audience, and enough identity to build an ethos, based on the notion of contributing to the development of a national culture. The BBC executive Oliver Whitley remarked in 1965 that the classic serial should educate the British people, most of whom were rather "culture-resistant". A 1972 book Television and the People congratulated the Corporation's classic serial output for rendering "obsolete the former divisions which stratified the public into high, low and middle brows".

This concern for cultural education (allied to the financial constraints placed on the Serials Department) significantly affected the ways in which James's novels were adapted for the screen. All directors and adapters were encouraged to keep as close as possible to the author's original intentions, both in terms of characterization and narrative. This technique is evident in the screenplays for The Portrait of a Lady and The Golden Bowl, which incorporate substantial passages from the original novels, and which unfold at a leisurely pace, permitting viewers to reflect on what they are seeing and—perhaps more importantly—hearing. Exterior locations are kept to a minimum—in The Portrait of a Lady, for instance, only one scene (where Isabel rejects Lord Warburton's proposal of marriage) takes place outdoors.

The viewer's attention focuses on the interplay between characters, with Cellan Jones's camera ruthlessly scrutinizing their reactions in close-ups or two-shots. Both adaptations make frequent use of visual symbols to facilitate the viewer's understanding of a particular sequence, and how it fits into the overall narrative.

It is hard to imagine Cellan Jones's approach recommending itself to BBC producers of today, in an environment where cost-effectiveness has become more and more central to decision-making, and where the economic logic has shifted from producer-unit to package-unit. In the past, producers could work on a variety of projects, secure in the knowledge that they would be scheduled at regular times, and attract a loyal audience.

By the 90s every adaptation was planned on the assumption that every aspect of an adaptation had to demonstrate marketing potential to ensure high audience figures and good overseas sales—whether it be the star casts, historic locations, or the meticulously designed sets and costumes. Commercial imperatives had always been important for Masterpiece Theatre on PBS in the United States (where Mobil provided the entire series budget of between $10m. and $15m. per annum between 1971 and 1998), but it was a new phenomenon for the BBC in the 90s. The $9m. production of Middlemarch filmed in the ancient town of Stamford, Lincolnshire, adapted by Andrew Davies, was widely regarded as a test case: "If the series was not a critical success, they threatened to give up adapting proper books altogether" (Giddings and Selby 89). The Corporation had no need to worry: Middlemarch was sold to 30 countries and recouped over $2.75m. in video/DVD sales.

With the BBC of the 60s and early 70s being less preoccupied with commercial imperatives and more with the quality of their output, directors had the freedom to develop their own idiosyncratic interpretations of a particular work. In the second part of this article, I will analyze Cellan Jones's representation of the female protagonists in The Portrait of a Lady and The Golden Bowl—Isabel Archer, Charlotte Stant and Maggie Verver—focusing in particular on their refusal to conform to what people expect of them. Isabel rejects a financially advantageous marriage to Lord Warburton, and chooses to return to England to comfort the dying Ralph, in defiance of Osmond's wishes.

On most occasions, however, she sustains her independence through less direct means, ones that Cellan Jones highlights televisually: he frequently frames her face in close-up as she chides her friends for asking too much from her, or expecting her to behave in a particular manner. Both Charlotte Stant and Maggie Verver in Cellan Jones's Golden Bowl opt for silence as a method of resistance. On the surface they appear to be committed to marriage, home and family, but no one really knows them. The on-screen narrator Bob Assingham makes repeated attempts to explain their motives; it is clear from his speeches, however, that his judgements are riddled with uncertainties. Cellan Jones's emphasis on female potential might now be considered sexist (it clearly reinforces women's position on the periphery of society); for first-wave feminists of the late 60s and 70s, however, this viewpoint was of paramount importance.

Carol Andreas's Sex And Caste In America suggested that a greater awareness of female potential could open up "new possibilities for freedom" for both men and women who hitherto had been "kept in anxiety about their worth and identity as human beings because they must 'make it' as a man or woman member of a sexist society". In Towards a Recognition of Androgyny, Carolyn G.Heilbrun exalted "feminine traits", in the belief that "since they have been so drastically undervalued, must now gain respect, so that a sort of balance is achieved among those in power, and within individuals".

Perhaps the classic serial of the 60s and early 70s was the ideal means of communicating these ideas to viewers who (in the directors' minds at least) were considered perfectly capable of listening to as well as watching what took place on screen. In a recent book on the history of British television, Stuart Jeffries waxed lyrical about adaptations such as Fay Weldon's Pride and Prejudice that included whole speeches from Austen's novel: "Such delicious circumlocution! Such English sang-froid! Such brightness of spirit and of intelligence!... we could, through watching adaptations of Jane Austen, imagine a time when all was well...". Jack Pulman's screenplay for Cellan Jones's Portrait of a Lady likewise incorporates large quantities of Jamesian text. In one sequence the action moves from the scene where Madame Merle promises to talk to Isabel on Mrs. Touchett's behalf to the moment where Osmond wonders what to do with Pansy. The dialog remains much the same as in the novel, save for the omission of Isabel's observation to Osmond ("I think that wouldn't do much towards making her resemble me").

This concern for the Jamesian text is equally evident in Cellan Jones's adaptation of The Golden Bowl. In one newly-written sequence Bob Assingham observes Maggie Verver waiting for her husband to return home: "So Maggie waited, her heart I'm sure beating very fast". The Prince returns without a greeting from Maggie. In the next scene Bob admits that "what she might have said, what she longed to say, I suppose, was...", followed closely by Maggie's own voice-over of a passage taken almost verbatim from the novel:

"Why have I made this evening such a point of our not dining together? Well, because I've all day been so wanting you all alone that I finally couldn't bear it, and there didn't seem to be any great reason why I should try to. You seem these last days, I don't know what, more absent than ever before, too absent for us merely to go on so. It's all very well and I perfectly see how beautiful it is all around. But there comes a day when something snaps and the cup flows over. That's it. The cup all day has been too full to carry, so here I am with it spilling over you, because it's my life after all, and I don't have to explain, do I, that I'm as much in love with you now as on the first hour we met, except there are some hours, which I know when they come because they frighten me, that you are even more so, and they do come, oh how they come, how they come."

The cup image is used earlier on in the novel, when James describes the Prince's eyes meeting Charlotte's on the balcony: "So therefore while the minute lasted it passed between them that their cup was full; which cup their very eyes, holding it fast, carried and steadied and began, as they tasted it, to praise". Charlotte subsequently observes that she feels "like a great gold cup that we [i.e. the Prince and herself] must somehow drain together". Cellan Jones retains Charlotte's line, but emphasizes the strength of her attraction to the Prince—

as expressed through the gold cup image—by having Mr. Blint play the love-song "Plaisir d'Amour" on the piano in the background.i The fact that Maggie is unaware of this, when she makes use of the golden cup image to express her feelings for her husband, renders her speech even more poignant.

Throughout Maggie's long speech the camera focuses on her expressionless face until Bob observes in a newly-written line that "of course she couldn't say that". In the novel the Prince talks about what he has been doing, then excuses himself with the phrase "I must go and bathe". The clear implication is that he seeks to cleanse himself of Charlotte's smell, leaving Maggie alone in the darkness as the scene fades to black. The entire sequence seeks to render the novel's interior states of being visible: viewers contemplate Maggie as she reflects on her husband's behavior, and comes to understand what he has been up to.ii The experience of watching classic serials of this kind was well summed up in Julian Critchley's review of The Portrait of a Lady: "James comes over well on television.

We concentrate not on action but on character, and watch with growing pleasure the application of a large talent to the very slightest of stories". Bearing in mind the likelihood that many viewers were encountering The Portrait and The Golden Bowl for the first time, Pulman and Cellan Jones tried to show how both novels were as much concerned with states of mind as character and incident. Little attempt was made to liven up both plots with gratuitous action: viewers had to listen to as well as observe what was unfolding on screen. In this respect, Bob's reflective monologues provide an experience analogous to that of reading James's novel. For those more accustomed to classic serials of the 90s, which take more liberties with the original texts, The Portrait and The Golden Bowl might seem flat and undramatic; nonetheless they provide excellent examples of how the classic serial at its best could educate as well as entertain television audiences of the late 60s and 70s.

Sometimes it seems as if Cellan Jones deliberately interrupts the narrative to enable viewers to reflect on the characters' behavior. Isabel's journey from Gardencourt to Italy is not described in James's Portrait (we only learn that she finds Italy "a land of promise, a land in which the love of the beautiful might be comforted by endless knowledge"). In the adaptation Isabel's voyage is symbolically represented by means of an interlude in which an etching of a ship at sea is shown onscreen, accompanied by Ralph's (Richard Chamberlain's) voice-over telling his father that he seeks to "get just the good I said a few moments ago I wished to put into Isabel's reach—that of having met the requirements of my imagination".

As studio time was limited in 1968, and most classic serials had to be recorded quickly, it is likely that sequences such as this were deliberately introduced to enable the actors to move from one set to another. Nonetheless this strategy—a legacy of the days when all BBC dramas were broadcast live—has a thematic as well as a practical function. Just like the artist who painted the ship, Ralph perceives Isabel as a canvas onto which he can project his dream of social success. This interlude also adumbrates the next scene in the adaptation where Madame Merle tells Osmond that drawing is his sole accomplishment, even if it does reveal his "adorable taste".

Such devices were no longer necessary by 1972, as the technology of video-tape recording had improved. However, Cellan Jones frequently interrupts the action to allow Bob Assingham to address the viewers direct to camera, or comment on the other characters through voice-over. On one occasion Maggie sits in a tea-shop staring into the middle distance while Bob tells us how she had been courted by the Prince. Later on—in a newly-written speech—he reflects on Charlotte's forthcoming marriage to Verver:

"I think in her own way she was bent on making the marriage work. When she thought about it consciously I think she meant all that she had said to Verver that day on the pier at Brighton. She did want to get married. She did like him; she was immensely grateful to him and perhaps at first she didn't know what was truly at the back of her mind..."

Writing in the London Times after the opening episode

was broadcast in May 1972, Leonard Buckley complained that the use of Bob as an onscreen narrator was "irksome", as Cusack's voice was not "the sort to sustain a long narration without grating". It is certainly true that Bob's voice-overs divert our attention away from the visual image, as we concentrate on what is happening mentally and emotionally rather than physically. But perhaps this is the most effective way of rendering James's exploration of his characters' state of mind explicit on screen.

Not all critics were happy with this style of adaptation, which had remained much the same since the BBC started transmitting classic serials on a regular basis in the years immediately following the end of the Second World War. Commenting on John Davies's 1972 War and Peace, one writer complained that the genre had become too predictable: "Sometimes you feel as if the same serial has been going on for five years. It changes title once every six months. Some time ago it was called Portrait of a Lady; then Pride and Prejudice. Still later they called it Middlemarch, and for the moment they refer to it as War and Peace".

Even a recent critic such as Lee Clark Mitchell, who was generally sympathetic towards Cellan Jones's Golden Bowl, described the production as "bare-bones... with restrained costumes, uncluttered rooms, shot in under-stated studio sets". Yet this style of presentation seems to be appropriate to a Henry James adaptation; by concentrating almost exclusively on the characters and their reactions, through close-ups, medium or two-shots, it can reveal (in Jonathan Freedman's words) how "human beings must not only reckon with the relations that construct them, but also work to build new, more efficacious ones". This certainly seems the case in The Portrait of a Lady. At one point Isabel admits in some newly-written lines that "if it hadn't been for the money, I'd never have married him ". Yet she refuses to take Henrietta Stackpole advice and end her marriage. Her reasons are plain enough: "Why—because I know him better now than when I married him. That would be a paltry thing to do. I must make him like me better. While it remains unspoken, there's a chance it may improve. I think I owe him that. I think I owe it to myself". The entire sequence is filmed in a series of medium shots and close-ups, with Isabel standing next to a large marble statue, its gleaming whiteness providing an apt metaphor for the sterility of her marriage. Her determination to try and make things better is also expressed symbolically, as she moves away from the statue and sits in a chair sipping tea in the shadow of a tree. Clearly she is searching for more fertile ways to communicate with her husband.

This quest proves futile, however, as Osmond accuses her of having played "a very deep game" in driving Lord Warburton away, and thereby preventing Pansy from contracting a financially advantageous marriage. Cellan Jones shoots this scene in a series of two-shots, with Osmond standing threateningly over Isabel. On at least two occasions the action cuts to a point-of-view shot of Osmond looking at his wife sitting on the sofa, with all of his ornaments (vases, bronze figures) illuminated by candle-light in the background. On the one level, this point-of-view shot stresses Isabel's confinement; she cannot evade Osmond's gaze, let alone leave his house. On another level, the shot suggests that Osmond treats her as just another item in his collection of antiques.

In The Golden Bowl Charlotte's burgeoning affair with the Prince is expressed through a close-up of their hands linked together. The Prince's head is seen on the right of the frame as he moves towards Charlotte; as he does so, the camera tracks backwards to show her smiling face. What makes this moment more interesting is that, as the action unfolds, we hear Bob telling us that his wife Fanny could not understand "whether anything was going on between them or not. One moment she thought there was, the next she thought she was mistaken". Clearly Charlotte and the Prince are thoroughly enjoying their affair—particularly when no one else appears to know about it. Later on Maggie's growing suspicion about their relationship is suggested in a sequence that begins with a close-up of Charlotte playing the piano.

The camera tracks backwards once again to a medium shot of the Prince, Maggie and Adam Verver, who are listening to her recital. Two medium close-ups of Maggie's face, her eyes fixed on the Prince, are separated by another shot of Charlotte playing "Plaisir d'Amour". Clearly this song, with its romantic message, alerts Maggie to the fact that it might not be intended for everyone's pleasure.

Another technique Cellan Jones employs to focus attention on the relationships in both adaptations is the use of visual symbolism. I have already shown how the marble statue functions as a metaphor for Isabel's marriage; the same image appears in the sequence where Isabel and Lord Warburton are shown walking in the grounds of Gardencourt—the only scene of location filming in the entire adaptation. This says a lot about Isabel's status in society; she is only permitted to walk outdoors when faced with a proposal of marriage. The two of them are shown sitting by a large marble statue placed in the center of an ornamental pond.

Clearly we are meant to understand that whereas the union might bring Isabel wealth and social position, it will prove as lifeless as the statue. She is thoroughly justified in telling Warburton "not to hope at all" for her consent. The most obvious symbol to appear in The Golden Bowl is the bowl itself. The Prince is the first to identify the flaw in its structure; as he considers whether this might be a bad omen or not, Cellan Jones cuts to a close-up of the bowl with Charlotte's fingers running round the edge. The same shot is used later on, once Maggie discovers the truth about her husband's infidelity, only this time it is Maggie's hand, rather than Charlotte's, which is shown running round the bowl.iii

So far we have concentrated mainly on Cellan Jones's approach to adaptation, showing how it was dictated by financial constraints as well as the need to fulfill the BBC's public service responsibility to inform, educate and entertain audiences. What we have not yet considered is how both The Portrait of a Lady and The Golden Bowl focus on the question of female identity—something that not only concerned feminists of the late 60s and early 70s, but Jamesian critics as well. Manfred Mackenzie remarked in 1972 that, once she marries Osmond, "Isabel is utterly displaced from her identity.... We must, I think, imagine that she has determined to suppress her revenge-feeling for the time being". A year later Lisa Appignanesi saw Isabel at the end of the novel as someone who had become "another masculine emanation, a static figure, whose outlines are complete, defined, and whose possibility for expanding the circuit of 'felt life' and attaining consciousness is closed". If these critics are to be believed, Isabel should have adopted a feminist perspective if she wanted to preserve her self-respect. Perhaps she should have followed Maggie Verver's example: according to Naomi Leibowitz in her essay "Magic and Metamorphosis in The Golden Bowl", reprinted in a 1970 anthology, she undergoes a transformation "from victim to saviour.... She breaks through the sentimentality of Fanny's picture of her 'brave little piety' to its truth in relationship".

In Cellan Jones's adaptations, however, neither Isabel, Maggie nor Charlotte have to choose between sacrificing their femininity or making a bid for independence through direct means. Rather, they endeavor to create a specifically feminine language for themselves which is irreducible to a masculine language based on unity and explicability. In Isabel's case, this is evident through her reticence, which renders her difficult to accommodate within the patriarchal order. To Ralph she is "a clever girl—with a strong will and a high temper", possessed of "a rare mind". He invites her to "be frank" about her marriage to Osmond, to which Isabel replies: "I didn't marry to please my friends, and I can't complain just to please them either". Cellan Jones cuts to a close-up of Ralph's crestfallen face—despite his friendship for her, Isabel will not give him access to her "rare mind".

On another occasion Lord Warburton admits that he cannot make out what Isabel is "up to", and suggests that her mind is "a most formidable instrument" that "looks down on us all; it despises us".iv Cellan Jones adds the following lines: "ISABEL: I do not like the picture you draw of me. WARBURTON: It might be exaggerated. Perhaps you're right. Perhaps we should join the others".

Creating a portrait of a lady—either physically or in one's

mind—constitutes a masculine strategy that imposes order and unity on her by capturing her for eternity in a particular attitude. Isabel resents this; she seeks to remain "perfectly free", and not have to justify her behavior to others, even if she could.

This is further emphasized at the end of the adaptation. As someone who has based her career on manipulating others for Osmond's benefit, Madame Merle might have expected some reaction from Isabel to the revelation that it was Ralph who had imparted "that extra lustre... to make you a brilliant match". James's novel implies that this is the case, as Merle observes "in a kind of proud penance" that Isabel is unhappy. In Cellan Jones's adaptation, Isabel remains silent, refusing to betray her emotions. After a few seconds, she turns away, delivering the line "I think I should like never to see you again" with a long pause between the words "like" and "never". She opens the door and quietly exits, leaving Merle alone, a pathetic figure whose scheming has left her with nothing—not even the pleasure of sustaining some kind of hold over Isabel. To anyone who trusts in Bob Assingham's judgement in Cellan Jones's Golden Bowl, Maggie Verver's and Charlotte Stant's behavior must seem equally unpredictable.

On one occasion Bob likens Maggie to a bird who "had flapped her little wings as a token of wanting to fly a little, not merely as a plea for a more gilded cage" (TGB 355, slightly rewritten). The result, according to Bob's patriarchal view of the world, was that Maggie "felt suddenly immensely alone". This summation is undermined by the events that follow, as Maggie admits that Charlotte has "always been so good, so perfect, to me—but never so wonderfully as just now.

We have somehow been more together—thinking for the time almost only of each other; it has been quite as in old days". Cellan Jones emphasizes the closeness of their relationship by means of a split-screen image, with Charlotte on the left of the frame, and Maggie on the right. Such contradictory impulses—where Charlotte chooses to remain close friends with someone who suspects her of having an affair with her husband—are beyond the scope of Bob's imagination. The strength of Charlotte and Maggie's friendship is further emphasized in a newly-created sequence when Maggie buys the golden bowl. The shopkeeper recalls the time earlier on when Charlotte looked at it, and asks Maggie whether Charlotte is her sister. Maggie's countenance is shown in tight close-up as she replies: "No—my friend".

Bob also attempts to explain Charlotte's motives, once the details of her affair with the Prince have been brought to light. In a newly-written speech delivered to camera he remembers that "When Fanny said 'Poor Charlotte', I knew exactly what she meant. For whatever you may think of Charlotte, it was the cruelest thing imaginable that could be done to a woman as much in love as she was. To leave her suspended in mid-air and just wondering.... She could sense the panic rising in Charlotte's heart, as if she were a bird in a cage, suspended in a room into which a cat had just walked. She saw the flutterings, the beating of wings, the trembling of feathers around the throat".

What happens next does not appear so dramatic, as Charlotte and Maggie exchange confidences on the Castledeans' balcony, as if nothing had happened. Charlotte guides groups of tourists round her husband's house, while Bob solemnly intones in a voice-over that she "knew what her doom was, that she was to be separated from her lover and to all intents and purposes never to see him again".

Charlotte neither confirms nor refutes his observations; like Isabel Archer, she appears to be enjoying "her cheerful submission to duty". The last we see of her in the adaptation is just before she departs for American City, where she stresses that "our real life isn't here [in England]" and points out, much to Maggie's chagrin, that she speaks both for herself and her husband: "Let me admit it—I am selfish. I place my husband first". While such brazenness is an act, designed to cover up her private anguish, it seems hardly characteristic of a woman fluttering like a "bird in a cage" and proceeding inexorably to her doom, as Bob would have us believe.v

Cellan Jones's adaptations can scarcely be considered 'radical', in the sense that they seek to re-evaluate existing television production practices. The narratives are predominantly constructed according to classical principles, whereby viewers are encouraged to identify with fictional characters. By means of these identifications, viewers are drawn into the adaptation, so that when the questions of plot posed by the narrative are resolved by its closure, the viewers seem 'closed', completed or satisfied. This structure is characteristic of what Annette Kuhn has described as "dominant cinema, classic Hollywood narrative in particular"; but is equally prevalent in the classic serial, where each episode ends with an unanswered question, the solution of which can only be found out by watching the next installment.

The treatment of characters in The Portrait of a Lady and The Golden Bowl may appear equally conservative. Feminists such as Jane Gaines have argued in general terms that the link between femininity and silence shifts attention away from rational male discourses to the linguistic in-between. This might also be the case in the two adaptations; but we have to bear in mind that both adaptations are the work of a male director, who could be trying to emphasize women's marginal position in a patriarchal society. Yet perhaps we should not be too critical: Cellan Jones's representation of women is very different from the kind of images that were characteristic of the majority of British film and television productions of the late 60s and early 70s. Sue Harper has argued that the film industry in particular was "in no position to respond to the changes in women's lives and consciousness" that were happening at that time, on account of "the industry's penury and cultural decline".

Many low-budget films which posited a radical view of women were either abandoned due to lack of money, or given very limited distribution. Consequently most female roles tended to be confined to familiar stereotypes: the patient wife, the harridan, the sex-object. I have shown elsewhere how The Nightcomers, Michael Winner's meditation on The Turn Of The Screw, can be seen as a response to the perceived 'threat' of feminism by depicting Miss Jessel as a sex-starved spinster who cannot resist Quint, even though she finds him repulsive.

While Isabel, Charlotte and Maggie appear to subject themselves to patriarchal authority, even if (in Charlotte's case) this involves a repression of her sexual desires, their refusal to explain themselves suggests some kind of repudiation of masculine values. Just like the readers of James's novels, viewers have to form their own interpretation of events, asking the same kind of questions, and reaching the same kind of tentative conclusions as the characters themselves. Like Bob Assingham, we might find our judgements disproved by events. Cellan Jones's view of James's novels was later articulated by critics of the 90s.

Alfred Habegger's "The Fatherless Heroine And Female Son" stresses that James was not fond of "the sort of liberty that is manifested in institutional reform—the emancipation of women in particular". The freedom that interested him particularly with Isabel in The Portrait of a Lady was "the internal kind, where the hands remain manacled, but the spirit somehow spreads its wings". More recently Martha Banta has drawn attention to the way the ending of The Golden Bowl "seems to snap shut", but "reaches no soothing conclusions, grants no stability to its gender relationships".

Jane Gaines argued in 1984 that an ideal feminist text should seek to "destroy the codes of mainstream entertainment and ultimately replace them with a cinema that provokes thought and encourages analysis". Her ideal approach was Brechtian-inspired, based on a refusal to allow audiences to identify with characters, and thereby provoke them into critical analysis of what unfolds before them. Cellan Jones's Portrait of a Lady and The Golden Bowl do not go that far; but by permitting the female protagonists to leave certain things unexplained, and thereby undermining the sense of closure in the endings, he prompts us to consider the limitations of mainstream classical narrative.

Both The Portrait of a Lady and The Golden Bowl are very much products of a particular period in British television history, with their studio sets, restrained costumes, and rather stilted visual style oscillating between medium shot and close-up. This essay has sought to suggest that this was deliberate, prompted partly by budgetary restrictions, and partly by the desire to make the viewer listen to as well as observe what took place on screen. In Alistair Cooke's view Henry James's "calm and wary analysis of the emotions of people" was "just what the small screen craves". Pulman and Cellan Jones stressed this in their adaptations, by showing how "television is not so much a miniature theatre as a powerful microscope for scanning the emotions concealed under gestures so small as a licked lip... or a defensive chuckle". At the same time both adaptations demonstrated how feminism had begun to penetrate mainstream television drama in the late 60s and 70s. The directors and writers might still be overwhelmingly male (and remained so in British television for another decade to come) but at least they were prepared to acknowledge that women might have a different way of interpreting events around them. The BBC producer Irene Shubik complained in 1970 that "one of the most disappointing things" about television drama at that time was "that if you try to do anything at all off the beaten track nobody seems to want to understand or know". I suggest that the very opposite was true; that directors like Cellan Jones explored the limits of the genre in an attempt to comment on gender relations of the period.

Chapter 14

Critical Essays

Observing Femininity: Peter Bogdanovich's Daisy Miller

Since its release in June 1974, Peter Bogdanovich's film of Henry James's Daisy Miller has attracted considerable critical interest. Opinions on its first release varied from qualified enthusiasm ("With middling expectations... I stayed to like Daisy Miller"), to intense dislike ("it's a historical film bereft of any feeling for history, and a literary adaptation that reveals a fine contempt for literary subtlety"). The film's reputation has improved somewhat over the last quarter of a century; by 1996 critics such as Brian MacFarlane argued that it should be treated on its own merits as a "drama of restricted consciousness" filtered through Winterbourne's point of view, and not simply as an "inferior" adaptation of James's nouvelle. Philip Horne has congratulated Bogdanovich on his handling of the material "with classic Hitchcockian precision... as though it were a thriller", while in the most recent essay on the subject, David Cross congratulates Bogdanovich on "his attempt to 'imply certain things that leaves unimplied' ".

In this essay, I want to consider Bogdanovich's Daisy Miller in relation to the principal debates over the representation of gender in the cinema, which emerged at the time of the film's release, and which retain their importance today. These debates focus on two specific issues — firstly, that women are expected to conform to a certain number of pre-determined roles; and secondly, that they have largely been transformed into passive objects for male viewing pleasure by male movie-makers. On the one hand, Daisy Miller suggests that Daisy's opportunities for self-expression are limited by her social circle (who expect her to observe certain "lady-like" standards of behavior) and by Winterbourne, who continually treats her as an object of his gaze. On the other hand Daisy resists such attempts to constrain her through sheer vitality and a determination to find new means of self-expression. Winterbourne may envisage her as a romantic heroine; cinema-going audiences are encouraged to respond to her very differently.

Some of the material in this part of the essay has also been covered by David Cross in his recent work on the film; his main interest lies in determining whether Bogdanovich has found an appropriate means to convey "Jamesian themes" and "the novella's tragic tones". My purpose is rather to suggest that Bogdanovich's point of view is limited by the conventions of the mid-1970s Hollywood film. Winterbourne remains at the center of the film's consciousness: many sequences end with him continuing to gaze while the other characters leave the frame. Daisy's resistance might encourage the audience to identify with her, but she ends up "paying" for her crusade with her life — in other words, conforming to the stereotype of a femme fatale. Joan Mellen observed in 1975 that this was a characteristic strategy of Hollywood films of the time:

When women cease to be "pure" in these films, that is, dependent and demure, they forfeit the protection given to domesticated women... After all, goes the accepted if unstated premise, she — the "free" woman — only gets what she deserves.

It was not until the late 1990s, when gender identities were perceived as more fluid, that a Jamesian heroine could successfully transcend such conventions, as witnessed in films such as Agnieszka Holland's Washington Square.

Following three enormous commercial successes (The Last Picture Show, What's Up Doc?, and Paper Moon), Bogdanovich decided to make a film which might not find too much favor with the movie-going public, but which appealed to him personally as an interesting subject. Originally he had wanted to film John Galsworthy's The Apple Tree, but changed his mind when he failed to obtain the rights. Having visited Rome in 1969, he had become intrigued by "the whole idea of an Italian versus American background", which prompted him to film Daisy Miller (quoted in Harris 1990: 160). James's story also appealed to Bogdanovich because it provided a starring vehicle for Cybill Shepherd — his current partner — and gave him the chance to reconsider the ways in which women were perceived in Hollywood films. Daisy Miller was an attractive personality for Bogdanovich — "a symbol of the vitality and life [characteristic of] the New World", who wanted to remain independent by refusing to conform to the expectations of the Euro-American "old world."

The finished film demonstrates how difficult it is for her to find opportunities for self-expression. Much of the action is filtered through Winterbourne's consciousness, as he observes Daisy or is photographed in such a way that we seem to be looking over his shoulder. In one sequence Winterbourne, down left of frame, with back of head to camera, looks up at Daisy who faces the camera in close-up as he tells her "I'm puzzled if you want to know", and his gaze is directed at her face for clues about how to "read" it. In another scene written especially for the film she is shown enjoying herself at the piano with Giovanelli at the Millers' hotel. Winterbourne enters and sits down on a red velvet chair, while Daisy sings two songs "Pop Goes the Weasel" and "Maggie", framed against the bright sunlight of the window. His expression, serious at first, melts into one of pleasure as he listens to her. She represents a vision of loveliness, both for him and the spectators; it is part of his tragedy that he is unable to express his feelings.

Such sequences represent Daisy as fundamentally passive, an object to be molded according to other characters' whims. At Chillon Castle, Winterbourne, "a man of imagination and... sensibility", looks at Daisy's "white dress and, on the great staircase, her little, rapid confiding step" and "felt as if there was something romantic going forward". Mrs. Walker — described in the nouvelle as "a very accomplished woman" — advises Daisy to refrain from walking with Giovanelli in the Pincio, to avoid being "talked about" or worse still, being considered "a very reckless girl" by her peers. The camera focuses on her face, then cuts to a two-shot of Daisy and Winterbourne, as Daisy asks "Does Mr. Winterbourne think that, to save my reputation, I ought to get into carriage?". After a few moments, Bogdanovich cross-cuts between Winterbourne, Mrs. Walker, Daisy and Winterbourne once again, implying that this represents an attempt to subjugate Daisy to the demands of polite society.

Later on, Winterbourne talks with his immediate contemporary Charles a character especially created for the film, who expresses many of the opinions expressed by James in reported speech ("these shrewd people [Winterbourne's acquaintances] had quite made up their minds that she was going too far"). Winterbourne's and Charles's dialogue shows their willingness to pass judgement on her, especially when she is not there to defend herself:

CHARLES: She's certainly pretty.

WINTERBOURNE: Yes, she's a mystery. I can't decide whether she's really reckless or really —

CHARLES: Innocent?

WINTERBOURNE: Yes — I suppose.

CHARLES: Well, no one can say you aren't gallant. I hear she's about all hours with that Italian and not always in the most refined surroundings.

WINTERBOURNE: Maybe she's just an American girl and that's that.

CHARLES: All right. What do you say we both go back to Geneva this summer?

WINTERBOURNE: Well, it's a hopeless puzzle anyway, and if there's anything I've missed about her, it's too late now. She's obviously carried away with Giovanelli.

CHARLES: I don't think you've missed a thing —

However, there are moments when Daisy seeks a more active involvement in the action. In James's nouvelle, the visit to Chillon provides an opportunity for the narrator to observe ironically that "Miss Miller's observations [on the castle] were not remarkable for logical consistency". Bogdanovich and his co-screenwriter Frederic Raphael change the emphasis of this scene with some newly-written dialogue that shows Daisy subverting Winterbourne's efforts to instruct her in local culture. Her insistent chatter reduces him, in John C.Shields's phrase, to "a panting, fondling puppy":

DAISY: Oh, what an awful hole!

WINTERBOURNE: It's called an oubliette.

DAISY: That's French.

WINTERBOURNE: That's right. Comes from the word oublier, which means to forget. They used to put a man down there and throw away the key.

DAISY: Do you have any brothers and sisters?

WINTERBOURNE: No, I don't.

DAISY: Oubliette.

At Mrs. Walker's apartment, Daisy and her mother continually reduce their hostess to virtual silence with their talk about Schenectady, Dr. Davis, Winterbourne's alleged meanness in refusing to remain at Vevey, and Daisy's intention to bring Giovanelli to Mrs. Walker's party. During this one-sided conversation, Mrs. Walker never once looks at Daisy in the face; from her expression it is clear that she disapproves, even though Daisy at the moment is blissfully unaware of this. Several critics also registered their distaste: John Simon described her as "a ponderous coquette — a verbal Lizzie Borden". By refusing to conform, however unwittingly, to the Euro-Americans' notions of polite behavior, Daisy is making her bid for freedom. She represents the new world of vitality and spontaneity; Winterbourne and Mrs. Walker, on the other hand, are victims of an identity crisis, trapped between the old and new world cultures. Daisy herself suggests at the beginning of the film that, for all his verbal sophistication, Winterbourne sounds "more like a German" than an American.

The contrast between Daisy and Winterbourne is re-emphasized later on, as the camera frames them in a two-shot while Daisy asks Winterbourne his full name. He replies "Frederick Forsyth Winterbourne", which prompts Daisy to run out of the right side of the frame, exclaiming "I can't say all that!". By refusing to stay within the frame, and participate in small talk, Daisy quite literally breaks with tradition; she resists any attempt either on Winterbourne's or the cinematographer's part to constrain her. I have already quoted the passage from the nouvelle where Winterbourne imagines that "something romantic" is developing between them; the film suggests that Daisy has a completely different view. On the Chillon ferry, the two of them are once again photographed in a two-shot as Daisy observes "You're funny". Intrigued, Winterbourne replies "Am I?"; Daisy mumbles "Uh-huh" before running out of the left side of the frame, leaving Winterbourne staring after her in astonishment. Clearly this is not how a romantic heroine should react.

Several critics praised Cybill Shepherd's attempts to convey Daisy's independent yet endearing nature. To Jonathan Baumbach she seemed a "chattering, spoiled princess", when compared to the Europeanized Americans. Yet this is part "of her peculiarly American innocence". The Movietone News reviewer Kathleen Murphy discussed Shepherd's interpretation in detail, drawing attention to her "direct and unshrinking" glance that so disturbed those who wished to manipulate her. This was part of the actress's "self-absorbed innocence... expressed so naturally since her modeling days". In a 1983 book Barry Putterman called Shepherd's Daisy "untutored [in European manners] but emotionally incisive".

However, the structure of the film also suggests that Daisy's bid for freedom is little more than an illusion. In a seminal essay, written in 1973 and published two years later, the British film-maker Laura Mulvey drew a distinction between the representation in mainstream Hollywood cinema of "woman as icon" and the active male figure who "controls events... The male protagonist is free to command the stage, a stage of spatial illusion in which he articulates the look and creates the action". In this construction, the female is "isolated, glamorous, on display, sexualised". Mulvey uses psychoanalysis to justify this distinction; for the male unconscious, woman represents a danger, her lack of a penis implying a threat of castration and hence a lack of pleasure.

There are two means to avert this threat — fetishistic scopophilia, or building up the physical beauty of the object, transforming it into something satisfying in itself; or voyeurism, asserting control and subjugating the guilty person — normally the woman — through punishment or forgiveness. Mulvey elaborates her argument with references to Vertigo and Rear Window.

Like Hitchcock, Bogdanovich makes use of both strategies in Daisy Miller; this comes as no coincidence, given the fact that he is a cinephile, whose film-making style has been heavily influenced by classic Hollywood directors. In interviews Bogdanovich compared Winterbourne's condition to that of James Stewart's paralyzed state at the end of Vertigo; he remains a voyeur, unable to engage with people on a personal level. Thomas Harris suggests that this is part of Bogdanovich's "distanced approach ", which suggests that "merely looking is no substitute for the real thing". This would seem to be the case in another scene which is not in the nouvelle, where Daisy and Winterbourne watch a Punch and Judy show. Bogdanovich intercuts between close-ups of Winterbourne staring at Daisy, and Daisy's face in profile, her white bonnet, blonde hair and delicate features illuminated by the sun. Winterbourne gives a small smile; Daisy smiles back, and turns her head once again towards the show. Winterbourne essays another glance; but this time it is returned by an unnamed woman coming towards him from the distance. Once again his reluctance to openly declare his feelings leads to disappointment.

However, Winterbourne is not as passive a figure as Harris would have us believe. James's nouvelle ends with an ironic comment on Winterbourne, who has returned to Geneva, from whence came a report that he is " 'studying' hard — an intimation that he is much interested in a very clever foreign lady". Clearly Daisy's death does not deter him from pursuing another socially advantageous alliance. The film omits this coda altogether, and ends with Winterbourne alone in the cemetery after Daisy's burial. As the camera draws away from this solitary figure, who gradually fades into a stark bright white nothingness, the song "Maggie"—first heard when Daisy was sitting at the piano with Giovanelli is played on a harmonica. On the one level, this sequence reiterates the theme of lost love; how Winterbourne cannot break his social shackles. On another level, the use of this music recalls Winterbourne's idealized vision of Daisy playing the piano, framed against the sunlit window – suggesting once again that even after her death, he is attempting to minimize her potential "threat" to his masculine identity through fetishistic scopophilia. Eric Birdsall suggests that "old Winterbourne has learned a painful lesson" in the last scene of the film, but the fact that he is the last person to be seen on the screen indicates precisely the opposite. Bogdanovich persistently controls the image in order to demonstrate how Winterbourne clings to patriarchal authority in his efforts to control Daisy. No doubt she would respond to the director in the same way as to Winterbourne ("You're too stiff", "too imperious").

Before blaming Bogdanovich for his reluctance to allow Daisy to elude the male gaze, even in death, we should consider more closely the socio-historical context in which the film was produced. He enjoyed his greatest success at a time when the so-called "Movie Brats" came to prominence — a new generation of cine-literate directors who were either film school graduates, and/or had served their apprenticeship in television. At the forefront of this group were Francis Ford Coppola, Brian DePalma, Martin Scorsese, John Milius, George Lucas and Steven Spielberg. Many of them were aware of auteur theory and of film history in general; and aspired to become auteurs themselves, working within the industry but at the same time establishing their individual personae. Lucas observed in an interview that they were wresting power from the studio chiefs:

We're the pigs... We are the ones who snuff out the truffles. You can put us on a leash, keep us under control. But we are the guys who dig out the gold.

For a while it seemed as if this claim was true, with the auteurists achieving financial success with one film and subsequently being given carte blanche to pursue projects of their own. Coppola's subsequent success was built on The Godfather Lucas's on American Graffiti and Star Wars, and Bogdanovich's on What's Up, Doc? and The Last Picture Show (which occupied numbers 4 and 6 of the 1972 list of top box-office hits). Daisy Miller itself was made by the Director's Company — a joint venture set up by Bogdanovich, Coppola and William Friedkin (whose main success was The Exorcist). Following the box-office failure of Daisy Miller the venture collapsed.

But just how much leeway did this generation of directors have to create films of their own? One inescapable fact remained: despite their pretensions to autonomy, their reputation depended on continued box-office success. Those who tried too hard to create unusual, personal films became marginalized: Robert Altman was a famous example with his work after McCabe and Mrs. Miller. The majority of directors respected the kind of structural conventions which had become part of the classical Hollywood narrative. Daisy Miller fits securely into this tradition, with its unified narrative in which a cause leads to an effect, and that effect becoming a cause for another effect, creating an unbroken chain across the film. At its simplest level, the chain might include Daisy's refusal to ride in Mrs. Walker's carriage, which results in her being excluded from the Euro-Americans' social circle, prompting her to walk at night in the Colosseum, which leads to her death. The screenplay also assigns each character a particular set of traits; the spectators' impressions of such traits lasts throughout the film as the characters behave consistently. Winterbourne is the voyeur; Daisy the social misfit.

In the early 1970s, conventional Hollywood wisdom dictated that the "Women's Movement" simply did not exist; there were only individual women who felt personally constrained. Martin Scorsese's Alice Doesn't Live Here Any More provides a good example. Alice, a widow, unsuccessfully tries to pursue a singing career, as a way of recovering her self-respect. She meets a non-oppressive man to whom she can relate on equal terms and with whom she can experience a satisfying relationship. On the one hand, the film's ending contains a certain ambiguity: we have no way of knowing whether this relationship will last, or whether it will bring Alice any lasting happiness. On the other hand, the ending also suggests that women have no need to seek independence, so long as there are strong protective males around to look after them. Their search for independence is accordingly reduced to a gesture, "an irrational 'feminine' whim", as Robin Wood suggests.

Bogdanovich's Daisy Miller proposes a similar point of view. Because Daisy refuses Winterbourne's protection, her desire for self-expression, for all its superficial attractiveness, remains nothing but a dream. In spite of his enthusiasm for her as an American breathing new life into a stale Euro-American society, Bogdanovich ends up by depicting her as a victim of her own stubbornness.

Even if he had been interested in current literary criticism of James — and there is no evidence to suggest that he was (in one interview he admitted that he was "making a movie... And whether or not I put in the movie what James means to say with the story doesn't really concern me") — he would have found that most interpretations depicted Daisy as a victim either of her own self-will, or of her inability to adjust to Euro-American society. Lyall Powers upbraided Daisy for refusing to accept Winterbourne's "friendly and unselfish advice" which precipitates her downfall: "He condemns the American failure to adopt expressive manners intelligently, and points out the folly of believing that a good heart is readily visible to all". Charles Thomas Samuels's The Ambiguity of Henry James took a different view. Daisy's behavior was "ambiguous" for the male observer at least; a "baffling mixture of innocence and seductiveness". Winterbourne yearns for an ideal world, free of ambiguity, where "love was perfectly innocent and sex benign"; because Daisy does not fit the roles he prescribes for her, he "literally kills... in an effort to purify her". It was not until the late 1970s that a fully-fledged feminist analysis of James emerged, with the publication of Judith Fetterley's "The Bostonians: Henry James's Eternal Triangle".

Since Daisy Miller opened in 1974 there have been

considerable shifts of opinion, both in the way women are perceived on the screen, and how it might affect one's reading of the film. Laura Mulvey herself wrote in a 1983 essay that "the either/or binary pattern" she used in her earlier work "seemed to leave the argument trapped within its own conceptual frame of reference". She proposed instead a model derived from the Bakhtinian notion of the carnivalesque, in which women could occupy a space "between silence and speech, the terrain in which desire almost finds expression"... could provide the basis for change". Other commentators have argued that the fetishization of the female body has the potential for producing the alternative pleasure of a masochistic relationship between the male moviegoer/voyeur and the female star. As this bond refuses the symbolic power of the father, masochism challenges established gender and sexual differences: the female star represents a power found in performance which transforms the pleasure and control of the male gaze (McDonald 1998: 189-90).

From this point of view, Winterbourne in James's nouvelle can be thought of as being involved in "a motion picture of his own life", in which he has retreated from the world of male competition, where Daisy is placed on a series of romantic pedestals of his own making. After her death, he looks at the "raw protuberance" of her grave "among the April daisies" — which according to one critic "suggests a swelling in two ways ironic. As a female swelling, it is an image of death in the place of pregnancy... As a phallic protuberance, it suggests death's cause and Winterbourne's stiff loss [of masculinity]".

Such views, I would suggest, were beyond the scope of Bogdanovich's film, which should be seen as an attempt to deal with some of the profound social changes of the time. On the one hand it uses James's nouvelle to deal with issues of women's rights, suggesting that they are often ignored. On the other hand, the liberalism of this message is contradicted by the suggestion that however justifiable or attractive their cause might be, women should continue to participate in patriarchal narratives. This I suggest is the consequence of Bogdanovich making his film in a Hollywood trying to accommodate a new generation of directors, yet determined to maintain the conventions — particularly concerning the representation of its male and female stars — on which its reputation had been built over the previous half-century. Douglas Kellner suggests that during the 1970s Hollywood film, "like society, was very much a contested terrain, with the future of society and culture up for grabs". Bogdanovich's Daisy Miller offers an example of one director's response.

Ghosts at the Windows: Shadow and Corona in The Ambassadors

Toward the end of The Ambassadors, accounting for his previous blindness to the commonplace truth about Chad and Marie's "attachment," Strether explains to Maria Gostrey: "`Of course I moved among miracles. It was all phantasmagoric'". To "phantasmagoric" we might add "phantasmic," "ghostly." James calls Marie de Vionnet an "apparition". The medium in which she floats is soft as a ghostly sigh, as soft and tantalizing as phosphorescence. Or, again, we might say it is like the light of Paris. In that light—"dear old light," says Miss Barrace—one sees "what things resemble", but we are not sure we see what they are. One night Lambert Strether waits, alone, "at the witching hour," asleep to one reality, of essential concern to him, but awake to another: "the great flare of the lighted city". He is under a spell, and for some time has been under a spell. "Ghosts" hover, metaphors of the doubleness in Strether's experience and in our experience of that experience: light-filled, wondrous, floating, yet dark and mysterious—dazzling.

Strether's awakening to his own inward Europe is what has thus set him afloat. At Gloriani's garden-party, Strether first confronts European possibility in all its richness and risk. The air swarms with phantasms, an "assault of images," a "sense of names in the air, of ghosts at the windows, of signs and tokens, a whole range of expression, all about him, too thick for prompt discrimination". He gives himself up to the flood. With "frequent instinctive snatches at the growing rose of observation," he surrenders himself to the flow of "scent and colour," ready to "bury his nose even to wantonness". Ghosts, like coronas, come from the eclipse of light. A shadow produces a shadow, in reverse polarity—light out of darkness. With a blink of the camera eye, the polarity reverses again, to negative, and darkness comes out of light. The ghost, like the corona, is in the eye of the beholder, a blurring at the edge of definiteness and at the edge of perception, inherently unstable, ready to reverse itself or disappear at every blink of double consciousness.

Hard outlines and definiteness are the antithesis of the ghostly. In The Ambassadors, our first hint of perceptual blurring comes at the outset when Strether moves, almost as if in a dream, to rejoin Maria Gostrey in the hotel garden. His "sense of himself" becomes oddly "disconnected from the sense of his past". He has all along had a "double consciousness", but now it becomes double with a difference. The palpable starts to shade into the impalpable. As he walks across the "small smooth lawn" toward Maria, the hard edges of both selfhood and perception soften, blur, and flow, setting him afloat, disconnected—"launched" into "the watery English sunshine". We too, as readers, caught up in Strether's consciousness, begin to float.

In the midst of this long, weltering paragraph, James takes us back five minutes. Strether, upstairs in his room, preparing for his tryst with Maria, makes "a sharper survey... than he had for a long time been moved to make" of the Actual, himself. Its solidity dissolves mysteriously into "elements of Appearance" in a "dressing-glass that struck him as blocking further, so strangely, the dimness of the window". Struck? With this eclipse of light we find ourselves struck with word after word. "Appearance," "window," and "dressing-glass" are words about light, but they have shadows, penumbras of carefully, even fastidiously, attenuated suggestion, suggestion that we are entering a world where objects, words, and perceptions vibrate in an elastic web. Ostensibly, "Appearance" here signifies the Actual, what is visible, solid, and inelastic: a closed, Woollett window. But capitalized by James it suggests the opposite: a window open to the illusory.

The word becomes a looking glass, a perhaps Hawthornian mirror, dimming the apparent window but opening another, onto perilous seas of what moves, trembles, and melts, so that "what seem all surface one moment seem all depth the next".

Now, as Maria Gostrey waits in the garden, drawing on her "singularly fresh soft and elastic light gloves," eyeing Strether, the gloves stretch in one's consciousness, all surface one moment, all depth the next, as a sign of the eternal female and of European flexibility, waiting to draw him in. In this scene, Maria is the self-assured, competent one. No wonder Strether, half-seriously, professes to be afraid of her. As she waits—waiting being what she does supremely well—she strokes her gloves smoother, professionally, appraisingly, giving him "the time he appreciated." Hesitating, he fumbles with his overcoat "to gain time"—in one of those marvelous, lingering, page-long Jamesian moments—as if rummaging in his subconscious "for something, possibly forgotten." The overcoat is actual, not even symbolic, but it is also one of those "elements of Appearance" that he has just brought under "a sharper survey," as if to find out what it is. He is experiencing, "so strangely," double consciousness; there is something there that he cannot put his fingers on, or in. He is clinging to the solid, to what he owns, stroking it, delaying his encounter with the shadows, just as a minute later he clings absurdly to his card, his own identity card, momentarily forgotten.

Well might he cling to it, for he is about to undergo a sea-change into someone else. Strether has "faced every contingency but that Chad should not be Chad", every contingency but that Strether should turn out not to be Strether. The Actual—himself—is in danger of being no longer there. Strether is stepping through the looking glass into a world where nothing adds up; everything multiplies and divides—images, meanings, truths, identities. The air in Chester is alive with doubleness, with double entendres. Maria's "expensive subdued suitability" is an essential aspect of her appeal, suggesting what can be counted on—"a perfect plain propriety" —but also its shadow-opposite, her dangerous desirability. Her very substantialness suggests to Strether that the substantial is giving way beneath him and that he is falling. She "comfortably" says, "`I think... you trust me,'" and he replies, "`I think I do!— but that's exactly what I'm afraid of. I shouldn't mind if I didn't. It's falling thus in twenty minutes so utterly into your hands.... nothing more extraordinary has ever happened to me.'" She says, alluringly, "`That means simply that you've recognized me—which is rather beautiful and rare'". Like a sybil in a cave, a shadowy, glinting "pirate's cave" as it turns out, she says, "`there's nothing I don't know'". A page later she demands, "`Will you give yourself up?'" and he replies, "`If I only could!'" She presses in: "`But you want to, at least?'" and he answers, "`Oh unspeakably!'".

Of course, they are not talking love but only talking about Woollett's and Strether's inability to loosen up and enjoy, yet if these quotations seem, out of context, to come from a love scene, that is precisely what James intended: to suggest the dynamic interaction of image and shadow without "stating." Those who, like Arnold Bennett, thrust aside The Ambassadors without finishing it, because of what Bennett called its "very considerable absence of passionate feeling", are missing out on a pervasive undercurrent of sensuousness in this novel that is all the more effective for its being simultaneously suggested and withheld, after the fashion of Emily Dickinson's "goblin bee that will not state its sting."

James, as he tells Hugh Walpole, refuses to do anything "so foul and abject as to `state'". For a man whose art took the form of dictating words to the sound of a clacking typewriter, James makes capital use of silences. One of the ways James keeps meanings dynamic is by creating shadows, resonances between the words—by "playing with the silence," to use his phrase from "The Altar of the Dead". James's ambiguity and significant silences have always annoyed some readers, but, I would contend, he can fascinate us most when he does not "state." It is the same with metaphorical ghosts as with "real" ones: people recoil from them yet pursue them for the withheld knowledge they are presumed to have. In story after story (The Turn of the Screw, "The Figure in the Carpet," "The Aspern Papers," "The Altar of the Dead," "The Beast in the Jungle,"

The Sacred Fount) protagonists fixate upon "ghosts," upon knowledge withheld. James withholds things from us deliberately from an occasional "ghostly" pronoun antecedent, to the tantalizingly absent boat scene that "should" have highlighted The Bostonians, to the question of what will happen to Strether, Chad, and Marie after the end of The Ambassadors.

This Jamesian habit of withholding meanings produces in some readers an anxiety, a desire to penetrate the veils. But the "signs and tokens" are "too thick," too profuse, for "prompt discrimination." Each light, each token, is associated with a shadow-opposite. Throughout The Ambassadors these thematic oppositions or polarities thicken the air: the stated/the withheld, light/shadow, sound/silence, innocence/experience, America/Europe, nature/art, past/present, fullness/emptiness, substantialness/insubstantialness, floating/sinking, actuality/appearance, security/insecurity, identity/non-identity, presence/absence.

In the Gloriani garden scene, for example, we encounter several of these polarities, including the past/present one. The phrase "nursery of young priests" shows James's way of releasing energy by an association of opposites—in this case youthful innocence and, for Strether, forbidden fruit: Catholic tradition. Gloriani's genius and "deep human expertness," which flashes upon aging but still-innocent Strether in the present moment, has been wrought like iron, by struggle, through "time" and "consecration." Strether contrasts young Bilham's still-present chance to "live" with his own failure to have done so. In the present moment there is a flicker of sunlight, "scattered shade," Gloriani's dazzling smile, chapel bells, a background hum of talk, and a twitter of "bird-haunted trees." As we wait in the garden with Strether, we expect brilliant conversation from Madame de Vionnet and the other European sophisticates; what we are perhaps more conscious of in the event is a shadow-opposite that James dramatizes but does not state: silence, their almost ignoring him. The measure of Strether's American innocence against Gloriani's European experience is that Strether asks himself, after

Gloriani "drop" him, whether "he had passed," since "he had been tested".

In a polarity, says Richard Hocks, opposites are "interpenetrating" rather than "juxtaposed" as in a dichotomy. Polarities are dynamic. As Owen Barfield says, explicating Coleridge's principle of polarity, "Where logical opposites are contradictory, polar opposites are generative of each other—and together generative of new product". When the sun is covered by its polar opposition, darkness, a new product seems to be generated: ghostly rays of light shoot out across the darkness like a thin veil. Reading The Ambassadors without smoked glasses, our eyes dazzle. The trees are "bird-haunted," our eyes assaulted by images. The opposites do not stand still; they are evanescing—endlessly complicating the work of those who think, with R. W. Stallman, that the critic's job is "to resolve ambiguities." My contention is that to read The Ambassadors we must do as Strether did: we must float with, not fight, the flow; we must relax into the tensions of opposites. We must accept a multiplicity that cannot always be resolved into a simplicity. We have to go with the ghosts.

Woollett-mindedness cannot abide ghosts, and the essence of ghosts is polarity. Ghosts are impalpable or "thin," yet thronging and "thick"; they are usually absent, yet called "presences"; luminous, yet called "shadows"; knowing, yet withholding knowledge; lurking silently by windows, yet assaulting through them; evanescent, fleeting, yet quiescent and still; associated with fear and insecurity, but beyond time and change. They float, just beyond our ken.

Combined with the thick/thin polarity is the America/Europe polarity. The assaulting images in Gloriani's garden, like James's meanings, are too thin and too thick—too insubstantial to grasp and "too thick for prompt discrimination." America is solid; it is also thin. Europe is thick; it is also ectoplasmic. The mind of Strether's Woollett clings to the rock-solid, to what can be counted, counted on, and accounted for, but it is thin, rigid, conventionally moral, unimaginative. As Strether opens to the shadows and sees his Woollett certainties vaporize, he has to learn that the thickness, the density of Europe is in a different way also insubstantial. Strether has to learn what Maggie Verver learns: the force of evanescence; the evocativeness of what is withheld and thus communicated; the mind-filling penetration—the excitement and danger—of a rose, evanescing in the darkness and making "the whole air medium".

"Thick," as applied to Europe, implies profusion, many-mindedness, moral flexibility, and sensitivity to suggestion, association, nuance. "All voices had grown thicker and meant more things; they crowded on as he moved about". "'The' thing was the thing that implied the greatest number of other things". "The air quite thickened, at their [Chad and Marie's] approach, with further intimations". James says in "The Art of Fiction," "I see dramas within dramas in that, and innumerable points of view". For writers like Browning and James, truth becomes a drama with many voices. The "bright Babylons" of Paris or Rome, with their vivid present and their reverberant past, become the ideal settings in which to project—in what is called in The Sacred Fount "a magnificent chiaroscuro of colour and shadow," "a bright confusion of many things" — the Jamesian sense of the mystery, the miraculousness of life.

To live in "a bright confusion of many things" is to take risks. But to become a complete person one must become, as James says in The Golden Bowl, "filled to the brim with the wine of consciousness". If Strether is not to stagnate in the Woollett backwater, he must give himself up, float with the stream of "colour and shadow."

Critics of The Ambassadors, in contrast, have usually felt that James's imagery suggests the dangers to Strether of his floating. Reginald Abbott sees mermaids lurking to pull unsuspecting males out of boats. James Wise associates floating with being adrift, floundering, being shipwrecked. John Paterson speaks of "perilous flood" and "drowning in the dining rooms". Robert Garis says that Strether's mind ends up floating "at the mercy of its conflicts".

But water can hold us up as well as drown us. Floating suggests uncertainty and the possibility of intellectual and moral disaster, but also ease, security, savoir-faire, and mastery. At the end, Strether simply lets go of abstract "truth" and floats: "`I have no ideas. I'm afraid of them. I've done with them'". When, near the end of The Golden Bowl, Maggie Verver says to her father that she seems often "`not to know quite where I am,'" James makes the very principle of her uncertainty into a source of her security:

"the suggestion as of a creature consciously floating and shining in a warm summer sea, some element of dazzling sapphire and silver, a creature cradled upon depths, buoyant among dangers, in which fear or folly or sinking otherwise than in play was impossible...."

On the other hand, one does not simply arrive at security and stay there. James's images of the sea and of light can suggest not security but disorientation and misconception. When Strether defends himself against smugly moralistic Sarah Pocock by saying that "`an inexorable tide of light seems to have floated us into our perhaps still queerer knowledge'", the "tide of light" flows not toward singleness and certainty but toward its shadow, toward breaking apart like a breaking wave, scattering. With the sly word "seems," the passage seems a Jamesian duplicity, even without the culminating irony of Strether's comeuppance for his Will to Believe in innocence. Strether's "knowledge" is not only queer but profoundly flawed by his assumption that what appears to be (the "virtuous attachment") is the actuality.

We might then ask the Woollett question: whether, behind such slippery surfaces, there is anything to hold on to, any "really" that can withstand Miss Barrace's ironic "Oh I like your Boston `reallys'!". Ruth Yeazell says that we are in a world of "epistemological vertigo" in which "we are left to float in a world seemingly without solid fact". For Strether, what has seemed palpable dissolves, each solid thing that he reaches for becoming one of the Appearances. At the end, the novel leaves us, with Strether, asking whether what began as appearance is not the actuality after all. To call Chad's attachment "virtuous" is not so much a dissembling as a recognition that "a sufficiently ambiguous language ensures that no hasty judgments can in fact be made, that all possibilities of vision and feeling must remain open".

The problem we face in James's slippery world is that Actual and Apparent are a polarity—opposites, yet unstable opposites. When we say "actual" we mean what is real, usually with the implication of palpability. When we say "apparent" we imply that the reality is different from what is on the surface. Yet, along with little Bilham, we can say of the "virtuous attachment," "'What more than a vain appearance does the wisest of us know? I commend you... the vain appearance'". As Strether ultimately decides, the attachment is at least virtuous enough to commend it to Chad as preferable to the vain appearances of Woollett and advertising. Yet, how much do we actually know? Do we know, for example, whether little Bilham actually intended to lie when he spoke of the "virtuous attachment," or do we know "only what those words can be made to mean" ? For us, as for Strether, Actual and Apparent dissolve into each other—ghostly, as in the Chester hotel mirror.

James's trafficking with ghosts and mirrors, his way of turning solid things into smoke and light and then back again, fascinated and annoyed his brother William, who tried to dispel the ghosts and yet dallied with them. William objected to Henry's creating

"the illusion of a solid object, made (like the 'ghost' at the Polytechnic) wholly out of impalpable materials, air, and the prismatic interferences of light, ingeniously focused by mirrors upon empty space. But you do it, that's the queerness!.... For gleams and innuendoes and felicitous verbal insinuations you are unapproachable, but the core of literature is solid. Give it to us once again! The bare perfume of things will not support existence, and the effect of solidity you reach is but perfume and simulacrum."

William wanted a novel with "no twilight" and with "absolute straightness in the style". Henry wanted twilight, ambiguity, luminescence, the tug of polarity—ghosts, endlessly suggestive. To him, what William was advocating was "that two-and-two-make-four system on which all the awful truck that surrounds us is produced". It is not that Henry James disparages solidity. He wants to transform it by putting things in dynamic relationship, stressing them against all they suggest. The result is an effect of energy and reserved power, leisured loitering and flooded consciousness, constant motion and stillness—each pole reflecting its opposite dizzyingly, beyond the limits of imagination.Thus, a window in a Chester hotel room can be a mirror, drawing our eyes both outward and inward. A mirror can block the light and yet reflect it, sending us careening down the sacred river, Alph. James says of Strether's final drift toward conclusion, his world turned inside out and dazzlingly self-reflective, that there would be a "reckoning to come," that "one would float to it doubtless duly through these caverns of Kubla Khan" in "a sweetness of vain delay". "Sweetness" and "vain delay" delicately float our minds outward to the plot of the entire book, which they suggest in miniature. From there we float back again, to the point where the words suggest only a minor eddy of anxiety: a polarity inside that larger one in which exotic Eastern pleasure domes reverberate with Western final judgment. In these resonating caverns, images bubble like the sea, which receives them inexhaustibly.

The pleasure dome, Paris, is also the city of the unstated sting. In it, identities, like Jamesian meanings, are veiled, dimmed, but new ones emerge from the obscuring-revealing mirrors between which absence and presence, identity and non-identity oscillate. Persons disappear, tantalizingly, and then reappear. Repeatedly, the people Strether wants most to see are out of town, and when he finds them they are not themselves. In the beginning, the long-awaited Chad steps through a door when least expected, and he has a surprising new identity. At the end, the mysterious woman Strether has pledged to find, but hasn't, materializes. She is, after all (or perhaps she is not), La Belle Dame or La Gioconda or Miss Jessel, rising mysteriously beside the waters, and with the unstated sting of ghostly knowledge, given and yet withheld.

One evening, in lamplight and shadows, Strether waits in Chad's apartment, unaware of the transformations in store for him. Out of stillness will come motion. Chad is absent. "Lemon-coloured" novels hang "as fresh as fruit on the tree" of the forbidden. Baptiste, "subtlest of servants," whose serpent-like function is to initiate the innocent, plucks them and pushes them for Strether's perusal "within the soft circle" of "the mellowest lamplight and the easiest chair": "the novel half-uncut, the novel lemon-coloured and tender, with the ivory knife athwart it like the dagger in a contadina's hair." Outside the window shines "the great flare of the lighted city, rising high, spending itself afar," extending the soft circle of enchantment outward, like a corona. The fullness, the light of Paris, is the more compelling because mediated through vagueness and shadows: "the vague vista of the successive rooms." Through the vista and the window throng the ghosts, as earlier through the dimmed window and its obscuring mirror in Chester, England. Now, in this Paris "witching hour," Strether "invoke, in Chad's absence, the spirit of the place" and is "in possession as he never yet had been". As Strether invokes the presences, which are the more present by being dimly absent, is he in possession or is he possessed?

Part of what Strether is possessed by, of course, is Marie de Vionnet, who sums up in her person several of the more ghostly polarities. She is luminous and dwells in shadows. She is changeable almost to the point of evanescence, yet perfectly poised and still. She is "an obscure person, a muffled person one day, and a showy person, an uncovered person the next". She talks to Strether with "no movement, in all her person, but the fine prompt play of her deep young face". Praying in Notre Dame Cathedral, she has a "supreme stillness", but when she emerges from the shadows she blossoms, as if a Rembrandt painting were in motion and were being transformed into one by Renoir. The light that emanates from her flickers, like the candle-filled chapel she has just come from. When she moves, one might say she "floats," as ghosts float.

The stillness of Marie de Vionnet is what fascinates Strether. From her, he learns the essence of what James intends to convey to us in his book: the extraordinary evocativeness of what is withheld and thus communicated. To hold still is to move, and be moved. Talking with Marie de Vionnet, Strether begins to move to the unheard music: "And what he didn't say—as well as what she didn't.... It ended in fact by being quite beautiful between them, the number of things they had a manifest consciousness of not saying". The intercourse between Strether and Marie is a minuet of shadows, a matter of not saying and not even thinking. In their final scene, Marie dangles before Strether the temptation of admitting what she has sensed: how much he cares for her. Offering Strether a cup that he can take by either of its two handles, she says, "'I happen to care what you think of me. And what you might,' she added. 'What you perhaps even did.'" But at this moment, when professions of love, or perhaps tears, poise delicately on the brim of the full cup, Strether deliberately empties the cup, making the moment the more poignant, the more full: "'I didn't think anything. I never think a step further than I'm obliged to'".

What is withheld gives not only speech but vision a new dimension. At Chad's party, in the city that runs "too much to mere eye", Miss Barrace, the quintessential observer, looks around the room with her lorgnette. Doing so, she "saw in an instant all the absences that left them free". James deliberately takes us out of the noise and lights and dazzle, into the shadows, here as elsewhere giving Strether distance enough for "temporary surrenders to irony, to fancy, frequent instinctive snatches at the growing rose of observation, constantly stronger for him, as he felt, in scent and colour, and in which he could bury his nose even to wantonness."

In this imaginary rose garden, Strether's sensorium is flooded "even to wantonness," but between nose and flower there has to be air to convey the perfume. By all the absences the imagination is set free.

The tension between sensation (light, movement, sound) and absence of sensation (darkness, stillness) produces a something beyond, which we might call imagination or transcendence. The "polar opposites are generative of each other—and together generative of new product." For example, Strether loiters one day in the "long dim nave" of Notre Dame

Cathedral. His senses are tingling but his "moral" sense is entering into a sleep, a floating, that we might call an awakening. By doing nothing he is moving, beginning to perceive something beyond Woollett's worldly moralism. In the cathedral he sees how "the things of the world could fall into abeyance" for the "refugee" from the "hard outer light." Then the direction of the paragraph reverses: to stand still, to take refuge from the world, with its choices between moral polarities, is "cowardice"—"probably." But then another reversal in direction gives back what has just been taken away. This should not surprise us. As Ralf Norrman shows, such chiastic reversals are typical not only of James's sentences, paragraphs, and plots, but of his whole pattern of thinking. To Norrman, James's "antonyms are mutually interchangeable" and therefore a choice between them "does not matter," since "both are equally dislikeable".

But I find a primarily positive effect, not that of self-annihilation but of engendering, in James's collisions of opposites. In the paragraph under discussion, as elsewhere, polarity produces ghosts, luminescence, in the mind of the reader. James, having suggested that in the cathedral one dodges, begs the question, sinks into "oblivions," concludes his paragraph by associating unworldliness with a positive image: a brightness, a unity, of multitudinous lights. "Justice was outside, in the hard light, and injustice too; but one was as absent as the other from the air of the long aisles and the brightness of the many altars". In the dim cathedral the light is soft, an inner light. The interplay between brightness and dimness suggests a something beyond the polarity. The light in the darkness is like the light of a blind person, whose imagination and other senses supply what is missing. As James says in The Golden Bowl, "It was like hanging over a garden in the dark; nothing was to be made of the confusion of growing things, but one felt they were folded flowers and that their vague sweetness made the whole air their medium". Out of the stillness comes a sense of profusion. From emptiness can come fullness, from darkness light.

Strether's awakening to the mysterious polarities is

therefore an awakening to the ghosts at the windows, the ghosts that are luminous and yet are called shadows. The windows are everywhere. In Gloriani's garden, in sunlight and "scattered shade," Strether's New England consciousness is assaulted, flooded, by these light-scattering, alien presences. This garden is an ambiguous garden, a supremely civilized one, "a chamber of state" in the middle of a city, not a place of innocence at all. Its glow is not from simplicity but from a complex doubleness: both from what is present and from what is past, only imagined or remembered.

Time and tradition and ecstasy and dedication and suffering have all tempered the radiance. Gloriani's very name is a sunburst, not of morning but of late afternoon: he of the "medal-like Italian face, in which every line was an artist's own, in which time told only as tone and consecration." Strether responds, as to a touchstone, marked and moved deeply, to "the deep human expertness in Gloriani's charming smile—oh the terrible life behind it," which was "flashed upon him as a test of his stuff". In the charming, terrible garden, amidst its thronging colors, lights, and shadows, its crowded present and its historic past, emerges Marie de Vionnet, like another Beatrice Rappaccini, the most beautiful and mysterious of its unfolding blossoms.

In the garden of Europe everything multiplies: images, words, events, people. As readers, we rub our eyes. We wonder if we can we be sure of what we are experiencing. The garden of watery English sunshine, at the outset of Strether's European adventure, deepens in its sensuous "references" until all Paris blossoms as a garden in Strether's consciousness, and in ours, for we are to be made willing participants, collaborators almost, in his enlargement of vision and his seduction, his "fall" from Puritan narrowness.

In our first view of Paris, Strether wanders by the river and past the tempting bookstalls into the garden of the Tuileries. Paris is fresh-sprinkled, cheerful, filled with morning sun, redolent of spring, yet brisk and bustling and ticking like a clock. James has presented to us the multiplicity of the city, but the city has one quality of The Garden: we can give ourselves up to it, with Strether, without fear. There is no day of reckoning. The "wonderful Paris spring" and "the prompt Paris morning" and the "sprinkled smell" are innocent and bright. The phrases bounce along—"bareheaded girls with the buckled strap of oblong boxes," "thrifty persons basking betimes," "blue-frocked brass-labelled officialism of humble rakers and scrapers"— creating a mood of innocence and festival. Mingling resonantly, as at Gloriani's, are light and dark, present and past, innocence and experience, the city and the garden. The deep, black "references" of the "straight-pacing priest" are set against the "sharp ones of a white-gaitered red-legged soldier". "References" denotes both the immediate sensory impressions—the sound of boots on cobblestones, the sway of priestly black against a grey background—and also things that are absent: "recalls of things imagined". Dimly in the background, providing a musical undertow, is the "irremediable void" of the remembered palace burned by the Communards in 1871.

What is drifts away like smoke, in the imagination of Strether, into what is not. In this evocation of morning and Paris springtime, the undertow of the past, subtly preparing us for the afternoon and evening of Strether's awareness, lulls us, rather than suggesting the disaster ahead. We experience what Strether is experiencing, an enlargement of consciousness, and we become his doubles. We can "tilt back a straw-bottomed chair" with Confidence. We can let ourselves drift with Strether as he floats "unspent" up the Rue de Seine. Strether is letting himself go, becoming one of the images; and slowly, subtly, inexorably, we are being made complicit, are being drawn along with him.

"'I never think a step further than I'm obliged to'" seems to be Strether's motto. He is looking for an inner light, a level of thought and light that avoids "the hard outer light" of the practical world and is like darkness visible. In his passivity and leisurely procrastination that is yet a determined act of choice, he is merging into a background, as if he were to merge into a painting on the wall.

Later, at the turning point of the book, Strether is

described as indeed "in the picture", a particular picture, a remembered Lambinet landscape. He opens a window in his mind as if it were a picture frame, and there it is and there he is. He lets himself go, gives himself up completely to impulse—"artless enough, no doubt," artfully comments James —the impulse of a journey through the French countryside "as securely as if to keep an appointment" with the image of the Lambinet. Sure enough, when he gets off the train, completely at random, the painting stored in the imagination has rematerialized, in "the poplars and willows, the reeds and river". The painted landscape blossoms, Appearance becomes Actual, and Strether himself—finally succumbing to Maria's initial demand, "Will you give yourself up?"—surrenders to the assaulting image. Instantly, he becomes part of the picture, diffused, atmospheric, as if resolved into light and projected in bits, in discrete flecks of color. Actual becomes Appearance. What is solid has become a ghost, yet palpable for all that. James's conceit is interesting: the more Strether gives himself to nature, the more he becomes locked in the frame of art; the more he gives in to impulse and romantic illusions, the more imminent is the shattering of his illusions.

What we see shifts, depending on which way we frame it, and that is much of what The Ambassadors is about. Looked at one way, this garden of the French countryside is static, reassuring, solid as paint: "the sky was silver and turquoise and varnish". But James nests multiple Appearances like Chinese boxes. Strether is in the frame of the novel. The Lambinet is outside that frame and also inside it, inside Strether's imagination. There, matter becomes energy; the Lambinet takes dominion everywhere, like Wallace Stevens's jar in Tennessee. It mirrors the sprawl of nature and by framing it turns the Actual into Appearance, into art. Within the frame of nature that becomes art and art that becomes nature, Strether loiters, both outside and inside the Lambinet, as if in a mesmerizing, comforting, bewildering labyrinth of mirrors. Caressed by the seductive images with their "subdued suitability," a shadow of himself, he drifts "comfortably" toward conclusion, where may lurk "the thing itself," propagating images, ineluctably multiplying. Now, in the lived-in Lambinet, in the inmost imaginary garden of Xanadu, at the moment when the natural and the artificial have most merged, around a bend in the river comes the boat bearing Chad and Marie, "caught." The parasol that Marie shifts momentarily, "as if to hide her face," is as filmy and yet solid as a few scattered flecks of paint—precisely the image, the highlight of color, the "pink point in the shining scene", required to complete the perfect impression, to make nature most perfectly artistic. James's irony is perfect and complete. All is palpable. There is a real toad in the imaginary garden. Yet it evanesces, floats, and escapes. The glaring light upon the newly revealed Actual hides as much as it reveals. All is blended, compromised, in equivocations and silences.

We may think we now know the truth about Marie and Chad, but we don't; we know only the image, the surface appearance. We have never seen into their minds, their history, their hearts, as lovers of each other. Like Strether, we are excluded from what is most important about them. We are locked out of their frame of reference in which their own "references" resonate.

We now see that over this scene as over the entire book, created by the very radiance of it—and this is surely one of the most light-filled, radiant books in all literature—hang the shadows of knowing and yet not knowing. As light came out of darkness in Gloriani's garden and in Notre Dame Cathedral, now darkness comes out of light and holds it in ironic tension. We, like Strether, have learned some things about doubleness and darkness and about the limits of knowing: each frame, each perspective, each angle of vision leaves other perspectives out; each advance in knowledge creates a further darkness just beyond it. Strether says his final good-bye to Marie de Vionnet in semi-darkness, in candlelight. She is like a ghost of the past, "dressed as for thunderous times... in simplest coolest white," reminiscent of Madame Roland "on the scaffold." As Marie moves "over her great room," she is literally and figuratively a double image, "with her image almost repeated in its polished floor." Her mirrored movement becomes one of the "deep references" of the priest and the soldier. History is the shadow of her shadow. Through the windows seems to come "the smell of revolution," "the smell of blood." The reverberations have deepened. They suggest not only richness and fullness—"a whole range of expression... too thick for prompt discrimination"—but also the shadows that the adventurer risks: devastation and emptiness, the potential anarchy of the flow-state, a breakdown of the psyche, a reign of terror. Strether is assaulted, ever so delicately, so richly, so quietly, by lights and shadows, by images and ghosts.

The "gleam here and there, in the subdued light, of glass and gilt and parquet, with the quietness of her own note as the centre—these things were at first as delicate as if they had been ghostly... ". Thus, inside of his knowledge of the limitation of knowledge, Strether has achieved something else: a sense of density and evanescence, of the rich tapestry of what is and what is not—or, we might say, of what is as fascinating, fearsome, and delicate as ghosts. In Europe, Strether has understood from the beginning that he is confronting "the vast bright Babylon" —the dangerous, exotic multiplicity that has floated before the Puritan imagination for centuries.

From the beginning Strether has associated Marie de Vionnet with it: "You might confess to her with confidence in Roumelian, and even Roumelian sins," and have "a moment of wondering... what sins might be especially Roumelian". He knows that he is in mortal danger, but he is fascinated and does not run from the fire before he has experienced it fully. He discovers that Babylon, the richness, is also, strangely, the thinness. Because he does not run away too soon, he discovers at the center that this woman, Marie de Vionnet, who is so full, the flower of civilization, a ghost at the window, is "the finest and subtlest creature, the happiest apparition, it had been given him, in all his years, to meet"—and that simultaneously she is unfilled, no more than human, "a maidservant crying for her young man".

At the end, Strether will wander forth from Europe, that paradise of phantasmagoric knowledge, marked in his own person by all the devastating and redeeming polarities; he will be full of experience and empty-handed, with all the world before him—free to choose, and nothing, it would seem, left to choose from. Yet, confronting this prospect, he is at peace with himself. He has learned to live with uncertainty.

But for us as readers, the limitations placed by James on our knowledge have often led to what Keats calls an irritable reaching for certainty. We call for more light, more light. James does not say, for example, what will happen to Chad and Marie after Strether leaves Europe, yet many critics profess to know what will happen to them.

The positiveness of such claims to knowledge, the lack of allowance for ambiguity, is surprising; but taking away the Jamesian veils can be a pleasant diversion, as when Stallman demonstrates that the mysterious product of Woollett is no doubt clocks or watches. Says Stallman, "to resolve ambiguities is the critic's function". Like Waymarsh diving into the jeweler's shop or like Strether fumbling with his overcoat in the Chester garden, we itch to have something definite, something we can put our hands on or into. Then, with the sense of mystery gone, we are left with the shabby actual; we are left like Waymarsh with time on our hands, sitting in a railway car at a forward angle through the "ordeal of Europe", the ordeal of James.

Opting for definiteness, E. M. Forster writes, "... Chad will tire of the exquisite Frenchwoman, she is part of his fling; he will go back to his mother and make the little domestic article and marry Mamie". In almost the same tone of voice, Sallie Sears echoes: Chad "emerges almost unscathed from his affair: he's off, apparently without remorse, to advertising, Woollett, and if not Mamie then some other sweet young thing at home". Philip Weinstein foresees an even less moral future: "Chad's marvelous youth has been transformed into a vast arena for future infidelities and 'affairs'".

Maxwell Geismar claims that Chad has already moved on, that he "abandons without even a farewell recorded in the novel." Later in the paragraph, Geismar even gets it backwards about who is saying what in Strether and Chad's final meeting. Richard Hocks assumes that Chad's fascination with advertising constitutes a "decision to embrace" it. Peter Stowell modulates Strether's "You'll be a brute... if you ever forsake her" into "Chad is not `refined', but is a `brute'". On the other hand, Laurence Holland considers Chad's future a matter of "patent uncertainty". Dorothea Krook emphasizes that the Jamesian method is one of "ensuring that the ambiguity shall remain totally unresolved" —although she applies this principle to Strether's perception of Chad, not to Chad's final attitude toward Marie. Similarly calling attention to James's pervasive ambiguity, Yeazell voices a warning that there is a "distance between a world of simple fact and the subtle realm which most Jamesian characters inhabit," a warning that in that realm "facts are never quite as simple—or even as knowable—as Bob Assingham or William James [or E. M. Forster, I would say] would contend".

To be sure, the idea that Chad will return to Woollett can be inferred from the text, but we might ask if it is also denied by what floats above the text. If Chad's "development" is all surface without depth, if the ending is simply an ironic reversal of Strether's earlier perceptions about Chad, then Strether's voice should be there with the critics, roundly condemning Chad to the perdition of marriage and advertising. If Chad is a bounder he does not deserve Marie de Vionnet. If he is only a "cold young fornicator who is ready to move on," as Charles Samuels says, then Sarah Pocock is more than righteous, she is right. Few of us, I suspect, are ready for that surprising conclusion. Finally, if Strether is indeed clinging to a delusion—that Chad's fading love affair is worth salvaging—we will have to give up what is often taken to be the donnee of the novel, the assumption that Strether grows in moral awareness, and join Samuels in calling him a fool. These are matters of some moment, affecting our whole view of The Ambassadors.

At the end of this book James wants, I suggest, closure without finality. "Agnes Whitney Cromwell, in talking with James about The Ambassadors, was asked whether she knew what had happened to Strether, Chad, or to Miss Gostrey after the book ended. When she answered in the negative, James admitted that he did not know either." As James said in his notebooks, "The whole of anything is never told... ".

If we can relax, with James, from our forward angle, restraining our Woollett-minded desire for definite knowledge, we can relish the ambiguity and not insist on having our Boston Reallys for breakfast the next morning. If Strether does not say that his labors over Chad have been wasted, that his audacious adjuration to Chad—to be good by continuing to be "bad"—has been a waste of breath, perhaps we can remain in suspense too.

We can float with Strether a while longer, with the tide of disorienting light and accumulating shadows, can cultivate negative capability and not stretch our claims to certainty beyond the limits James sets. Floating, not swimming, is the way to savor this book. The Ambassadors sustains a delicate balance between what might be or might not be. A crude and positive striking out for shore disturbs the float, the sense of the miraculous.

"It was all phantasmagoric," says Strether at the end. The words might be applied to The Ambassadors itself. Its "solidity of specification" is beaten into an airy and delectable something by that "white-capped master-chef," James. All the absences leave us free. James gives and then takes away, takes away and then gives. Light and darkness, what is there and what is not, interacting dynamically in the imagination, result in what is beyond either—an evanescence, a halo, a mere perfume if you will, that makes the whole air its medium. It is a little like Shakespeare's evocation of the "bare ruined choirs where late the sweet birds sang."

The assertion is of an emptiness, but what we are conscious of is doubleness: a fullness and an emptiness, a movement and a stillness—the birds singing against the November sky. As we look through the mind's windows, into empty space, the shadows hover.

NOTES

- Hocks discusses, at length, in relation to The Ambassadors, only two of the particular polarities I mention, namely America/Europe and nature/art.Stallman writes, "The Ambassadors builds on contraries, contradictions, ambivalences arising from poles of opposition. Consequently, identities and scenes overlap, one image or vision impinging on another. Thus we are never in Paris but what simultaneously we are also in Woollett."

But he calls this a "device of juxtaposition", and his "poles of opposition" seem to lack either Hocks's "interpenetration" or the dynamic quality that I stress.Light/darkness in The Ambassadors has been little discussed at any length except by Schneider, who sees the light/darkness pair as a dichotomy, not a polarity, and associates darkness with evil: "But beneath the bright surface is darkness, the abyss, a moral jungle.... " He presses this so far as to say—of James's light, playful metaphor of nature as a "white-capped master-chef" that "The white cap conceals an unspeakable darkness of slavery and automatism".

- Cf. Derrida: "The activity or productivity connoted by the a of differance refers to the generative movement in the play of differences". Readers may find this similar to the dynamic interplay of polarities and the "floating" for which I argue; but floating, with its suggestions of joyous freedom and outward-moving possibility, is the antithesis of Derrida's verbal ingenuities, in which concrete reference to anything real and recognizably living is replaced by a mirage-world of highly abstract words, turning in upon themselves endlessly, "ineluctably multiplying the supplementary mediations that produce the sense of the very thing they defer: the mirage of the thing itself" (Of Grammatology 157).
- Veeder, on the other hand, relates floating to Strether's "progress toward moral mobility". Stallman writes, approvingly, "the river is the agent of life-the-unpredictable, that which upsets all theories about it".

In Defence of Henry James

Ramaswamy R. Iyer

I

This note examines certain criticisms of Henry James which have come to be uncritically accepted by many and which have a degree of influence even on admirers of HJ. I find elements of those criticisms obscurely lurking even in my thinking. This examination is therefore partly an attempt to exorcise the demon.

A widely prevalent view of HJ is that his characters lacked flesh and blood, that they did not inhabit the real world, that apart from verbal sparring nothing really happened in his novels, that he was completely oblivious of social and economic issues, that there was an absence of physicality in HJ?s work, that his late style represented a degeneration, and so on. It is not merely the middlebrows and non-intellectuals who hold such views: even intellectuals, literary critics, and many who admire him are affected to some extent by that perception. Leavis?s view of the later novels of HJ was coloured by it; Edith Wharton, a friend, admirer and benefactor, asked HJ why he suspended his characters in the void, leading to his bewildered response ?my dear, I didn?t know I had!? H.G. Wells wrote a parody of HJ. Max Beerbohm?s cartoon of HJ is well-known. HJ?s own brother William James was perhaps his most ?consistent critic, patient misunderstander." And more recently, Naipaul has described HJ as ?the world?s worst writer."

All this is of course completely wide of the mark: it represents a failure of understanding (Edith Wharton, William James) or sheer perversity or a kind of blind spot (Leavis in so far as the late novels are concerned) or plain stupidity or crassness. Henry James was a very great novelist, among the greatest in the English language. There are indeed a couple of questions that one needs to confront in relation to his work, though they do not call for a substantial qualification of the overall view of his stature expressed above. This article will go into those questions in sections IV and V.

II

Let us first take note of five aspects or dimensions of his work.

- As a novelist ? like all other novelists-he was the creator of imagined life (people, relationships, situations, developments).
- He was a self-conscious artist, theorist and technician. He was a careful planner and constructor of his novels and had a deep interest in questions of technique and craft (a narrator; a controlling 'point of view?, i.e., seeing everything through the eyes of a certain character; 'dramatic action?, i.e., making the novel come close to drama; indirection and obliquity, i.e., what is said in the dialogue being less important than what is left unsaid; and so on).
- Allied to that preoccupation with technique and craft was an exalted notion of 'the Artist? and of creativity, and mystical evocations of the Muse.
- At the heart of his work lies an acute, powerful moral vision, a deep insight into equivocation, moral shabbiness, pettiness, meanness, and evil. Conrad?s description of James as the ?historian of fine consciences,? which occurs in an elaborate tribute, may be misread by some to mean that HJ wrote only about sensitive, scrupulous, self-questioning people. That may be true of some of his characters, but he also wrote about mean, devious, unscrupulous, strategy-practising, evil people.)
- There is of course the famous change of style from the early to the late work. This is often attributed to the fact that all his later work was dictated, but one must go a bit deeper than that.

III

Let us now return to the criticisms. James was of course very different from Dickens and Tolstoy, but is it true that his characters lacked reality and substance? Think of Isabel and Madame Merle (The Portrait of a Lady), Catherine and her father Dr. Sloper, Lambert Strether in The Ambassadors, Kate

Croy (The Wings of the Dove), Charlotte Stant, the telegraphist girl, even the not so central or major characters such as Mr. Wentworth, Henrietta Stackpole, the journalist George Flack and Francina?s father Mr. Dosson, and so on. Many other names can be mentioned. All these are solid, real, credible individuals ? as real as characters in the novels of other great novelists.

Is it true that ?nothing really happens? or that there is a lack of vividness? Think of the central confrontation between Isabel and Madame Merle in The Portrait, and the several confrontations between Isabel and Osmond; or the two contrasting scenes of Graham Fielder?s encounters first with Mr. Abel Gaw and then with Mr. Betterman in The Ivory Tower. These seem to me to be among the most dramatic and vivid scenes in English literature. Those are only two examples; many more can be cited. As a matter of fact, James was particularly good at proceeding towards a dramatic climax or denouement. Leaving aside the well-known novels (Chad?s volte face in The Ambassadors, for instance, or the denouement in Washington Square), we can see this in "The Author of Beltraffio" (the death of the child) and in the smaller or lesser works such as The Reverberator, In the Cage, "The Altar of the Dead," or "The Bench of Desolation." (I must add that I am very fond of In the Cage, but I have some reservations about the last two.) To add one more example that comes to mind, think of the denouement in The Outcry.

Absence of physicality? Certainly, James did not write about genitalia or sexual intercourse or excretory functions or menstruation or sweating. However, think of What Maisie Knew: sex is a constant presence in that novel. It is also present in The Awkward Age. An even more striking example is the chapter in The Wings of the Dove where after long deferment Kate Croy has visited Merton Densher and gone. James does not specify what happened during the visit, but the vivid description of what that room comes to mean to Merton, how everything in that room stands transformed by the visit, is one of the strongest things in the novel. If that is not 'physicality? what is?

Blind to socio-economic realities? How can one possibly say that unless one forgets or deliberately ignores The Princess Casamassima? Nor was that novel an oddity or an aberration. Social realities are very much there in What Maisie Knew. Class relations are central to In the Cage. The Ivory Tower is about two bequests, and the greed and treachery that property and possessions inspire; in it we see James?s profound misgivings about the great American fortunes ("the black and merciless things that are behind the great possessions"; ?the hideously rich?; resources ?so dishonoured and stained and blackened at their very roots?).

IV

I turn now to a couple of questions that trouble me. First, I am a very great admirer of HJ, but at the risk of being considered middlebrow or a philistine, may I venture to say that his interest in the art and craft of the novel is a trifle overdone? I am not saying that his preoccupation with the formal, structural and presentational aspects was unimportant. These are indeed among his strengths, and one can admire the enormous skill with which The Awkward Age or What Maisie Knew is constructed. Structure and form have interested other novelists too (for instance, Thomas Mann?s The Magic Mountain or Dr. Faustus, Joyce?s Ulysses, practically all of Nabokov?s novels, and in particular Pale Fire). A proper appreciation of these aspects is essential to an understanding of those novels; so too with James. Nevertheless, it seems to me ? and I state this for possible contradiction by the reader ? that HJ attached a degree of importance to such questions that the reader may but need not fully share: what he referred to as ?the quantity of finish that it stows away? (a remark about The Awkward Age in his Preface to Vol. 9 of the New York Edition, 1908) seems to me less crucial to an understanding of a novel than the author might have thought.

(May I add in parenthesis that while reading James?s famous invocation to his Muse — ?causons, causons, mon bon ?.? (HJ's detached notes to The Ivory Tower, Jan. 4, 1910)—I experience a mild sense of anti-climax when it finally ends with a reference to "a little organic and effective action.") There are indeed several novels or stories of James in which form, structure and presentation are integral, ineluctable parts, and we cannot understand or properly respond to the novel or story without understanding them. However, it seems to me that this is not true of all his works: surely, taking even the later works, one can respond adequately to The Ambassadors, The Golden Bowl and The Wings of the Dove (i.e., to the characters, situations, conflicts, motivations, dilemmas, nuances, and so on) without excessive interest in form, structure and technique.

V

The second question that I need to tackle is that relating to HJ?s later style. There is indeed a problem here, but it is not a simple case of a good style degenerating into a bad one, nor is it simply a change from a taut and structured written style to a loose, flowing spoken style, the structure of which is unclear but can be brought out by reading aloud. It was a case of the evolution of a special style that best expresses the delicate probings, the nuances and slowly emerging insights, the dim perceptions developing into clear understandings, the tentative verbal formulations and indirections ending in an epiphany. It is difficult to imagine the Jamesian explorations being performed in any but the Jamesian style. While there is indeed a difference between the early style and the late style, there are similarities too: the characteristics of the late style were there in the early work, but became more pronounced and pervasive in the later work. From the beginning James was groping his way towards a style that would correspond to his content, and found it in his later novels.

Not everyone would agree with that statement. Broadly speaking, four criticisms can be-have been ? made of the late style:

- The dialogue is unrealistic; people don?t talk like this; all characters speak like Henry James.
- There is a lot of verbal sparring; the communication between the characters is indirect and oblique; what is not said matters more than what is said.

- The language is dense and incomprehensible; one has to work hard at the meaning.
- It is verbose and often highly coloured, even florid.

We cannot dismiss these points out of hand; we must consider them. Unrealistic dialogue: Jane Austen and Dickens created conversations that could have taken place in real life. The dialogues in James?s novels are not of that kind. However, that can be said of other writers as well. Think of George Eliot or Conrad or even Lawrence: are their dialogues wholly 'realistic?? Except in a few cases, dialogues in novels are not exactly like conversations in real life: they are stylized, with varying degrees of similarity to what one actually hears in the world. James?s dialogues are more stylized than most other novelists?. That by itself is not a fault.

(In painting, leaving aside abstract or non-representational painting, consider Canaletto, El Greco, Rembrandt, Goya, Velasquez, Vermeer, Turner, Reynolds, Whistler, Sargent, the Impressionists, Amrita Sher-Gil, Nandalal Bose, Jamini Roy, and so on: you have a range from photographic realism to a high degree of stylization; and even the most 'realistic? works are stylized in some degree.)

The more important point is: how characteristic is the utterance? In Shakespeare?s Macbeth, Lady Macbeth?s dialogue is not 'realistic?, but everything she says is completely true to her character: she could not have spoken in any other way and no other character could have said the things that she said. The same holds true of Cleopatra in Antony and Cleopatra. The dialogue creates a real human being. Similarly, in Eliot?s Murder in the Cathedral, the dialogue is not realistic but true to character, and creates credible personalities. Judged by this criterion, the dialogues in James are true to character at every step: they create real human beings. Their speech is theirs.

Indirection/Obliquity: This is not a defect but a necessary means used by James for his probing and exploring. There is no need to discuss this further.

Density, Difficulty: Yes, the reader has to work at the late style. Joyce was difficult too; so was Eliot?s The Waste Land when it first appeared. Once again, this is exploratory, experimental writing. This is quite clear in the case of Joyce and Eliot, but not so obvious in the case of James. He fashioned a special language for himself, but superficially it looks like conventional, even old-fashioned English. We can parse the words and analyse the sentences: they work, grammatically and syntactically. So we are misled into thinking that this is conventional English made needlessly convoluted and obscure ? in other words, bad English (as Naipaul thought it was). That is a serious error. The later novels are written in a new language developed by James using English, to express his explorations and discriminations with precision. As I said earlier, it is difficult to imagine the Jamesian explorations in any but the Jamesian style.

Verbose, Florid? That brings me to the last point. What we have here is not verbosity but deliberate excess ? a wheeling and circling towards the meaning; HJ goes round and round and then lands on the exact spot. Again, what we have in the late style is not 'highly coloured? or 'florid? (the analogy of a magician pulling out an endless stream of multi-coloured ribbons out of his mouth has been suggested by someone), but the poetic use of language. Just as Shakespeare wrote poetic drama, James evolved from the straight prose of the early works towards a poetic novel. (Let me make it clear that I do not mean 'prose poetry? of the Tagore translation kind.) A combination of surface density, relative obscurity, use of image, symbol and simile, and striking and colorful turns of phrase, gives us a prose that from time to time comes close to poetry.

A special characteristic of the late Jamesian style is that he deliberately chooses what one might call 'soft-focus? writing (it may seem fuzziness to some) which creates a dim surface through which the meaning gleams and glimmers (as he himself might have said), and then suddenly sharpens the focus and heightens the mellow light into bright luminosity. The effect is very powerful.

This is not special pleading or an apologia for the much-criticised late style. Many people ? intelligent ones ? find the style off-putting. That was clearly not James?s intention. Joyce for instance deliberately made it necessary for his readers to work hard at his writing. That cannot be said of James. He followed his Muse and wrote in a manner that would best express what he wanted to say, but he did not set out to be difficult and obscure.

e wanted a large readership and was disappointed when that did not happen. Unwittingly he erected a barrier between the readers and his writing. From the low sales of his books, and from the criticisms that he heard (not least from his brother William), he must have known the effect that his later style had on readers. However, he probably did not quite realize what an effort he was demanding of his readers. Granting the need for indirectness, obliquity, circlings and wheelings, the alternation of soft and sharp focus, perhaps he could still have cut the prolixities and reduced the obscurities to some extent; but he did the opposite when revising his works for the New York edition. The result is that many intelligent and sensitive people who might have found the later works enormously interesting are turned away by the formidable barrier of language. This is indeed a problem that cannot be glossed over.

VI

That is not the note on which to end. We must return to his greatness. Graham Greene puts him in the company of Shakespeare. Even if that seems an over-statement, it is clear enough that James is a towering figure as a novelist. To conclude on a personal note, I started reading Henry James when I was a student at Elphinstone College, Bombay, in the 1940s, have been reading and re-reading him ever since, and continue to do so in 2007.

Henry James and a 'Sense' of Place: The Modalities of Perception

By John D. Ballam
University of Bristol and Open University

In an article entitled, "Social Geometries: Taking Place in Henry James", Mark McGurl poses this amusing conundrum:

Where does fiction take place?... could, one supposes, be

said to take place anywhere an author says it does and, yet, since it is fiction, could as easily be said to take place nowhere at all.

Either way, the apprehension of fictional realities by readers demands the existence of a framework of real time, within which sequences of perceptions may be said to occur. The management of those sequences devolves into a tripartite arrangement involving the interaction of three "senses" of perspective, belonging to the reader, the narrator and the characters themselves. For each, the possibility of ascertaining information about the existence of a "place" depends upon locating a temporal order through which contact, however limited or imagined, might occur. There are thus, three streams of time descriptive of fictional places. They are that belonging to the real time experience of the reader (holding a book as she sits in a chair); that of the narrator (who "holds" the entire story simultaneously in suspension and revelation); and that of the characters (who hold narrative events in a sequence of past-present-and-future which is, although concurrent with the narrator's, possessed of a sequence that is altogether different in kind, insofar as many aspects conforming to the narrator's perspective are either hidden, denied or simply latent. But the manner in which an author's narrative strategy allows or fosters insight into these diverse perspectives remains an interlocking one. In reading fiction, as in reading Life, we may ask, "What could he do?" "How should she have acted?" Or, with the voice of an assumed narrator, we may suggest that, "They ought to have known." Or, again, suspending disbelief, we may share the burden of choice with characters who ask, "How will I be able to survive?"

The strategy I am referring to here is one of the subtlest ones — and hence probably least consciously employed — that we possess. It is the manner in which we enable ourselves to recognize the multifarious dimensions of reality — concrete existence — through the momentary intellection of alternatives with which they compare. Thus we know a dog from a cat with virtually no pause for analysis of probabilities, yet faced with the spectacle of differentiating between a young kangaroo and a full-grown wallaby, most of us would require some time to arrive at an answer. "It could be a kangaroo..." And the vital factor I wish to isolate is that moment of suspension which occurs in narrative time when figures (character or narrator) enforce a pause to embrace the essential indeterminacy of perception. I have called this vital, because what happens in that interval is a conditioning of expectation that encourages a limiting of fictional realities, while simultaneously confessing that such limits are arbitrary. The key to understanding this process lies in the author's use of modal verbs.

There aren't actually many modal verbs in English: can, could, dare, may, might, must, need, shall, should, will, would and the modal constructions, be able to, ought to and be allowed to. And my focus upon Henry James is taken in the belief that James is peculiarly alert to the range of options available to the sensitive mind as it comes into the proximity of experiences with which it has little to condition its expectations. For this reason, James is singularly cautious in offering single, or definitive options for his characters' reading of their circumstances. To highlight some of the differences in James's approach, I have chosen two texts wherein the expository style can be seen to be contrasting, not least through the different stances to authenticity proposed by their different genres. These texts are English Hours (published in a revised form and as a collection in 1905, although largely written in the 1870s), and What Maisie Knew.

The fundamental difference between these two books is that What Maisie Knew is a novel, and English Hours is a collection of travel articles about England largely written for American magazines. Yet while one occupies that indeterminate place that McGurl has postulated, and the other the historical world of James and his contemporaries, in both the characters and narrators are disinclined to trust the veracity of the sensory data they are presented with. In English Hours James finds many impressions that hover about him, refusing either to be fixed or to admit the possibility of distinct recognition. In "Wells and Salisbury" he writes, "the place seems always to savour of a Sunday afternoon", "it seems densely embroidered by the chisel", "the general atmosphere... seemed peculiarly luminous and sweet", "the mild grey seventeenth-century deanery and the other dwellings... seem to reflect in their comfortable fronts the rich respectability of the church"; and in Glastonbury, he says "a savour of hooves and hide seemed to accompany me"; while in a very strange construction — and my own favourite — he says of Salisbury cathedral spire, "it grew to seem to me the least bit banal". In every case, something seems to be "true," and yet, as James admits, may just as easily not be so. Probably central to James's method here is the emphasis he betrays in that last passage, whereby he acknowledges the filtering process of recollection. That is, the making of realities in the mind is a gradual process, involving delay and re-structuring, while the worth of immediacy in sensory impression is something akin to Walter Pater's "transcendental materialism," which conceives of surfaces (vision, touch, sound, smell) as the meeting-place of spirit and matter. Within James's prose, this is figured as a perpetual re-embodiment of the narrator/character within the context of their own imagined sense of places, or the artist refashioning him/herself with every new work of art and its incorporation into consciousness. The metaphor James frequently uses to explain this process is the relative positions of audience and stage. Or, as he writes of Canterbury cathedral, "I can, in my fear to pretend to dabble in the esoteric constructional question... speak only of the picture, the mere builded scene." Thus, like Pater, and like his brother William James, it is not the facts of the situation which hold any interest for James, rather it is the uniquely gained truth of an individual perception, however much such a perception may resemble the flattened perspective of a post-Impressionist canvas. (This comparison is made by McGurl.) Or to extend this spatial metaphor, the quest for a truly individual perception represents the search for a Jamesian "centre of consciousness" where limitation will be understood in the modalities of perception; where modality represents the unknowableness at the centre of character even as it posits its own relation to either real or fictional externals. Even beyond these considerations, modality can be seen to mediate between narrator and reader. In one of the earliest articles from English Hours, James writes of "the brave little walls of Chester":

There could be no better example of that phenomenon so delightfully frequent in England — an ancient property or institution lovingly readopted and consecrated to some modern amenity. The good Cestrians may boast of their walls without a shadow of that mental reservation on grounds of modern ease which is so often the tax paid by the romantic; and I can easily imagine that, though most modern towns contrive to get on comfortably without this stony girdle, these people should have come to regard theirs as a primary necessity. For through it, surely they may know their city more intimately than their unbuckled neighbours — survey it, feel it, rejoice in it as many times a day as they please. The civic consciousness, sunning itself thus on the city's rim and glancing on the little swarming towered and gabled town within, and then at the blue undulations of the near Welsh border, may easily deepen to delicious complacency.

"The good Cestrians may boast" (that is, they ought and probably do); and "I can... imagine"; although "these people should have come to regard theirs as a primary necessity" (but then, perhaps they haven't); "they may know their city more intimately"; "the civic consciousness... may deepen to delicious complacency" (but just as easily may not). In any case, the reality of the matter is an open question.

If this is beginning to seem a trifle pedantic, then consider the alternative. In his article, "Abbeys and Castles" James simultaneously emphasizes the volubility of the dominant narrative voice while demonstrating the permeability of perspectives as his description is re-centered within his reader:

This entertainment is inexhaustible; for every step you take in such a house confronts you in one way or another with the remote past. You devour the documentary, you inhale the historic.... You may lie upon the grass at the base of the ivied fragment,... You seem yourself to have hollowed the flags with your tread, to have polished the oak with your touch.... The massive step by which you ascend to the threshold is a trifle crooked, as it should be;... You look up and down the miniature cloister before you pass in;... After dinner you are told that there is of course a ghost -... Then, when you take your chamber candle and go wandering bedward by a short cut through empty rooms, you are conscious of an attitude toward the which you hardly know whether to read as a fond hope or as a great fear.

You may "devour," you may "inhale," you may "touch," you may "look," you may be "told" — but although you will become "conscious of attitude," you will not be able to "read" it with any certainty. In addition to McGurl's question, "Where does fiction take place?" in reading this passage, we might ask ourselves, "What space do we occupy within it?" We might ask, or we might not.

To summarize a bit, and to borrow a further metaphor from James, modality is a window between characters and their own sense of their surroundings, as well as being one between ourselves and those characters. Without modality, fictional action and/or sensation is dispossessed by its narrator and becomes merely so many "facts" without temporal relation. And more importantly, without temporal relation, there is no causation. We may have bread and we may have rain, but if we did not have rain, we could not have bread. If there is no narrator actively determining precedence among a balance of alternatives, causation would be ineluctable, and motivation implausible (that is, ALL options would remain equally preferable).

But it is at this point that the temporal hiatuses that modality suggests most clearly represent the struggle between the narrator and the author's sense of mastery (or of being an author in the Foucauldian sense). However we choose to describe a story in its pre-compositional state (or even pre-sentient, pre-conscious state) its being as a story necessitates a negotiation between supposed options, for which the narrative voice is ultimately persuasive. Seen in this way, modality is a species of rhetoric — offering, as it were on oath, a single alternative as probable, while acknowledging opposites as co-existent. It is in order to address certain questions of how that rhetoric may be used that I now want to turn to What Maisie Knew.

It isn't uncommon to read What Maisie Knew as a species of bildungsroman — the story of Maisie's emotional and intellectual development at the hands of her divorced parents, and the subsequent machinations of their various partners and surrogate-figures, is undoubtedly the core theme of the novel. Adrian Poole, in his recent introduction to What Maisie Knew, underlines this aspect of the story, but in addition he points out the evident insecurity felt by the narrator as Maisie's maturation advances. This is a position with which I concur — that the narrator is not altogether certain of details which, in a different context, might be stated as objectively knowable — but my reading of the problematical position of James's narrator (telling a story s/he doesn't altogether "know") is founded upon differing criteria.

For example, I began by asking whether James's grammatical modality is being used predominantly to suggest a fragmentation of perceptions, ("It could be true.") or to enforce cohesion, possibly with a teleological aim ("So much ought to be true.") What I found undoubtedly supports the view that the story of Maisie's growing-up is completed, in a sense, by the narrator's tacitly acknowledging that her understanding of her role is superior to anyone else's; and this understanding is one that she gains through a series of penetrating insights into her surroundings. There is, in fact, something like confusion in the portrayal of simultaneity across an unspecified period, with the result that Maisie's interior development is given a pace wholly unlike that of "exterior" events. This is something that Maisie herself eventually becomes cognizant of:

So the sharpened sense of spectatorship was the child's main support, the long habit, from the first, of seeing herself in discussion and finding in the fury of it—she had had a glimpse of the game of football—a sort of compensation for the doom of a peculiar passivity. It gave her often an odd air of being present at her history in as separate a manner as if she could only get at experience by flattening her nose against a pane of glass.

The phrase "she could only get at experience" suggests that agency for the things Maisie observes cannot be understood as subject to the same conditions of temporality that Maisie herself "experiences," and that she must construct a framework of time suited to reading her surroundings. This process takes up nearly a quarter of the intervening narrative, and the stages of its completion can be marked in the increasingly evident inability of the narrator to discuss those affairs of Maisie's inner thoughts in anything except the crudest spatial terms. Thus a few chapters later, "an idea at the back of her head shifted its place to her lips", leaving, as it were, the small time-piece the narrator later calls the "more comfortable place was Maisie's light little brain, it hummed away hour after hour". One result of this gradual bowing-out of the company of Maisie's thoughts by the narrator, this retreat into the narrative equivocation made possible by grammatical modality, is that besides demonstrating the apparent intractability of knowledge centered on space and time, the narrator questions almost inadvertently the actual worth of "knowing" as much as s/he "supposes."

This lateral movement by the narrator – a shrinking in authoritative stature even as Maisie grows in independence – is the gradual projection by Maisie of her mental configurations onto the world around her; in effect, a colonizing of external spaces, and through the assignment of significant images, a re-making of those places in accordance with her reading of them. Even in a book as concerned with whereabouts and relocations as this one is (as well as what one learns from such movement), it is striking that one of the most notable locations for this activity is Maisie's schoolroom. The figure that comes to preside over this scene, transfixed in unchanging two-dimensionality, is Sir Claude:

Miss Overmore...drew from a table-drawer the photograph of Sir Claude and, standing there before Maisie, studied it at some length.

"Isn't he beautiful?" the child ingenuously asked.

Her companion hesitated. "No—he's horrid," she, to Maisie's surprise, sharply returned. But she debated another minute, after which she handed back the picture. It appeared to Maisie herself to exhibit a fresh attraction, and she was troubled, having never before had occasion to differ from her lovely friend. So she only could ask what, such being the case, she should do with it: should she put it quite away—where it wouldn't be there to offend? On this Miss Overmore again cast about; after which she said unexpectedly: "Put it on the schoolroom mantelpiece."

A few pages later and, "This pleasing object found a conspicuous place in the schoolroom". In this instance, James's narrator intrudes upon the conversation, replacing direct speech with narration, and offering modality as a means of gauging worth: what should Maisie do with the photograph? The question hangs momentarily before the reader as much as it does before Miss Overmore. Some might sense in this a type of materialism, or concretizing of things held dear in the mind, so that their worth can be made public. That is, What IS the photo worth? And there is a brief acknowledgement by the narrator that this could be part of the motive here:

Mrs. Wix had put up a Japanese fan and two rather grim texts; she had wished they were gayer, but they were all she happened to have. Without Sir Claude's photograph, however, the place would have been, as he said, as dull as a cold dinner. He had said as well that there were all sorts of things they ought to have; yet governess and pupil, it had to be admitted, were still divided between discussing the places where any sort of thing would look best if any sort of thing should ever come and acknowledging that mutability in the child's career which was naturally unfavourable to accumulation.

But it is noticeable that the narrator takes no credit for this position — it is as "he" said, it is "governess and pupil" who are divided. Yet as tempting as it is to read this delight in the imagining of material changes as a consumerist exchange of new ideals for old, I think a more adequate reading is to see Maisie's re-figuring of her external world in terms very similar to those I used earlier to describe the travel narrator of English Hours. Maisie's makeover of her surroundings is accomplished because of her need to gain possession of them spatially. Given the instability of her existence, it is altogether psychologically plausible that she should wish to do so. But it is curious, and sometimes amusing, to see how Maisie projects her series of schematics on to the people and scenes that make up her world:

Here indeed was a slight ambiguity, as papa's being on Mrs. Beale's didn't somehow seem to place him quite on his daughter's. It sounded, as this young lady thought it over, very much like puss-in-the-corner, and she could only wonder if the distribution of parties would lead to a rushing to and fro and a changing of places. She was in the presence, she felt, of restless change: wasn't it restless enough that her mother and her stepfather should already be on different sides?

But as well-observed as James's description here seems — a child's mind re-arranging the adults surrounding her very much as counters in a board game — it is fitting that Maisie's growth to confidence and insight should be accompanied by a real measure of anxiety on her part. As quaint as it seems, or more cynically as manipulative as it might appear, Maisie has a real need to arrange the figures in her world, as well as her place among them, with something like a measure of certainty. Without this she is conscious, as the narrator acknowledges, of being adrift; a feeling that comes to the fore as she travels to France:

It was singular, but from this time she understood and she followed, followed with the sense of an ample filling-out of any void created by symptoms of avoidance and of flight.... Maisie had known all along a great deal, but never so much as she was to know from this moment on and as she learned in particular during the couple of days that she was to hang in the air, as it were, over the sea which represented in breezy blueness and with a summer charm a crossing of more spaces than the Channel.

As a traveler, Maisie exhibits many of the characteristics observable in James's travel narrators, particularly in her management of visual impressions. But what is significant for the story of Maisie's development is her discovery that such impressions of places can be fixed in time in the same manner that Sir Claude's photograph fixes him in her apprehension, allowing her to view the wider surroundings in terms of the relation thus created. Movement, or the range of temporal options more generally, is shrunken by selectivity to establish a personal nexus of meanings describable, to the observer at least, as "true." The proprieties of the senses thus establish dominance upon their environment, outside the demands of linear time. As Brigette Bailey describes it, "Pictorializing a scene and exercising the connoisseur's play of aesthetic and sentimental responses across its surface turns the scene into a temporal possession". With this power over the present, comes a consequent power over the future, and a concomitant abandonment of modality in narrative structure:

The place and the people were all a picture together, a picture that, when they went down to the wide sands, shimmered, in a thousand tints, with the pretty organisation of the plage, with the gaiety of spectators and bathers, with that of the language and the weather, and above all with that of our young lady's unprecedented situation.

For Maisie, there is a period of heightened mental activity combined with a sense of increasing clarity in her perceptions: "There was literally an instant in which Maisie fully saw — saw madness and desolation, saw ruin and darkness and death." As this competence develops on Maisie's part, the narrator's own urgency increases in a manner I've noted occurring frequently in James's fiction. That is, there is a repetition of a particular word or phrase over a short space, on each occasion giving the words a slightly different emphasis, as if, on the one hand, to give evidence that a variety of contexts have been considered — from the trivial to momentous and on the other, to demonstrate that a particular turn of mind is dominating a character's thinking. On this occasion, James's narrator gives particular prominence to Maisie's thoughts about the exact placement of things. For example, in the short space of six pages he repeats this idea seven times: "it seemed to give a reason for papa's behaviour and place it in a more favourable light"; "she bounded in her place"; "shaking a feather into place"; "the coachman... turning in his place"; "another of the places on her list"; [among the wet places] "there were dry places as well"; "Nothing more remarkable had taken place". Trifling as these examples are, they give a clear indication of the fact that, barred from her motivations, the narrator's gaze has turned in the direction of Maisie's own observation of her world and its small details. But given her early ascertaining of the circumstances of her own predicament based on visual clues — and her continual refinement of her perceptive abilities — it is not surprising that Maisie comes to regard her eyes as ultimately capable of penetrating surface appearances. Seeing is not simply believing, it is the irresistible key that opens all secrets. For example, late in the novel, in the midst of her doubts about Sir Claude:

Maisie felt that however they talked she must see him, but she said nothing more for a time, a time during which she conscientiously finished dressing and Mrs. Wix also kept silence. It was as if they each had almost too much to think of, and even as if the child had the sense that her friend was watching her and seeing if she herself were watched. At last Mrs. Wix turned to the window and stood—sightlessly, as Maisie could guess—looking away. Then our young lady, before the glass, gave the supreme shake. "Well, I'm ready. And now to SEE him!"

The conclusion suggested by this emerging pattern is that a growth in maturity — a growth in perception — includes a commensurate loss in speculative reasoning. More specifically, as Maisie comes to know the adults who inhabit her world, and the texture of those surfaces masking their actions — a growth in apprehension made possible by her literal movement from place to place and group to group — her knowledge of the variables affecting both human behavior and perception becomes such that her reading of her surroundings is noticeably less cautious. At the same time, as if check-mated by this rising independence on Maisie's part, the narrator's becomes more so. Several passages underline this. When Maisie has her longed-for interview with Sir Claude, he attempts to paint an imaginary portrait of the future for her, but the timidity of his description, and the rather frail mood he seeks to establish, show that such thinking is juvenile, and no longer suited to the person Maisie has become:

My idea would be a nice little place—somewhere in the South—where she and you would be together and as good as any one else. And I should be as good too, don't you see? for I shouldn't live with you, but I should be close to you—just round the corner, and it would be just the same. My idea would be that it should all be perfectly open and frank.

Well may Sir Claude ask her, "Don't you see?" as it is vital to Maisie's matured understanding to have this firmly verifiable existence in her mind's eye. A few pages later and it becomes evident that Maisie is no longer willing to indulge her senses in an imagined future, preferring the solidity of the present:

She saw nothing that she had seen hitherto—no touch in the foreign picture that had at first been always before her. The only touch was that of Sir Claude's hand, and to feel her own in it was her mute resistance to time. She went about as sightlessly as if he had been leading her blindfold.

She "saw nothing" and there was "no touch" in this future; but mutely and "sightlessly" she would seek, briefly, to resist time. It was a strategy that, changed as she was, she soon abandoned.

Ultimately I am left with attempting a summary that is capable of illustrating how perceptions of the geographies of these two books compare — geographies that are both non-fiction and imagined, that exist to project, construct or repair aspects of several independent senses of place — yet which is also able to demonstrate that tripartite division of time I spoke of at the outset. In both English Hours and What Maisie Knew there is the possibility that James is employing grammatical modality to construct a fantasy of "otherness" where none is in fact possible or, at least, probable. As readers, we find ourselves crossing the temporal gulf between our worlds and those of fiction (or re-imagined non-fiction) without ever being entirely certain of how we came to set foot on the bridge. We are, in common with the narrator, perpetually aware of a fictional "future" that is simultaneously "present" – the narrator "knows" the story, and we embrace its ending between the covers of the book. Where we, as readers, differ from the narrator in most cases, is in the extent to which we, like the other characters, must wait for future events to occur, with the narrator holding ultimate authority over that information. Thus the five minutes it takes to read of the passage of twenty years are different in relative durations, but not in kind. However, what distinguishes these two books, and James's writing more generally, from much of his contemporaries' Realist fiction – is that James's narrators lack omniscience in certain clearly observable areas.

The voice of English Hours wants, hopes, believes, imagines, deduces and so forth, but is generally reluctant to offer certainties even about the sensory data that underwrite the observations gathered there. The narrator of What Maisie Knew initiates an alliance with the reader, possibly over-emphasizing certain features to mask uncertainty, yet clearly framing Maisie's experiences within a landscape where choices and variables exist, and over which relationships the narrator exercises some competence. But as Maisie's own reading of these surroundings grows, her perceptions come to marginalize, if not altogether exclude, those of the narrator. The immediacy of Maisie's intellection (seeing, hearing, touching) supersedes the narrator's time-keeping (could see, would hear, should touch). One is left to wonder, given that this is a primary factor in Maisie's progress to adulthood, whether this recession of the narrator is a shirking of adult responsibility for what has occurred in the real time of the reader. Certainly, we are left like the other characters and like the narrator to wonder exactly what Maisie knew.

Imaginative Architectures

"On her long journey from Rome her mind had been given up to vagueness; she was unable to question the future. She performed this journey with sightless eyes and took little pleasure in the countries she traversed, decked out though they were in the richest freshness of spring. Her thoughts followed their course through other countries‹strange-looking, dimly-lighted, pathless lands, in which there was no change of seasons, but only as it seemed, a perpetual dreariness of winter. She had plenty to think about; but it was neither reflexion nor conscious purpose that filled her mind. Disconnected visions passed through it, and sudden dull gleams of memory, of expectation. The past and the future came and went at their will, but she saw them only in fitful images, which rose and fell by a logic of their own."

This passage, from the last chapters of The Portrait of a Lady, strikes me as one of the most brutally sad moments in the entire novel. Here Isabel, who has defied Osmond[1]s wishes that she defer to the Œsanctity[1] of their marriage has, with a solemn and ghostly nod to the liberty and independence that has characterized her throughout, come to be beside her cousin Ralph as he dies. What makes the passage so effectively tragic is that in its tone, language and imagery, it picks up on notes that have been sounded again and again from the beginning of the novel; at the same time, however, we cannot fail to register the differences in the workings of our heroine[1]s mind as she tries to make sense of what has become of her.

Much of the poignancy of the above-quoted lines comes from the way in which they contrast with James[1] earlier descriptions of Isabel[1]s mentality. It is surely part of her aptness as a protagonist that from the very beginning of the novel, her mind is constantly and sparklingly alive: "Her imagination was by habit ridiculously active...". The most fertile ground for her imagination is her own life: "She was always planning out her development, desiring her perfection, observing her progress." (It is interesting to note, here and elsewhere in the novel, the way James often has Isabel treat herself in her own mind as an external, abstract, almost objectified subject: James might well have written Œher own development[1] or Œher own perfection[1], but chose not to, leaving us with the subtle impression that she is somehow disconnected from herself in her own mind.) Given these first descriptions of Isabel, it is hard not to register the simple power of the statement that, "she was unable to question the future"‹she, and by natural extension the reader, has been deprived of one of her liveliest faculties, and James has ensured that we feel the immensity of this momentary loss.

Another thing to note in this passage is James[1] metaphorical use of landscape. In the opening chapters of the novel, we are told of Isabel: "Her nature had, in her conceit, a certain garden-like quality, a suggestion of perfume and murmuring boughs, of shady bowers and lengthening vistas, which made her feel that introspection was, after all, an exercise in the open air, and that a visit to the recesses of one[1]s spirit was harmless when one returned from it with a lapful of roses." Now that her narrative is no longer an abstract question before her, her thoughts move through "other countries‹strange-looking, dimly-lighted, pathless lands, in which there was no change of seasons, but only as it seemed, a perpetual dreariness of winter. " Compared with the seemingly infinite openness of the initial descriptions, this new landscape is bleak indeed. The passage quoted at the top of this paper continues, picking up another metaphorical thread that is woven through the fabric of the novel: "...now that she knew something that so much concerned her and the eclipse of which had made life resemble an attempt to play whilst with an imperfect pack of cards, the truth of things, their mutual relations, their meaning, and for the most part their horror, rose before her with an architectural vastness."

Like physical landscape, architecture figures prominently throughout The Portrait as an index of internal workings. The first detailed Œportrait[1] in the book is of Gardencourt, and from that moment on, we learn to take important cues from James[1] elaborate descriptions of structures of all kinds.

Perhaps one of the most pointed examples is our first encounter with Osmond. As at the opening of the novel, we get a detailed view of the home before the inhabitant:

"The house had a front upon a little grassy, empty, rural piazza which occupied a part of the hill-top; and this front, pierced with a few windows in irregular relations... this antique, solid, weather-worn, yet imposing front had a somewhat incommunicative character. It was the mask, not the face of the house. It had heavy lids, but no eyes... The windows of the ground-floor, as you saw them from the piazza, were, in their noble proportions, extremely architectural; but their function seemed less to offer communication with the world than to defy the world to look in. They were massively cross-barred...."

With this brief image of Osmond[1]s house comes a definitive, palpable change in mood; whether we are aware of it or not, the consequent introduction of our new character is colored at the very root by the somewhat sinister language of this description. Our information here diverges from that of our heroine, and so, long before Osmond[1]s full nature is revealed to us, we cannot fully Œget behind[1] him as the man that should cause Isabel to "drop to the ground." Now, late in the novel, when James has Isabel relate the great trick played on her to architecture, it resonates with all the times throughout the book when people, and especially our heroine, have been metaphorically linked with houses and structures. To draw again on a quote I have already used in part: "Her imagination was by habit ridiculously active; when the door was not open it jumped out of the window. She was not accustomed indeed to keep it behind bolts..." A little further on, in Ralph[1]s musings about his cousin, James writes:

"He surveyed the edifice from the outside and admired it greatly; he looked in at the windows and received an impression of proportions equally fair. But he felt he saw it only by glimpses and that he had not yet stood under the roof. The door was fastened, and though he had keys in his pocket he had a conviction that none of them would fit."

In returning to the architecture metaphor as Isabel runs to the Œsanctuary[1] of Gardencourt‹"She had gone forth in her strength; she would come back in her weakness..."‹James only too vividly draws the contrast between Isabel[1]s initial freedom and her eventual imprisonment within the secretly and malevolently-built structure of her marriage.

It is with one word that James sums up the central tragedy

of Isabel's story when, fitted with this new, terrible consciousness, she concludes: "The only thing to regret was that Madame Merle had been so‹well, so unimaginable." Once again, James strikes a note that has sounded again and again over the course of our reading. Indeed, imagination is in many ways the novel's primary subject, as it is our heroine's ruin; by the end of this almost unspeakably cruel and sad story, we can only hope that it will be her redemption and transcendence as well.

The Portrait of a Lady and Dr. Breen's Practice. Discuss

THE Atlantic may fairly claim to have exercised its critical function upon the just completed novels by Mr. James and Mr. Howells before the reader had begun to enjoy them, and to have reserved the right,when the reader should be in full possession, of explaining why and how much it liked them.

Yet a book has, after all, a life distinct from the interrupted existence of a magazine serial, and it is quite possible to take up these comely volumes and receive a new impression of the integrity of the stories which they contain. Possibly, Mr. James's novel (The Portrait of a Lady, by Henry James, Jr. Houghton, Mifflin & Co. 1882) suffers less than some others might from being read in fragmentary form, for the minute finish of touch with which the lines in the portrait are applied meets the reader's eye with new power every time that he takes up the story after a fall upon other work; yet this very refinement of manipulation may lead one to overlook the larger consistency of the Whole figure. It is worthwhile to step back a few paces, and fail for a moment to see each individual stroke of the brush.

Come, then, since we have been looking at the portrait of Isabel from the near point of monthy chapters, let us seat ourselves before the book, and, armed with an imaginative tin opera glass to shut out all other pictures, renew our acquaintance with the portrait. How does it strike us as a whole? What is the impression finally left upon our minds? Have we added to our dream of fair women?

Return to Flashback: Henry James and The Atlantic

Monthly. See more Classic Reviews from The Atlantic's archive. The artist gives us this advantage, that all the elaboration of his work looks distinctly to the perfection of the central figure. One can repeat almost in a single breath the incidental story of the book. That is dissolved immediately, if the incidents deposited are the critical ones of Isabel's meeting with her aunt, her rejection successively of Goodwood and Lord Warburton, her accession to wealth, her marriage with Osmond, her temporary separation, and her final return. A person hearing the narrative might be pardonned if he failed to see the making of a great novel in it, but only when one has recited it does he become aware how each step in the fatal series is a movement in the direction of destiny.

By a fine concentration of attention upon the heroine, Mr. James impresses us with her im-portance, and the other characters, involved as they are with her life, fall back into secondary positions. It is much to have seized and held firmly so elusive a conception, and our admiration is increased when reflection shows that, individual as Isabel is in the painting, oue may fairly take her as representative of womanly life today. The fine purpose of her freedom, the resolution with which she seeks to be the master of her destiny, the subtle weakness in to which all this betrays her, the apparent helplessness of her ultimate position, and the conjectured escape only through patient forbearance, — what are all these, if not attributes of womanly life expended under current conditions?

The consistency of the work is observable under another aspect. Mr. James's method is sufficiently well known, and since he has made it his own the critic may better accept it and measure it than complain of it. What renders it distinct from, say, Thackeray's method, with which it has been compared, or from George Eliot's, is the limitation of the favorite generalizations and analyses. If the reader will attend, he will see that these take place quite exclusively wirhin the boundaries of the story and characters. That is to say, when the people in the book stop acting or speaking, it is to give to the novelist an opportunity, not to indulge in general reflections, having application to all sorts and conditions of men, of whom his dramatis personae are but a part, he has no desire to share humanity with them, but to make acute reflections upon these particular people, and to explain more thoroughly than their words and acts can the motives which lie behind. We may, on general grounds, doubt the self-confidence or power of a novelist who feels this part of his performance to be essential, but there can be no cloubt that Mr. James's method is a part of that concentration of mind which results in a singular consistency.

Yet all this carries an intimation of what is curiously noticeable in his work. It is consistent, but the consistency is with itself. Within the boundaries of the novel the logic of character and events is close and firm. We say this after due reflection upon the latest pages. There can be little doubt that the novelist suffers more in the reader's judgment from a false or ineffective scene at the close of his story than he gains from many felicitous strokes in the earlier development of plot or character. The impatient, undiscriminating objection, It does not end well, although it may incense the writer, is an ill-formulated expression of the feeling that the creation lacks the final, triumphant touch which gives life; the sixth swan in the story got a stitch-weed shirt, like the rest, but in the hurry of the last moment it lacked a few stitches, and so in the transformation the youngest brother was forced to put up with one arm and to show a wing for the other.

Isabel Archer, with her fine horoscope, is an impressive figure, and one follows her in her free flight with so much admiration for her resolution and strong pinions that when she is caught in the meshes of Osmond's net one's indignation is moved, and a noble pity takes the place of frank admiration. But pity can live only in full communion with faith, and we can understand the hesitation which a reader might feel before the somewhat ambiguous passage of Isabel's last interview with Goodwood. The passage, however, admits of a generous construction, and we prefer to take it, and to see in the scene the author's intention of giving a final touch to his delineation of Goodwood's iron but untempered will, Isabel's vanishing dream of happiness, and her acceptance of the destiny which she had unwittingly chosen. We suspect that something of the reader's dissatisfaction at this juncture comes from his dislike of Goodwood, the jack-in-the-box of the story, whose unyielding nature seems somehow outside of all the events.

To return to our point. This self-consistency is a separate thing from any consistency with the world of reality. The characters, the situations, the incidents, are all true to the law of their own being, but that 1aw runs parallel with the law which governs life, instead of being identical with it. In Andersen's quaint story of the Emporer's New Clothes, a little child discovers the unreality of the gossamer dress, and his voice breaks in upon the illusion from the outer world. Something of the same separation from the story, of the same unconscious naturalness of feeling, prompts the criticism that, thougth these people walk, and sit, and talk, and behave, they are yet in an illusionary world of their own. Only when one is within the charmed circle of the story is he under its spell, and so complete is the isolation of the book that the characters acquire a strange access of reality when they talk about each other. Not only so, but the introversion which now and then takes place deepens the sense of personality. In that masterly passage which occupies the forty-second section, where Isabel enters upon a disclosure of her changed life, the reader seems to be going down as in a diving-bell into the very secrets of her nature.

What is all this but saying that in the process of Mr. James's art the suggestion always seems to come from within, and to work outward? We recognize the people to whom he introduces us, not by any external signs, but by the private information which we have regarding their souls. The smiles which they wear — and one might make an ingenious collection of their variety — do not tell What is beneath the surface, but we know what they mean because we already have an esoteric knowledge. Mr. James is at great pains to illustrate his characters by their attitudes, their movements, their by-play, Yet we carry away but a slight impression of their external appearance; these are not bodily shapes, for the most part, but embodied spirits, who enjoy their rnaterialization for a time, anti contribute to a play which goes on upon a stage just a little apart from that great stage where the world's play, with men and women for actors, is carried forward....

Daisy Miller: Cultural Differences

In "Daisy Miller" by Henry James readers are challenged to take a look at an American girl mainly from the viewpoint of Winterbourne. Daisy is portrayed as extremely beautiful and fairly innocent. Winterbourne's infatuation with this typical American girl, in fact, reveals the differences between the highly-developed European upper crust culture and the newly developing American culture. Even though Winterbourne is American, he shows readers what European culture is: civility, gallantry and apparent gap among social status etc. Winterbourne's sophisticated manners contrast with Daisy's relatively poor education, innocence and crudity. Therefore, the way Winterbourne's aunt criticizes about Daisy's vulgarity symbolically indicates European high-minded pride over fledgling American culture. The dominant image concerning Daisy throughout the entire work is that she seems to be frank and thus never tries to conceal her inner mind like the typical European girls with a view to arresting attention from men. However, that prevailing image is bound to be changed by the last twist of plot. At the moment of death, Daisy's wish is that Winterbourne should know that she is not engaged with that Italian guy. Then, why? Actually, it is quite ambiguous; none the less, her wish can be interpreted as her desperate trial to overcome the European prejudices against shallow American culture. In other words, behind her vulgarity and innocence, there is a fundamental desire to appreciate and enhance one's dignity even in love affairs, which is not vulgar at all, and which makes Winterbourne study hard.

The Turn of the Screw-A Look at a Criticism

There are many different ways to interpret The Turn of the Screw, by Henry James. Many critics over the past century have voiced their opinions about the story. Each critical analysis of the story disagrees with the beliefs expressed in another. Robert B. Heilman is a critic who wrote in the mid-twentieth century. He interprets The Turn of the Screw to be a representation of the conflict between good and evil. Heilman's points are clear and obviously well thought out, but there are flaws in his argument that make his interpretation questionable.

In his 1948 essay, Robert Heilman explores the suggestion that The Turn of the Screw is a symbolic representation of the conflict between good and evil. Heilman interprets the apparitions of Peter Quint and Miss Jessel as evil forces. He explains that the ghosts only appear to the governess because evil lurks in subtlety before it strikes. It is the duty of the governess to "detect and ward off evil." She must protect the children from the awful ghosts. The governess describes Miles and Flora as beautiful little cherubs whose only fault is their gentleness. Heilman views the children's beauty as a "symbol of the spiritual perfection of which man is capable." Heilman explains the ghosts' attempts to reach the children by explaining that evil forces will always try to conquer and possess the human soul. Heilman continues to draw from the descriptions of Miles and Flora to support his theories. He points out that the two children are described as having an "angelic beauty" and a "positive fragrance of purity". The governess describes them as if they are perfect and beautiful in every way. This repeated vision of beauty, radiance, and innocence parallels the image of Eden. The house at Bly also resembles this image, "I remember the lawn and the bright flowers...". The governess makes mention of the "golden sky" and of Flora's "hair of gold," which Heilman believes connects Bly and Flora with these images of golden hues.

Robert Heilman perceives that the ghost of Peter Quint is a direct representation of the serpent that plagues the Garden of Eden. Heilman supports this with the description of Quint found in the text, "His eyes are sharp, strange- awfully;... rather small and very fixed. His mouth's wide, and his lips are thin." Heilman points out that these characteristics are those of a snake. The demonic presence of Quint poisons Bly just as the serpent in the Garden of Eden poisons Adam and Eve's home. The fall of innocence occurs as the seasons change from spring to autumn. On one evening, the governess notes that she "...listened to lash of the rain and the batter of the gusts". After the storm, the weather continues to be "damp and grey". When the governess and Mrs. Grose find Flora at the lake, Flora is playing with a piece of withered fern. At this point in the story, the governess is convinced that Flora has run off with Miss Jessel and that Miss Jessel has corrupted Flora. Heilman sees this as not only the change of season's before the end of the year, but as "the end of a cycle: the spring of gay, bright human innocence has given way to the ark autumn-or rather, as we might pun, the dark fall. The decaying foliage suggests the decay of Eden and the fall of Flora and Miles.

By the end of the story, Heilman states that the governess "emphasizes Mile's freedom and sorrowfully gives up 'the fiction that I had anything more to teach him.'" He suggests that this is because Miles has eaten from the tree of knowledge. Heilman points out that as the innocence of the children is spoiled, their health deteriorates. However, the story does not end here. The governess still adheres to her duty as protector and savior of the children. Heilman states, "The governess's priestly function is made still more explicit by the fact that she comes ultimately to act as confessor and to use every possible means to bring Miles to confession." In the ending scene, the governess must protect Miles from the evil force. However, when Miles tries to confess his sins, the horrible face of Peter Quint appears at the window. The governess ultimately fails as "Savior" and Miles is lost forever.

I find Robert Heilman's essay to be fairly convincing, but it does have its weaknesses. For example, the governess speaks of Miles's charm and angelic nature as a cover-up for the awful deed he has committed at school. Even before she meets him, she believes that Miles is "an injury to others". How can Miles represent Adam before his fall if he is already guilty of sin? Also, Heilman states that the governess's duty is to protect Miles from evil. How can she protect him from something that she already believes has overtaken him? The question that the governess asks herself at the end of the story does not support Heilman's notions that the governess is a "savior." She asks, "It was for the instant confounding and bottomless, for if he were innocent what then on earth was I?". This brings to light the governess's realization that she has been at fault throughout the story. Heilman completely fails to address what the fault of the governess is. He does, however, believe that the governess failed as a Savior because Miles dies without having confessed his sins. As I stated earlier, Heilman suggests that the devil, as Peter Quint, succeeds in taken Miles when he fails to confess. However, the ending quote of the story reads, "...and his little heart, dispossessed, had stopped,". If his little heart is dispossessed, then how is it possible that the devil won? The governess also declares that the monster has lost Miles forever and that she now has him. How has she failed if Peter Quint has lost Miles forever?

Robert B. Heilman's arguments are strong, but I can't fully agree with his interpretation of The Turn of the Screw. His ideas are well thought out, but the text does not always support his theories. Henry James wrote The Turn of the Screw in such an ambiguous manner that it is open to many different interpretations. However, it appears that no single interpretation has the ability to cover every aspect of the story and explain it in a way that is convincing to all.

Unrequited Love in the Turn of the Screw

In "The Turn of the Screw" by Henry James, the central character, the governess, feels so isolated that she will do anything necessary to quench the feeling. She decides that the way to do so is to be in love. Unfortunately, because she is located in Bly, such a desire is not possible to actualize. When the governess realizes this she begins to manifest her unrequited feelings in the shape of ghostly apparitions. Her point of view also plays an important role in how the reader observes the ghosts. Subconsciously, the governess has chosen to be an unreliable narrator, seeing fantastical phantoms which participate in an enamored relationship allows her to feel as though she herself was a part of it. When the governess becomes tired with these ghosts, however, she turns to other characters to fulfill her aspiration.

The governess sees ghosts in order to satisfy her yearning desire to be in love. The young governess is instantly attracted to the "handsome, bold and pleasant" bachelor uncle of the orphaned children by whom she is hired. This overwhelming feeling was the original motivation for her accepting the job as governess. The reader's introduction to the governess' most basic feelings shows the reader that this is one of her primary concerns at the point in her life that the novella begins. The governess' craving to be cherished by a man is induced by the uncle's "charming ways with women". His graciousness gives her a taste of how she would like to be treated in life. When the governess leaves to accept the position she is at an undeveloped age, with a background consisting of country poverty and only one position related to children prior to the event at hand. This results in a lack of knowledge as to what she wants from life. The gentlemanly uncle gives her an 'ideal' to aspire towards.

The governess is an unreliable narrator; her dreams to be in love become so realistic to her that she actually begins to see apparitions. Her first sighting occurs only a moment after she is dreaming about how it would be "as charming as a charming story suddenly to meet someone". The word 'story' implies an innocent, child-like, fairytale view of the emotion she experiences, this diction choice demonstrates her inability to deal with the emotion maturely. When Peter Quint appears on the tower at that point her imagination is taking over and giving her the 'love' that she has been dreaming about since she arrived at Bly. The governess' mind shows her Quint as a ghost because subconsciously she knows it's unreal and therefore unattainable, that he is a ghost is her rationalization of the situation — mental self-preservation. The governess' initial sighting of the second ghost, Miss Jessel, is of the same nature as her original sighting of Quint; our narrator wishes for, or in the second case, "becomes aware that has an interested spectator", before seeing it, leading the reader to conclude that the ghosts are manifestations of her thoughts.

She sees the ghost in her mind's eye and because of her imagination is then able to transfer the image to visual. For her to be able to have a relationship with 'Peter', the above describes the next logical step in her dream: to again allow her mind to take over and invent a 'Miss Jessel'. Miss Jessel and Peter Quint had "everything between them" according to Mrs. Grose, this supports the romantic relationship the governess conceives Quint to be involved in. Miss Jessel represents what the governess wants to be, a woman who is in love with someone who feels mutually towards her. The reader is forced to question the governess' narrative reliability, and because it is written in first person it difficult for the reader to accurately assess the feelings and opinions of other characters.

The governess' arrival to the setting in Bly is a logical place for her unrequited feelings of love to emerge. Her arrival in Bly at the start of the narrative is accomplished only after "long hours in a bumpy, swinging coach". This carriage ride is the physical process that brings her away from civilization and to a place that allows her imagination to run wild. On a psychological level the journey can be interpreted as a journey of her mind; it takes her away from her 'ego' and 'super ego' and into the deeper realms of 'id' (which covers such primal, instinctual feelings as the need to have sex, coming only as a result of having a male character with whom to interact). Her first impressions describe Bly as having "open windows, fresh curtains, bright flowers, a golden sky, and impressive rooms with great beds, full draperies and long glasses". The place is in such a state of perfection that the reader gets the feeling it is covering up abominable secrets of the past including taboo deaths and Miles' ambiguous expulsion. During her first night in Bly the governess considers with "uneasy suspicion" the "guarded" way that Mrs. Grose treats her. Such negative underlying emotions could result in an even stronger need on her part to escape to such a positive emotion as love.

The narrator looks for love in Bly, as her necessity becomes more and more frantic she looks to different, and all, male characters to satisfy it. It begins with a reasonable attraction towards the uncle, then her displaced emotion moves to the fictitious Peter Quint for the most part of the novella. In the last chapter she even looks to the boy, Miles, for a reciprocating feeling, this is shown in his adult diction and actions in her narrative of him, in her struggle to attain love she actually smothers Miles to the point of death. Finally, it is implied in the preface that after our account of the story ends, she turns the demand on Douglas.

The Turn of the Screw: Ghosts

Lawrence Kramer poses some interesting ideas about Henry James' The Turn of the Screw mainly by discussing the ghosts in the story. He refers to the ghosts as revenants; "a specter, a ghost, a phantom, one who haunts, who returns, who walks again." First, he implies that these revenants can only work when a person believes they exist. There must be something that makes a former person want to return to the living world from a state of death. However, this longing by the former person is not enough to make it a worthy revenant. Someone in the living world must believe that the revenant is actually there. Because of the feelings of "dread" and "desire" a revenant creates when it appears, most people find it difficult to disbelieve in this apparition. Therefore, it is fairly easyfor a revenant to work. This is critical to the story because in order for the revenants of Quint and Miss Jessel to work, the governess must believe that they exist. Because of the governess' belief, the revenants can work effectively. Although the governess wants to take away the power of the revenants, she does not realize she is the sole cause of their power. "Offering herself as the medium of [the desire for the children], she revives in a new, substitutive form the transgressive desires that the ghosts shared in life." According to Kramer, if she does not believe that the revenants exist, then the revenant will have no power or control. Next, Kramer goes into a short discussion describing the revenant of Peter Quint. His image involves clothes that are not his own, and he does not look like any one the governess has seen before. This creates a paradox. The familiar clothes give Quint a familiarity that the governess recognizes, and yet his features are not like anything she can distinguish. "Quint... is always familiar and yet alien." He possesses both familiar and strange qualities.

His name creates another controversy because it can be used as the nineteenth-century "formula for homosexuality." Somehow his name was used to refer to someone with homosexual qualities. He becomes a stereotype of the "predatory child-molesting degenerate." Kramer accuses Quint of causing the end of Miles's childhood or innocence. This implies that Quint could have sexual molested Miles while Quint himslef was still alive. The final exercise of the revenants' power comes when Miles dies. Miles dies while the governess is harassing him about what he saw at the window. She wants Miles to admit that he can see and has seen Quint. He replies that he sees nothing, but she keeps on pushing. Because of her involvement with the revenants, Miles dies and the revenants' desires of getting Miles are fulfilled. In the end, the governess causes what she has been trying to prevent.

Finally, Kramer discusses the historical aspects of the novel. Supposedly, during the Enlightenment period, ghosts were driven from walking on the earth to only existing in people's minds. However, "mental revenants" prove to be more destructive than actual revenants. When they were walking on the earth, these revenants could be avoided just by avoiding the places they existed, but one cannot avoid a revenant in his or her own mind. This becomes the problem of the governess. She cannot avoid these revenants because they exist in her own mind. This also explains why know one else sees them. This historical data that Kramer presents provides a new understanding about why the governess is the only person to admittedly see these ghosts. In a quick recap, Lawrence Kramer provides new insight into what revenants are, where they come from, and what they mean. This new insight helps aid with understanding difficult parts of The Turn of the Screw.

Turn of the Screw

In Turn of the Screw by Henry James, there is a question

of whether the ghosts of Peter Quint and Miss Jessel are real. They seem to only appear to the governess and she is the only one who admits to seeing them. F. W. H. Myers recognized apparitions as "a manifestation of persistent personal energy, —or an indication that some kind of force is being exercised after death which is in some way connected to a person previously known on earth." This fits the story perfectly for the ghosts appear to be nothing, just a "manifestation." The governess swears that Miles and Flora see the ghosts too, but that they refuse to admit it. She says, "whatever I had seen, Miles and Flora saw more— things terrible and unguessable and that sprang from dreadful passages of intercourse in the past." They are scared or intimidated. Some of the places the governess appears show many parallels to the sightings of the ghosts as well. The governess sees Quint in the glass door and up on the tower, a place where Mrs. Grose notices the governess. And the governess sees Miss Jessel sitting at her desk. She recalls, "In the presence of what I saw I reeled back upon resistance. Seated at my own table in the clear noonday light I saw a person..." These reflections of herself upon the ghosts portray an idea that she is a ghost or it is in her conscious and Bly is driving her mad. This leads the reader to believe that the governess is actually a reflection of the ghosts. When she sees the ghosts, it's like a mirror image. And mirrors ultimately just show you yourself in full, obvious form. They are an ultimate reality. When the governess sees Miss Jessel across the lake, it could be her mirror image reflected in her mind. "Miss Jessel stood before us on the opposite bank..." the governess recalled. "Where on earth do you see anything?" replied Mrs. Grose. However, sometimes mirrors show you what you want to see, for example, in Something Wicked this Way Comes. Or mirrors could portray a brutal reality like in Fall of the House of Usher. Reflections other than mirrors have the same meaning, for example, seeing yourself in water. In the end, neither the governess nor we the reader are certain that these ghosts are out to get the children. Being the one who sees them, the governess might actually be the victim.

Bibliography

Alter, Robert. "*The Novel and the Sense of the Past.*" Salmagundi 68-69 (1985): 91-106.

Andres, Sophia. "*Narrative Instability in The Portrait of a Lady: Isabel on the Edge of the Social.*" Journal of Narrative Technique 24.1 (1994): 43-54.

Ash, Beth Sharon. "*Frail Vessels and Vast Designs: A Psychoanalytic Portrait of Isabel Archer.*" New Esssays on The Portrait of a Lady. Ed. Joel Porte. The American Novel (AmNov), New York, NY. Cambridge: Cambridge UP, 1990. 123-62.

Auerbach, Nina. "*Alluring Vacancies in the Victorian Character.*" The Kenyon Review 8.3 (1986): 36-48.

Balsamo, Gian. "*Henry James and Emma Bovary.*" Canadian Review of Comparative Literature/Revue Canadienne de Litterature Comparee 18.4 (1991): 547-56.

Bamberg, Robert D. The Portrait of a Lady: An Authoritative Text; Henry James and the Novel; Reviews and Criticism. New York: Norton, 1975.

Baris, Sharon Deykin. "*The Lady or the Scholar? Contending Lights in James's Portrait of Isabel Archer.*" Hebrew University Studies in Literature and the Arts 18 (1990): 48-80.

Baris, Sharon. "*Gender, Judgment, and Presumptuous Readers: The Role of Daniel in The Portrait of a Lady.*" The Henry James Review 12.3 (1991): 212-30.

Baris, Sharon. "*James's Pyrotechnic Display: The Book in Isabel's Portrait.*" The Henry James Review 12.2 (1991): 146-53.

Bauer, Dale M. "*Jane Campion's Symbolic Portrait.*" Henry James Review 18.2 (1997): 194-96.

Baym, Nina. "*Revision and Thematic Change in The Portrait of a Lady.*" Modern Fiction Studies 22 (1976): 183-200.

Bazzanella, Dominic J. "*The Conclusion to The Portrait of a Lady Re-Examined.*" American Literature 41 (1969): 55-63.

Beauchamp, Andrea Roberts. "'*Isabel Archer': A Possible Source for The Portrait of a Lady.*" American Literature 49 (1977): 267-71.

Bell, Millicent. "*Refractions of Isabel Archer.*" 'Union in Partition': Essays in Honour of Jeanne Delbaere. Eds. Gilbert Debusscher and Marc Maufort. Liege, Belgium: L3-Liege Language and Literature, 1997. 59-69.

Bentley, Nancy. "'*Conscious Observation of a Lovely Woman': Jane Campion's Portrait of a Lady.*" Henry James Review 18.2 (1997): 174-79.

Berkson, Dorothy. "*Why Does She Marry Osmond? The Education of Isabel Archer.*" American Transcendental Quarterly 60 (1986): 53-71.

Bigliazzi, Silvia. "*Limina: T. S. Eliot's Silhouette of a Lady.*" Rivista di Letterature Moderne e Comparate 50.3 (1997): 287-96.

Birkerts, Sven. "*Reading and Depth of Field.*" Philosophy and Literature 20.1 (1996): 122-29.

Blodgett, Harriet. "*Verbal Clues in The Portrait of a Lady: A Note in Defense of Isabel Archer.*" Studies in American Fiction 7 (1979): 27-36.

Bloom, Harold. Henry James's The Portrait of a Lady. New York: Chelsea, 1987.

Bloom, Harold. Isabel Archer. New York: Chelsea House, 1992.

Bobbitt, Joan. "*Aggressive Innocence in The Portrait of a Lady.*" Massachusetts Studies in English 4 (1973): 31-37.

Bochner, Jay. "*Life in a Picture Gallery: Things in The Portrait of a Lady and The Marble Faun.*" Texas Studies in Literature and Language 11 (1969): 761-777.

Bollinger, Laurel. "*The Ethics of Reading: The Struggle for Subjectivity in the Portrait of a Lady.*" Criticism: A Quarterly for Literature and the Arts 44.2 (2002): 139-60.

Boren, Lynda S. "*Undoing the Mona Lisa: Henry James's*

Quarrel with da Vinci and Pater." Mosaic: A Journal for the Interdisciplinary Study of Literature 20.3 (1987): 95-111.

Bosquet, Marc. "*I Don't Like Isabel Archer*." Henry James Review 18.2 (1997): 197-99.

Boudreau, Kristin. "*Is the World Then So Narrow? Feminist Cinematic Adaptations of Hawthorne and James*." Henry James Review 21.1 (2000): 43-53.

Brody, Selma B. "*Dorothea Brooke and Henry James's Isabel Archer*." George Eliot-George Henry Lewes Studies 20-21 (1992): 63-66.

Buchanan, D. "*'The Candlestick and the Snuffers': Some Thoughts on The Portrait of a Lady'*." The Henry James Review 16.2 (1995): 121-30.

Budick, Emily Miller. "*James's Portrait of Female Skepticism*." The Henry James Review 12.2 (1991): 154-58.

Buitenhuis, Peter ed. Twentieth Century Interpretations of The Portrait of a Lady: A Collection of Critical Essays, 1968.

Buitenhuis, Peter. "*Americans in European Gardens*." The Henry James Review 7.2-3 (1986): 124-130.

Chandler, Karen Michele. "*Agency and Social Constraint in Jane Campion's The Portrait of a Lady*." Henry James Review 18.2 (1997): 191-93.

Choi, Kyong-Do. "*Pragmatism and American Realism*." The Journal of English Language and Literature 35.2 (1989): 235-258.

Collins, Martha. "*The Narrator, the Satellites, and Isabel Archer: Point of View in The Portrait of a Lady*." Studies in the Novel 8 (1976): 142-57.

Connaughton, Michael E. "*American English and the International Theme in The Portrait of a Lady*." Midwest Quarterly: A Journal of Contemporary Thought 22.2 (1981): 137-146.